Renata

— enjoy

PRAISE FOR JON COURT BOOKS

DO ANGELS BLEED?

DO ANGELS BLEED ?

Jon Court

ISBN: 0692489045
ISBN 13: 9780692489048
Library of Congress Control Number: 2015947330
Do Angels Bleed ?, Hancock, ME

CHAPTER ONE

VIRGINIA

<u>SEPTEMBER, 1862</u>

For eighteen months the American continent bled as the North and the South chose a field of honor to settle a mortal debate. For year and a half, the North fought a war it could not lose and the South a war it could not possibly win. Only McClellan and Lee waited to challenge this logic. When night fell, the stream called Antietam was thick with blood. Twenty-four thousand men carpeted the slopes.

High on a wooded bluff, John Spencer could hear only the muffled sound of bullets and cannon thunder. Sudden flashes of white, and tails of black and grey marked the road from Dunker Church where the young died.

As he watched, dusk blurred the pattern of military movement. The brilliant sparks grew fewer. Blackness quieted the day's terror. He imagined the war machine as some vast organism with a skin of flesh and steel sprawled out over the landscape. The creature, its energies spent, would sleep, heal its wounds, so that in the morning, it could awake and quake over the land.

Only the ambulance carts continued to move. Open wooden wagons. Closed cars with high sides and flat roofs. Even makeshift platforms on artillery cradles. The thick snake of vehicles, tail low in the valley, writhed, and with each twist, disgorged a vomit of crushed and dead in front of him.

The young doctor was a gentle man. In earlier days, he had seen men die ....but never with the violent blood-letting of brother against brother. For a day and a half, he watched the 21st Massachusetts Regiment being winnowed.

Now it was time for him to play God !

The *selection* area was a large clearing just to the left of the Hospital Tent. As each cart approached the field, litter-bearers identified the dead for railway transport home. The living were removed and laid out on the ground in neat rows. They waited there for the Triage Officer to tell their future.

Some sat upright. Others remained twisted in strange shapes. Some, driven by a lingering sense of duty, tried to stand up and present at attention. Kerosene lights hanging from tilting poles cast a flickering orange light. The soldiers were pale, tremulous. Their eyes had a vacant look. One and then another would scream as pain broke through the numbing shock.

Spencer waited in the canvas-draped doorway of the Hospital Tent. The physician was tall. He walked with a fast lanky motion. His shoulders were broad, his hips narrow. Wiry red hair covered his head and curled over the tops of his ears. Unlike his compatriots, he was close-shaven, except for a two-day stubble. His face was long and lean. Heavy cushions of red hair topped blue-green eyes sunk in darkened sockets. His chin was sharp, cut by a faint cleft. Had he smiled, creases encircling the corners of his mouth would have made his plain face almost handsome.

His Surgeons Assistant, Martin, had already peeled away the first soldier's right trouser leg. The ankle bones were shattered, replaced by a pulp of clotted blood, earth and fabric. Spencer did not look at the soldier's face. In a low tone, he instructed, "Amputation. Below knee."

He quickly moved to the next. The boy was trying to sit up, using one hand to support himself in a hunched-over position. The other hand clutched a square of stained linen to his chest. As he struggled to breathe, a foam of blood-tinged saliva collected in the corners of his mouth.

Spencer gently drew the boy's hand away. The bullet had pierced the chest under the right nipple. There was no exit wound. The bullet was trapped inside. John tried to visualize the bullet's path. It had to have pierced the lung. Probably hit the great vessels, too. The aorta? The vena cava?

The boy's pulse fluttered like a wounded bird's wings. His skin was covered with a fine layer of chilled sweat, even though the air was still warm.

Blood loss....? Where?

Martin helped lay the soldier out flat. Spencer examined the abdomen. His long fingers made cracking noises as he felt air which had escaped from the ripped lung. Spencer pressed deeper into the lacerated liver making the soldier scream. Spencer looked at Martin and his lips moved silently. Abdominal hemorrhage. Torn lung and liver. He did not have to say anything else. Even as he moved to the next patient, litter bearers were carrying the boy to the rear, where laudanum would ease his death.

The next. Left arm torn off at the shoulder. The arm? Lying somewhere in the valley below. John nodded to Martin. The boy was transported to the Hospital Tent for a pressure dressing.

The next. A soldier trying to speak through a face that no longer existed. Choking on blood that ran down into his lungs. To the rear.....laudanum.

The next. Left arm amputation. The wrist bent at an odd angle with shards of bone breaking the skin from a compound fracture.

The next. Right arm amputation. Spencer could see the dirty blue wool creased into the boy's flesh where a blunt-nosed lead Minnié shell had cracked his forearm.

Next. The soldier cradling his intestines with his two arms like a mother sheltering her new born. His eyes pleading. He received a grin of assurance. He left for the rear, to die, clutching his healer's sacred promise.

Spencer moved up the first row and down the second. Poking. Probing. Percussing. Lifting bandages. Feeling for bone chips, ruptured organs, rapid pulses. Always, that mask of faith and hope behind which the young doctor hid his shame and helplessness.

Still the wounded came. The tumbrels with bodies spilling over the tailgate. Dumping their cargo on the ground. The horses snorting from the climb to the top of the ridge.

Bodies. Limbs. John wondered…. if you collected all the bits and pieces and put them into a giant box and shook it, would the bodies that emerged have four intact limbs? For how many years after the War would the farms and city streets be populated by armless and legless men?

The last of the ambulances appeared over the crest of the hill. With a prayer of thanks, John Spencer entered the Hospital Tent for the Surgery. Suddenly, a sharp pain gnawed deep in the pit of his stomach. He stumbled slightly as the peptic cramp caught him up. Martin knew the doctor had not slept since the battle started two days ago. He had dragged himself from the *Triage Field* to Surgery and back. He had existed on countless cups of coffee and captured Kentucky Whiskey to dull the ache. They only made it worse.

He shrugged off Martin's offer to delay the Surgery. "I will be fine, " he insisted, "Just another cup of your coffee. That's all I need." He cocked his head at the dwindling sound of cannon fire, "Maybe tonight will be the end and we <u>all</u> can sleep,"

The grassy field was rapidly emptying as other physicians sifted the quick from the dead. He could not blink the tears away fast enough. He shook his head sadly.

"At least, <u>we</u> will wake up in the morning. Martin," His voice was flat and toneless. " God allows man to kill....yet, he made doctors to heal.

Is it possible that the Almighty, in His wisdom, intended to keep the healers one step behind? " His face grew stern, "I can't believe that. Someday, we must be able to restore life with the same ease we can end it."

He raised his head towards the horizon. A last shimmer of light brushed the hills as the earth rotated swiftly into night.

"Someday physicians must achieve parity, I cannot accept a world and a God otherwise," His voice softened. "My father .... that was different. He could. He had that special faith. Not me. Perhaps that is why I became what I am, and not what he wanted." He paused for a moment. "Martin, you know what saddens me the most?"

The short balding aide turned for the answer.

"It is that I will not be here when that day comes." He pointed through the tent door. " Even sadder, neither will they. I wonder how many more will die until the Father of our Christ balances the scale?"

CHAPTER TWO

The Surgery Tent was crowded with litters shunted over from the selection area. The grey-haired surgeon looked up with a weary sigh at his replacement.

"Be through in a minute," he cheerfully called out as he probed an eye socket with a long steel tenaculum that he had just used on another patient. Carefully, he pinched off the crushed optic nerve. The doctor reached into a large bale of cotton batting on the floor. He poked the lint into the open cavity to stop the bleeding. He raised the young boy to a sitting position and wound several rolls of linen over the side of the skull."

" That's a good lad. Now about you," He gently helped the patient off the table. Two assistants moved the patient to a chair and gave him a large tin cup of whiskey to drink.

"They're all your's, John. " He saw Spencer's hollow stare. His lack of response. He added, "It must really be bad out there."

The young doctor nodded mechanically.

"You know, John, I haven't been out of here for ten hours. When will the damn thing stop?"

The young doctor moved aside to let the surgeon leave the tent, then took his place at the table.

The amputations started again

One arm.

One wrist.

A leg.

A hand.

Another leg.

The limbs tossed into a long wooden box on the floor.

Each patient placed on the same unwashed table, fully clothed.

The same instruments.

The same unwashed skillful fingers.

John operated swiftly as Martin directed the never-ending flow from the waiting stretchers.

The white cloth cone over the patient's face to hide his human identity. The slow drip....drip....drip.... of ether sulfate. Then, when the ether supply ran out, chloroform. The convulsive twitching until deep anesthesia.....blessed sleep.

The surgeon took his carved bistoury, sharpened it on an Alabama hone stone kept in his pocket and etched a sharp incision around the damaged extremity. The blade slashed deeper as Martin held the limb out straight. Spurts of blood shot up whenever the knife cut a major artery. John would insert his fingers into the wound and pinch off the bleeding vessel. Then, with his other hand, he would take one of the dangling horsehair threads looped around the top button of his jacket and tie off the bleeder. He did not cut the ends of the ligatures. He left them untrimmed. The long tails dangled from the stump like a cat-of-nine-tails. The bone was severed with rasping short saw. The limb off, the plaster strips in place, the man was awakened and moved.

Another. The head of a three-inch shell in his abdomen, pressing against the spine. Removed without more damage. The skin edges brought together with linen strips....sealing in the battle filth.

Another. The bullet piercing the skill. Augers grinding a two-inch hole. A trephining unchanged since the days of the pharaohs. Spencer's fingers ran lightly over the brain, gently teasing away fragments of bone, clotted blood and hair, and a large piece of the man's cap. The cranial defect covered with linen plaster.

Still they came.

Amputations.

Wound packings.

Amputations.

One soldier, his abdomen sliced open by a Confederate bayonet. As hard as he tried, John could not replace the intestines. Despite anesthesia, the abdominal muscles remained in spasm. Spencer instructed Martin to take the patient by the head and another grab the patient by the heels. They lifted the boy off the table and let his buttocks drop to the floor, jackknifing him in the middle. Using a pair of silver spoons, Spencer forced the intestines back. The incision was closed with wide-spaced sutures and collodion adhesive.

When the last patient left the table, the floor was slippery with the blood of Massachusetts's finest. The crimson had congealed on the tired doctor's jacket, his face and hair. He could taste it in the back of his throat. His ears still heard the cries...the pleading. He wiped his hands on his pants. He still had one last duty before sleep.

The front had shifted so quickly that the 21st had been unable to set up a Hospital Tent for a surgical ward. A small white frame house on the other side of the woods was commandeered. If the front stabilized, civilian nurses recruited by the United States Sanitary Commission would arrive. For the moment, the men lay in the abandoned farmhouse, on blood and urine soaked straw, still in soiled battle uniforms and stinking of vomit and feces.

Assistants moved among them casting silent shadows. To some, they offered whiskey, soup, and water. To others, the universal panacea.....laudanum.

John Spencer knew that there was nothing more he could do. In two hours, he had exhausted the entire store of medical wisdom accumulated over the centuries.

If shock and hemorrhage were overwhelming..... the soldiers would die.

If bowel and kidney fistulas drained fluids....... they would die.

If gangrene took hold .... they would die.

If amputations were placed too close to the site of trauma, the stumps would rot and ....they would die.

If bowels perforated .... they would die.

If the latrines drained into the well-water....they would die.

if the lice jumped from one body to another, diseases yet to be named typhus and dysentery would triumph, and ....they would die.

If all these things did <u>not</u> come to pass, and, life was preserved, they would return to the world ......as cripples.

John Owen Spencer knew all this. Yet he pretended not to, as he moved along the rows, bending down to touch each in turn. Martin followed like a faithful shadow to record the treatments.

Patients burning with the fever from hidden pus...... strong enemas.

The speeding pulse from blood loss........repeated blood-letting, almost to the point of death.

Pain of exposed flesh.....laudanum.

Pain from festering sores....... laudanum.

Laudanum.

Laudanum.

By mouth.

By rectum.

Mixed with whiskey.

Mixed with rose water.

By itself alone.

Always…….. that wonderful, wonderful distillate of opium.

Pain…. and laudanum.

John gave wry laugh. Morphine and quinine. Monk's bark and the poppy.

An apology from God for the banishment? Two plants from the Garden of Eden. Did God toss them out along with Adam and Eve? Where were the others, he wondered ?

John stopped by the side of his last patient. The pale light revealed a handsome young man. The quality of his uniform showed wealth. Why had he not purchased his way out of conscription for $300 like so many other rich sons?

His face was square with hazel eyes and a prominent thrust of his jaw. Spencer knew the lad never asked for special treatment. He refused to be separated from the wounded under his command. He was a soft-mannered boy who somehow had wandered into the War. Now, maimed for life, he was finding it difficult to justify his decision, yet unwilling to admit he had been a fool.

An exploding land mine had shattered his body. Spencer amputated both legs above the knees. Hot shrapnel had ripped away his genitals. Both testicles were found dangling by shreds of skin. They were cut off with the crushed penis, leaving a female hole to urinate through.

He lay there in torment, throbbing stumps elevated on a dirty block of wood. As John bent closer foul vapors rose from the dressings. Twisted lengths of black silk hung underneath the linen. A slow drip of fluid ran down their lengths into a rusty iron cup.

Spencer gently removed the dressings. The ends of the stumps were alive with hundreds of swollen white grubs. The patient's eyes quickly darted downward. He let out a shrill shriek and cringed back, trying desperately to remove himself from what he saw. His hands seized the doctor's arms, terrified.

"Matthew, they look evil, but they do no harm. They eat only <u>dead</u> flesh." He held onto his smile. " They will clean up the wounds and keep them fresh. They do a better job than those men," indicating the assistants moving around the room. He continued to stroke the boy's hands.

"Matthew, Matthew. Do not be afraid of them. Perhaps God sends these foul little insects to help us in a strange way. Do not pick them off the stumps like the other men. Please, trust me, son."

The boy's fright slowly gave way to the soothing reassurance. Spencer picked up the right stump and untangled the ligatures. He gave the first thread a gentle tug. It did not budge. He repeated this with the second strand. The same result. The third suture parted easily from the leg. John was relieved to see no gush of blood. He continued, testing every thread. Finished, he hooked seven more sutures around his jacket button for the next patient.

John could see the patient wondering about what he was doing.

`"Matthew, these ligatures tie off the blood vessels. The stump will never heal properly until all the silk is removed. If we take them too early the artery will bleed . .

He patted the boy on the shoulder, "You are doing just fine, Matthew,"

The boy said nothing as he watched the surgeon uncover the mutilated remnants of his manhood. John inspected the cruel emptiness between his legs. His eyes surveyed the virile thighs and pelvis, the wide chest and muscular shoulders, the handsome face. The physician kept his tears inside for the waste.

As he left, Spencer could see the boy's eyes drawn like a magnet to the maggots at the ends of his fore-shortened trunk. Perhaps, knowing this, he should not have been surprised the next evening when the boy was missing. During the night Matthew Harcross had pulled out the sutures from both stumps. Without even a prayer to his Maker, he bled slowly to death. Spencer's assistant handed the surgeon the silk ligatures from the body. John stared at the strands, still knotted at one end.

John Owen Spencer was twenty-four years old.

CHAPTER THREE

MASSACHUSETTS 1862

Z ebadiah Harcross was not a man to wonder. He did not reason why the Almighty caused the sun to heat the tropical oceans. He did not ask why the vapor-laden air swept north four thousand miles to the American continent to condense upon the granite mountains of Vermont. As snow in the winter and rain in the spring, water joined in rivulets, then streams, finally to thunder into the rocky bed of the Quabbin, its source shrouded by haze curtaining the horizon.

Zebadiah was not a man of doubt. He did not question this powerful energy. For him, Nature existed to be wrestled to the ground until it pleaded for mercy, and then enslaved.

Zebadiah Harcross was not a man of religion. He was a man of faith. He believed he was placed upon the earth to crush the devil. To make of the wilderness a Garden of Genesis. He believed that if he labored and his sweat was crowned with gold, he would be guaranteed the Grace of God as his eternal reward.

Zebadiah Harcross was a proud man. Short and stocky of trunk, he stood with thick legs straddling the basalt ridge overlooking the Quabbin River. His square face was framed by dark brown sideburns tinged with grey. The same hair covered his head. Fierce tufts sheltered eyes which constantly scanned in all directions. His prominent chin, clean- shaven, thrust out from under thin tightly compressed lips. He was pleased with what he saw.

He wore a tall stove-pipe hat whose black felt gave off shimmers of heat, a dark frock coat with large velvet lapels, grey trousers, and shoes which laced higher than the shins. Despite the warmth, his neck was encased in a high starched collar which folded over a black moiré cravat.

He strode back and forth with short impatient steps, beating the sides of his thigh with a long roll of papers. For eleven years, Zebadiah Harcross had fought to bring the Quabbin to its knees. He had almost won. There remained only a single blow.

He was fifty nine years old. How many more years did he have? He had one son. His heir. Harcross's eyes squinted against the glare of the sun as he traced the river north until he found what he was looking for. The final battle was to be fought….<u>there</u>. He pursed his lips in a gesture of determination. One remaining shackle to rivet onto the river….. and it would be his. His and Matthew's.

Eleven years ago, on a yarn-buying trip for his textile mill in Lowell, Zebadiah had stood for the first time on this very spot. He had ridden for hours, cursing each time his horse stumbled on the hills overlooking the Quabbin River in central Massachusetts. As he picked himself up for the third time, he glanced down into the valley. It was a clear day. The green banks set off the ribbon of water as it flowed south.

Zebadiah Harcross was not admiring the beauty of Nature but the unusual course of the river. It made almost a complete loop back on itself, a perfect ox-bow enclosing a large spit of land which lay like a green pendant surrounded by blue. However, what caught his attention was a rough patch of white in the river bed which meant only one thing .... rapids.

Excited, he rode for miles, up and down on the banks, jotting figures on a piece of paper, until the setting sun forced him to stop. Satisfied with his calculations, he entered the small town perched at the tip of the pendant and transacted his business. Three weeks later, he was back. This time, two men accompanied him. One represented the Whiting mill owners of Lawrence. The other a Brewster of Boston, whose family money from the slave trade was available for a price. Within one month, the entire pendant had been bought and transferred to the newly-formed Cromwell Water Power Company, along with rights to the river for a distance of twenty miles above and below the loop. Two months later, three thousand Irish immigrants from Boston were brought to Cromwell. At a cost of fifty-two Roman Catholic lives, a dam was thrown across the river where the loop started.

Harcross knew that the rapids meant only one thing. The river dropped a one hundred and twenty seven feet as it bent around the oval peninsula of land. They built the dam and blocked the river before it made its descent. The dream came true when a canal was dug across the pendant connecting the two arms of the loop. The water now surged through the flat heart of Cromwell generating enormous amounts of power as it fell the distance. One year later, a second canal was built. Within five years three canals crisscrossed this once green jewel. Six-story mills replaced pasture. Deep in the cellars, horizontal water turbines spun, night and day, as water rushed to a lower level. Blocks of cheap housing packed tightly against the mills to eliminate waste time between the sixteen hour shifts, six days a week, from the age of fourteen until death.

By the time of the outbreak of the Rebellion, Zebadiah had acquired the majority of the Cromwell Water Power Company shares. If the War lasted long enough, he have them all. A cornucopia of riches, given by God to him and his son, for as long as the sun and the winds and the mountains existed. Even now, the old river, weary and polluted, robbed of its energy, and cheated of its past, retained its heritage only in the Indian name which meant 'place to walk with the stars'. By now, all the stars were locked up securely in Harcross strong boxes.

Elizabeth Harcross watched her father with a tolerant smile. She knew only restraint of character kept his pride bottled within. The shackled river. The fertile fields along its banks. The lumber yards above the dam slicing rafts of pine and fir floated down from the north. The textile mills converting soiled rags into rivers of pure white writing paper. The soot-drenched foundries casting the mighty turbines which sucked power from the canals. The huge multi-bladed rotors changing this frantic kinetic energy into 30,000 horsepower. The miles of leather belts whirring and slapping from cellar to roof. All paid tribute to the Master of the Quabbin.

To Elizabeth, the number was not a mathematical abstraction. As by a wizard's wand, the Quabbin was changed into thousands of straining beasts who needed no wages, no food, no lodging, who worked night and day, without demanding a day of rest. Her father had fulfilled this destiny. He expected his tithe for the proud deed.

Each spring and fall the rains raised the river. The excess spilled in a wasted torrent over the dam top despite extra flood boards. In winter, under the ice, the current flow continued at maximum pressure. Only when the hot summer days merged into fall, did the headwaters of the Quabbin dry up and the canals run half empty. The power in the canals fell to an unprofitable 17,000 horsepower. In the cellars of the mills the turbines turned sluggishly. The leather belts turning looms fell slack. The ground-rents charged by the now Harcross Water Power Company dropped by half. Zebadiah would curse the cloudless skies. The water to feed the canals had disappeared over the flood-boards months earlier.

The missing 13,000 horsepower. Zebadiah Harcross's crown of thorns.

Elizabeth was tall like her brother, her height accentuating her large-boned frame. Even the full swelling of her breasts could not counter the almost masculine width of her shoulders. She walked with an easy carriage, as confident as the sweating stallion by her side. Her face was broad with high cheek-bones. Flowing tresses of hazel complimented her brown eyes. The curse of the Harcross genes, the thrust of her chin, could not deny a strong beauty.

She knew she did not have the soft graces admired by the male sex. She carried herself as if hoping that perseverance and shrewdness were an adequate substitute. Sadly, it was an unprofitable exchange.

Elizabeth stood there at the edge of the cliff, oblivious to his stare, pelvis thrust forward, her head arched back to catch the wind. The sun beat full on her face and touched her hair with bronze and red. The stallion by her side snorted white foam from the climb. Its muscles shivered from evaporating sweat. When he moved, two fleshy globes swung under his rectum like bell clappers. His mane sent wild streamers into the wind.

Zebidiah watched his daughter. He thought of Matthew. Could nature have confused the mold?

"Elizabeth!" His voice was harsh against the wind. "What do you think?"

Her finger traced the course of the Quabbin. Moving upstream, it circled Cromwell, measured the water backed up behind the dam, continued north as the river became again a thin line eight miles higher. Elizabeth followed the valley to locate the spot.

"Pulpit Rock," she pointed.

"It must work, Elizabeth. A second dam at Pulpit Rock will back up enough spring to run the three canals...." He gave a sly grin, "maybe .... even ....enough water for.... a fourth."

Elizabeth raised her head. She could see the high brick chimneys scratching the sky to trap the draft winds. Even now, dirty smudges of smoke were rising through the clear air. Her expression turned bitter. It would never be hers. Why wasn't she born the male heir instead of the weakling who rebelled against Zebadiah's dream and fled into the Army?

Matthew. If <u>only</u> he....

The thought was shameful.

CHAPTER FOUR

I n the valley below, a horse-drawn cart was slowly making its way along the high edge of Pulpit Rock whose sheer sides squeezed the waters white and turbulent. The driver was in no hurry to return home to the Flats along the lower canals. The brown and white blotched mare stopped, grateful for the respite.

Patrick Francis O'Connell let the reins drop. With a painful half-jump, he hopped to the ground. He patted the horse and reached into his pocket for a sweetened biscuit. In the underbrush, insects buzzed, playing out their frantic life cycles. Through the screen of trees, he could hear the water tearing against the granite crevasse.

Millennia ago, Nature had split the land for the Quabbin River. Only Zebadiah Harcross would have wished to snap together the river banks and block the water's passage. For this prematurely aged Irishman of forty seven, the natural wonder was a thing of beauty which the Lord had made for all.

O'Connell's chest and trunk were doubled over by a crooked spine. Childhood rickets had twisted his ribs and bowed his legs out so wide that when he walked, he tilted from side to side. Each step pained as his hips rotated in eroded sockets. He had lost all his teeth years ago from malnutrition. His jaws had receded. When he talked, which was seldom, his cheeks sucked inward, cracking his face in two. His hair grey. Rough stubble covered his face. He wore a collarless shirt, limp with sweat. Around his hollow buttocks, trousers hung, held by a pair of worn green suspenders. He made his slow way to the crag which projected out over the river like a lectern, giving the site its name, Pulpit Rock. The young girl who climbed spritely after him was as fair as he was ugly. For the O'Connells, Nature had balanced its books.

Kathleen 0'Connell was two or three inches taller than her father. She stood erect with her bones straight and strong. Her skin, perhaps a bit too pale, was set off by jet black hair. She took off the hat and shook her head. A carpet of ebony rippled down to her shoulders. Her green eyes were spaced widely with long lashes. Eyebrows kissed in the depression above the tiny nose. Her lips were large and touched with red. When she smiled, sunlight caught the flash of glistening white teeth.

Patrick looked with pride at his daughter. He reached to help her. She laughed him away. Picking up her long skirt, she leaped ahead with a carefree grace and strength. Her father could not help catching a view of the shapely calves and thighs, the flush from exertion, the fine bead of perspiration on her upper lip. Her eyes were bright. Her color high.

His eyes dropped to her breasts which was confined by the tight lacing of her cotton bodice. He saw the tiny waist and hips which could be encircled with barely two spans. If he had the urge to hug her tight and run his fingers through her hair and rest her head on his shoulder and express his love, he restrained himself. He recalled the memory of Kathleen's mother, as young and beautiful when he married her as was her only child.

Mother and daughter. The Lord had made them both. Now he possessed only one. The Church had won.

Should he have saved the mother at the price of the child, assuming God even allowed such a bargain? Should the doctor have ground the augur into the skull of the unborn? Should he have deserted Christ to save his wife instead of Kathleen? His bride of one year, whose soft thighs he had loved. The virgin he violated with his manhood and who received his seed. He murdered her and gained a daughter whose mother's beauty brought tears.

He raised his head, but the sky gave no comfort. His fists clenched. Did God keep physicians ignorant to force a test of faith, like Abraham and Isaac? Why was God so cruel when His Son had been so unselfish? Why could not the physicians have saved them both?

Kathleen knew her mother died in childbirth, but Patrick refused to reveal more. She would catch him looking at her in a strange way.

Patrick feared the young men who came to pay court. If the suitor expressed serious intent, he would turn hostile and forbid further entry. Kathleen knew that there was locked up within her father a frightening secret which involved her mother.

She gave him a kiss on the cheek. "Father, the day is too beautiful to look so sad."

They sat there, steeped in the warm fall day. Occasionally, Kathleen would throw some pebble into the crevasse. If she leaned far over the edge, spray would land on her face and she would rub her cheeks, making them blush red.

The air was incredibly still. The winds which swept from the west, skipped from the bluff to bluff, never dropping into the hot valley below. Darning needles and green flies buzzed aimlessly above the vegetation, hop-scotching with the Monarch butterflies and grey-beige moths. The mosquitoes annoyed as they sought a moist patch of skin for blood.

Suddenly, Kathleen saw Patrick reach for her,

"What is it, father?"

"Kathleen, girl," he answered, " be a good child. Go back to the wagon and bring the bottle of whiskey under the seat. Don't worry. Everything will be alright."

His body started convulsing. His teeth chattered, "G., , go...to.. the...wag....," He rocked back and forth, losing his balance. His face was red. Sweat beaded and ran down his neck. His eyes were bloodshot. A vise of pain squeezed his temples. He struggled to breath. He drew his legs tight and wrapped his arms around his body as his temperature climbed to almost deadly levels.

She returned almost instantly. She raised his head so that he could drink. His lips were swollen. Most of the liquor dripped on the ground.

"Thank you...Kate..." He forced a smile. "Don't be afraid, girl," His breathing became easier. His limbs relaxed. He managed to sit up.

"Its the ague. Three years since I've had an attack. Give me a minute and you can help me back to the wagon. When we get home, the Jesuit tree extract will help. It will take more than the fever to carry old Patrick O'Connell away."

His smile vanished as quickly as it had appeared. He turned ashen. Kathleen pulled him toward her, preparing for another attack of shakes. He tore away and ran as fast as he could to a clump of bushes. The flux tore at his bowels. He vomited the stomach's contents. Then came the diarrhea. Patrick tried to stay out of his sight as he dropped his trousers.

Kathleen could hear the retching. She cried out for something that she could do Patrick did not answer. When he returned, she could smell the foul odors on his clothing. He had tried to clean himself with tufts of straw and grass which stuck to his trousers. He walked with his body turned away, ashamed of the soiling.

"The sickly season has started. It will be with us until the frost. Some years the shakes come and others it don't. You can never tell. Some never get it. Others catch the ague and chill and shiver and vomit. The flux comes upon them until they feel their insides have been purged to death. Most recover. Some... die. I've had it seven seasons. Last time you were too young to know. Each time I suffer until the cold cleans the air."

Kathleen did not understand.

"There is something about the air that brings the sickness. Never in the winter. It seems to get worse when new Negroes come. Escaped slaves from the south, or freed Negroes from the Indies. The black people move into the shanties along the river. Then we get another sickly season. I don't understand because some years the shakes come without them."

He doubled up in a paroxysm of coughing which ended by spitting up a plug of blood-flecked sputum.

"But, Kate I have seen it worse. Before the swamps were drained outside of Boston, that was the worst. Every year, man, woman and child, came down with the chills. Cromwell, is better. The farms are high and dry above the river." He hoisted himself onto the buckboard. "Most people here are safe. Especially the quality up in the Highlands." He pointed to the estates of the mill owners high on the west bank of the Quabbin, secure along the windy ridge.

" They never get the sickness. In the Flats we still do, but only some years and less each time. As long as the river flows narrow and swift and hard through the valley, we are safe." He thought of a time only he could see. "Someday, the sickness will disappear forever, and your childr..." he caught himself stumbling over the simple word, " Someday...all of us will be safe."

Patrick took one last look at Pulpit Rock before snapping the whip over the mare's back.

"Some people say, it is only a rumor, that Zebadiah and that daughter of his are planning to dam Pulpit Rock." His tone somber." The reservoir will flood the land upstream. The banks are low there. The water will spread out for miles. He plans to release the spring water in summer and fall when the canals run dry. You know what that will leave behind?" He warned, " Miles of wet swamps."

" The sickness will get worse." He shivered though the sun was hot. "Not only the ague like mine, with the shakes that grind your body into pieces, but the other!" His voice shook in fear. " The black water fever, the sickness that <u>kills</u>. Not up in the Highlands. Not for those bastards like Harcross who will get richer from the extra water power. No, Kate. We will get the yellow fever and die!'

Patrick gathered up his energy for the drive home. He could feel the shakes starting again. He drove the mare faster, with desperate lashes. He was no longer thinking of Zebadiah Harcross. His only thought was for the bottle of bitter black medicine of the Jesuits. He did not notice the grey speck which landed on his forearm and paused for the briefest second before flying off.

The wagon trundled along the half-deserted streets leading into Cromwell. It clattered with wood planks for Patrick's funeral home. Those who saw the wagon driven by the hunched over father were struck by the beauty of the daughter. The wagon wheels hit a deep rut in the roadbed, stirring up a cloud of dried horse manure. Patrick gave another moist cough.

The cart passed the Irish church. Patrick O'Connell was not a religious man. He had left the Church after Rachel's death. However, he quickly crossed himself. He had only one prayer to the Virgin. One wish. He asked for his daughter's life.

CHAPTER FIVE

Part One

POLAND 1862

For fifty million years, the bird had not changed. Even the lice in its feathers were untouched by evolution. Although the species had different members, they all shared the same compulsion ..... the urge to kill.

The bird had no charms for the poet. It was no swan or peacock. The dull brown feathers were streaked with mottled grey. The eyes could not even rotate in their sockets, forcing the head to make short jerky movements. Moreover, for a predator, its forward vision was a tiny window.

This predator never killed for pleasure. Only food. It could go for days without raw flesh. But, when hungry, it climbed the sky to seek and destroy.

The hawk was not a reasoning creature. It never knew the abstraction known as freedom as it soared for hours over bogs and coves. It avoided bodies of water, seeking hot currents rising from the land. Like magic, with wings wide, the bird would mount the column of air and rise vertically until out of sight.

This particular male hawk could never be free. From birth, a rigid code of obedience had been taught by a two-legged master. A leather restraint trapped the legs. A leather hood blinded it. It could not escape bondage. Each day, it was carried on a heavily gloved fist for training. It learned not to be frightened of man.

The September air was cold. The setting sun lit the sky with orange pink. The hawk had not been fed for five days. It was desperate for food. Then, so far below that it appeared a moving speck, the predator spied prey.

No conscious thought was needed. Instinct pulled the wings close in.

Gravity reached up with a vicious tug. It fell…. faster and faster. Diving with a shrill scream, talons stretched wide, beak open, the eyes were fixed on the humans below.

It hunted as it had done for millennia.

Mordechai Ringelblum could see the day was ending. He lashed the mare pulling the heavy cart. It was Friday night. Soon his wife would be lighting the Sabbath candles, a ritual so ancient it did not need his presence. He looked at the young soft-complexioned boy at his side and shrugged in despair. Sabbath. The candles. Everything his fathers before him had suffered to preserve. For what? For an only child, a clever boy, who ignored his heritage? Give him a chance to carouse and drink with the goyim. To make a zloty, he would spit on the sacred Ark itself. The rabbi said it must be a punishment from God. He whipped the horses in frustration. Mordechai searched his soul for his sins.

Avram could see his fathers impatience. Sunset. Sunrise. Sabbath. Who cared? A few more miles, A quick meal. He would take the horse from the dung pile called Biala-Poliaska, to Dzerzhinsk, There, he would find a woman who, for a coin, would forget he was circumcised and had dangling side-burns. Maybe, if he was lucky, without the coin.

His face was smooth with dimples when he smiled. Long black curls spilled down both cheeks. Silken eyelashes gave him a deceptively feminine appearance. His shoulders were narrow. His hands slender. His torso and trunk had not yet hardened. Only the large swelling in his crotch proved the end of adolescence.

He thought of last Friday night with Sonja the youngest in the whorehouse on Chabot Street. She was no more than fifteen with tiny pink nipples and blonde pubic hair. After fondling him, she wrapped a ribbon around his swollen shaft like a leash and showed him off to the other customers like a bobbed stallion.

Back in her bed, Avram struggled to insert his organ between her legs. The door flung open. Other couples crowded in to watch. They wagered bets. They lashed his buttocks with their belts to spur him on. They toasted champagne when he finally speared her belly.

Avram relived the erotic memory. His penis sprung up. He dropped his arm between his legs and pressed hard, letting the wagon's rhythm massage the sensitive head. When he finally came with a silent shudder, he bit his tongue rather than cry out. Finally, he relaxed against the wagon back and took the same somber expression of his father.

The cart gave a sharp turn onto the dirt road along the west bank of the Neris River. The setting sun gave the air a rare iridescence. In the distance, streamers of smoke signaled the outskirts of his village. Seventeen years watching his father sweat to make furniture from over-priced lumber the merchants in Minsk sold and then bought back at shameful prices. The taxes which bled away what was left.

It made no difference whether Biala-Poliaska was owned by Prussia, Poland, or the Tsar. It was always the same. The Landsteiners ruled the territory, collected the taxes from which they were exempt, and passed the gold on to whoever's troops were stationed outside of Minsk.

There were rumors in the village that Moscow was sending soldiers to crush the rebellion against the new forced army conscription. Avram heard his mother and father talking in whispers. They feared as if the Tsar's army would destroy his Jewish soul. The army did not scare Avram. Only that the draft would interrupt the pleasures his new prosperity had bought him.

Avram had talked Mordechai into selling the products of his cabinet shop directly to the farmers, keeping the profit which had gone to the middle-men from Minsk. Avram bought his lumber directly from the farmers. Valuable oak or maple, walnut, cherry, wherever a field had been cleared for planting.

The jingle of zlotys and even a stray Russian ruble or two made a pleasant sound in his pocket as the wagon rumbled over the wooden bridge into Biala-Poliaska. Avram was still in a relaxed mood from his discharge. Neither he nor his father could hear the high-pitched screech dropping out of the sky towards the two Sabbath chickens tied to the top of their cart.

The hawk tore at the hens, claws immobilizing the birds. With one easy bite, it severed the spines. For a moment, neither Mordechai nor Avram realized what was happening. When they saw the hawk tearing the carcasses to shreds and feathers, they tried to fight back. Avram grabbed a board. He scrambled on top of the wagon and hit the bird with the club end. The hawk flew at the boy, catching its claws in his scalp and trying to rip his eyes and face. Mordechai was stricken with terror. He threw himself on the bird, tearing it away from his son's body with his own bare hands.

The hawk turned on him, slashing his head. The blood excited the animal. It flew from one to the other, escaping their blows.

By the time the two horsemen reached the wagon, the Ringelblums were huddled under the cart, with the hawk seated on top finishing its meal. The Count and his son were dressed in English riding habits with jodhpurs and jackets soiled by dust. The father was short and heavy set, with dark sideburns and a coarse face with pox scars. He swayed back and forth in the saddle, taking swallows from a silver flagon strapped around his shoulder.

The son was not drunk. He swung down from the horse in an easy glide. He walked over to the cart and climbed on top. Both of his hands were encased in brown leather gauntlets which flared above the elbow. He reached his left hand out for the bird and secured the hood over its head. Holding the docile falcon before him like a lighted torch, he jumped lightly off the wagon.

Casmir Landsteiner was short like his father. His face was covered covered with a black beard. His lips were thick and fleshy. He constantly ran his tongue over them. His nose was long and narrow like his fathers. The heavily-lidded eyes were half-closed. He walked with a swagger.

"Alright, Jews. You can get out!" he sneered at the pair still cringing under the wooden cart for protection.

Avram emerged first. As he crawled out he saw the Count's son standing in front of him, legs spread apart, with a look of contempt. Avram gave a frightened start when he saw the hawk fluttering on the gauntlet. Casmir reached out and gently stroked the bird while uttering soft cooing sounds.

Avram helped his father get up. Avram tore his shirt into strips and wrapped them around his fathers wounds. He found a flask of water and gave it to him.

The Count watched the Ringelblums with several noisy belches. Whiskey ran down the front of his shirt onto the dusty ground.

Casmir stopped his stroking and started back to his horse. Avram forgot his pain. All he could see was his father, trembling from shock, the dead chickens, the blood, the callous indifference of the Poles. His eyes narrowed with hate. He grabbed Casmir by the shoulder.

"You bastard! Look what you have done," he shouted.

The son stepped back. He raised his left arm and threw the bird at the boy's face. Avram uttered a shriek and dropped to the ground, holding his hands about his head for protection.

Casmir let out a howl of pleasure. His father, watching, laughed at the young boy's terror.

"He is <u>still</u> hooded, Jew." He retrieved the hawk which was as frightened at being thrown as was the victim. "Remember, scum, never touch me again….. unless……."

He stood back to examine Avram. His eyes ran up and down the half-naked body. He touched the skin, the down-covered cheeks, the soft lines of the hips and thighs, the genitals which strained the thin fabric. He licked his lips with the tip of his tongue. "Unless……" His voice faded to a half-whisper.

Avram watched. He did not flinch. Mordechai was still traumatized by the vicious attack, scared of the Landsteiners, and willing to accept his wounds and even the loss of his chickens, just to get home, to see Sarah, and make the Sabbath benediction. He pleaded with his son. If Avram would keep quiet and let the Count and his son go, they could avoid more harm. One did not play games with the Christian nobles and expect to win.

Casmir started to leave, but his bladder was pressing. He hoisted himself off his horse and undid the side buttons of his pants. Leaning against his mount for support, he pulled out his penis. It was short and thick, the head covered with a long hood of skin. He stripped back the foreskin and started to piss. A stream of yellow sprayed out in all directions.

Mordechai turned his head away in shame.

Casmir reached into his pocket for a handful of small gold coins.

" Here, Jew, " he smiled and threw them in the puddle of urine. " Jewish blood and Polish piss. They are worth about the same." He gave a shrill sound like a horse whinnying.

Mordechai's hand tightened on his son's arm. To his surprise, Avram walked over to the Count's son. He was unexpectedly calm. He knelt down and picked up the coins. He dried each in turn, rubbing them on his crotch. Casmir watched. Here was another game he liked to play.

Within the week, the Landsteiner steward visited the poor Jewish workshop. The tall balding flunkey strode through the work shed. His riding crop touched the furniture he wished to buy, though his face never left the real object of the visit. It was obvious the man had negotiated often for his young master.

" The price is high." Avram stared at the man without flinching.

" How much ?"

"One hundred gold crowns."

Mordechai was dumbstruck. He would have asked one crown. He would have settled happily for half that amount. The steward was upset by the exorbitant figure. He was accustomed to pocketing the difference between what he paid and the amount he told Casmir. This Jew with the child's face was going to be difficult.

"Five,"

"Five?" Mordechai burst out. He rushed forward to kiss the Pole's hands, dazzled by his good fortune.

"No. It is one hundred. For that price, I will deliver the merchandise to your master..,.." casting his eyes down in mock humility, "in person,"

"Twenty-five," The leonine-faced man threw his hands up in a final gesture. For fifty zlotys, he could buy the village butchers son who had been copulating with the steward's cow.

"Seventy-five." Avram knew the steward could not go back without him.

"Fifty," the Steward parried in a low tone.

"It is fifty, then," He held on to his soft smile.

The Pole turned to the father.

"Your son is to deliver the furniture tomorrow to the old game-warden's cabin in the forest." He was angry at being cheated out of his usual profit.

"Yes....yes...." Mordechai stammered, still awestruck by his son's witchcraft.

Throughout the next day, the father kept pulling his beard and muttering to his wife,, "I don't understand. I don't understand."

It was late in the afternoon when Avram approached the shingled lodge on the west side of Biala-Poliaska. Casmir's horse was tethered in the front yard. The animal was shivering from the twilight chill. The weeds growing through the stone path, the dirt-clouded windows, the roof where the timber had cracked over the second floor dormer, all showed the building's neglect. Through the window, Avram could see the glow of a fire. The door was open.

"Come in, Jew."

For an instance, Aveam felt like turning back. The vision of his father, bloodied and scarred, the contempt of the Landsteiner pissing on the coins, kept him there.

Casmir was sprawled on a pile of pillows on the floor. Empty liquor bottles were scattered. A kerosene lamp on a nearby table gave a narrow circle of light. He waved the boy closer.

"Ah, yes. Fifty crowns. That was what you squeezed out of Anatole, wasn't it ?" He ran his hand up the boy's leg, kneading the thigh muscle until Avram winced with pain. "What makes you think you are worth it, Jew?"

Avram did not answer. Instead, he took off his clothes and folded each garment neatly. As he lowered his trousers, he turned shyly away from the son, shielded by the shadows. Casmir savagely cracked his riding whip across his buttocks, raising an angry red welt.

Avram cried out and raised his hand to strike back. Casmir gave a high-pitched laugh.

"No, no, my little Jew. <u>You</u> do not hit <u>me</u>. Not for fifty crowns."

Casmir ground the handle deep into the boy's testicles until he screamed with pain. He reached up and stroked the boy's penis until it enlarged. He wrapped the whip around it in a tight spiral. He pulled the boy towards him, then lowered the whip to the ground, forcing Avram down like a dog.

"Yes.." he purred, touching the saliva in the corners of his mouth. "Perhaps you <u>are</u> worth fifty crowns. But... we ...shall .... have....to see."

Avram grabbed a hold of the leather handle.

"Fifty crowns. Where are they?"

Casmir ripped the whip off with a quick lash slicing the skin "There," he pointed in back of him.

Avram squinted in the darkness. He gave a start. Hidden in the shadow was the falcon, his feet lashed together. By its side was a velvet pouch, half open with gold coins. The bird's head arched from side to side at the sight of the strange figure.

"Now, it is time for you to earn your pay." Casmir's voice cut through the still air.

Over the next hours, Avram did not moan as the Count tore through his body, lacerating his rectum. He uttered not a sound as he tasted the pollution the son discharged. Not a whimper as his flesh was whipped and beaten until blood flowed. Avram only smiled as he cradled the Pole's head and plied him with more and more liquor.

In the early hours of the morning, the Polish aristocrat could no longer think of a new torment. He lay back in a drunken slumber. Avram stood up and shed the servile crouch he had assumed for hours. He rubbed the crusts of blood and serum where the whip had raked his skin. He brought in from his cart heavy rope and tied the Pole's hands and feet. Once or twice Casmir twisted in pain as the bindings dug into his skin. Avram stroked his cheek and helped him swallow more brandy.

Avram went over to the falcon. The bird snapped at his wrist. By now, the boy was indifferent to pain. He threw a heavy scarf over the bird's head and carried the hawk over to the count's naked body. Avram took his heaviest rope and lashed one end around the Pole's testicles. He tied the falcon's feet to the other end. He uncovered the bird's eyes. Avram unloaded the purchased furniture and placed it neatly around the room. Finished, he sat down and waited until the snoring victim woke up.

The sun was high in the sky by the time Casmir finally stirred. At first the Pole wondered why he could not move. He looked about in a daze. He saw the young boy watching him. He could not understand why the hawk was tugging on his body.

"Let me loose, Jew," he snarled, trying to break free.

Avram waited until Casmir was exhausted by his efforts. The boy stood over him, naked body straddling his head, and calmly urinated on his face. The Pole twisted to escape the flow of urine which splashed into his mouth and his eyes.

"That was Jewish piss."

Avram took his knife and avoiding the falcon's beak, seized the son's penis and slashed off the foreskin.

The Pole gave a shriek as the knife sliced his flesh cutting the artery.

"That was Polish blood." Avram tossed the skin to the falcon, agitated by the smell of blood.

Avram took the kerosene lamp and tilted the brass base so that oil splashed over Casmir's body. He touched the flame to the Pole's skin and watched the fire grow. The victim screamed in agony. His thrashing only frightened the trapped bird and spread the flames.

34

The raptor was desperate from an instinctive fear of fire. It tried to escape. The rope grew taut, but held. Its eyes darted, blinking rapidly. The flames grew closer. It could feel the heat and taste the blood. It could not reason, but deep in its brain, an age-old reflex told what it must do. The fire consumed the room in a cauldron of orange and red as Casmir's falcon ate its way to safety.

Avram could hear the screams through the woods. Casmir's horse trotted docilely, tied to the back of the wagon. Avram counted the gold twice. Fifty crowns...as agreed. Casmir was a true gentleman.

When he reached his home, Avram's parents were not there. He could not wait for them to return from the market. He divided the gold and left half in his fathers money box. He gave one last glance around his home knowing he would never see it again.

For the first and last time in his life, he cried.

CHAPTER FIVE

Part Two

Avram Ringelblum buried the saddle with Landsteiner crest. Each jostle of the horse brought back the pain and humiliation he had suffered from Casmir. Below Minsk, the Neris entered the Neman for its final journey to the Baltic. Where two waterways joined, Avram stopped in a small farming village and sold the horse, adding to his hoard. He purchased some cotton fabric and fashioned a binder into which he sewed the gold coins. He cut off his sideburns and the Orthodox fringes dangling from his jacket. He made his way to the river-front and looked for a job on one of the provisioning skiffs accompanying the log rafts to the coast. He had no difficulty getting a berth by working for food and passage.

The Neman River was the border between Russian-occupied Poland and Prussia. Government troops were stationed on all bridges to intercept revolutionaries trying to enter Poland and youths escaping in the other direction from conscription. The ragged flotilla of logs slowly drifted down the center of the channel past the guards.

For the first time since he had fled Biala-Poliaska,   Avram relaxed. His wounds healed. The barge keeper and his wife, two good-natured Latvians, accepted the boy as a substitute for their son who had been killed at Warsaw during the riots of the year before. Only when one of the bearded Ukrainians working on a raft approached Avram with the same desire he had seen in Casmir's eyes, did he fear. He was a refugee who had murdered. He had to get to the sea. He agreed to the man's demands, for a price.....paid in advance.

Late that night, after his body was defiled with the sweat and semen from the illiterate peasant, Avram lowered himself in the flowing water and washed. Then he slit the drunken man's throat and dumped him overboard. He watched the black shape rise and fall in the raft's wake. It twisted in the moon-glow like a stray log until it stayed under.

For the rest of the trip, Avram was never molested. If anything, he was accepted as if he had passed some initiation. He helped the men on the rafts. His muscles grew thick from the work. He learned to keep his balance on the slippery logs. The men shared their vodka with him.

As the Neman drew close to the ocean, peat bogs stretched out on both sides.   Settlements of migrants could be seen cutting the turf. Ponds of stagnant water scarred the land where they had stripped the surface. The current slowed as the river broadened. Clouds of mosquitoes rose from breeding grounds in the bogs. The men cursed and slapped and bled and grew irritable.

Avram was anxious for the trip to be finished. At the port of Memel, he could taste the salt-tinged breezes from the Baltic. People brushed by, oblivious to the Polish refugee with stolen money strapped to his abdomen. Avram had no illusions should the Landsteiner gold be discovered. It was a constant worry during the river trip. Fortunately, the raft dwellers' disdain for personal hygiene protected his secret as he never removed his clothes to bathe.

It took him only half a day to solve the problem. Every seafaring port has its alleys of scavengers, money-changers, thieves. Avram wandered through the streets, bumping into prostitutes, street-hawkers, examining the dirty shops until he located one with a *mezzuzah* on the door. He spoke Yiddish to the proprietor and exchanged his gold for English currency. The old Jew squinted in the dark room. Where had the baby-faced *gonif,* gotten the gold coins? Avram gave the man little time to be curious. He seized the notes and lost himself in the crowd.

Avram got a berth on a sailing vessel bound for Liverpool with racks of leather hides and barrels of tallow. In England, he emerged from the bowels of the ship and purchased new clothing. Spending more of his dwindling supply of money and communicating with difficulty, he managed to obtain a cabin on the next ship leaving for the United States. The purser who took the bribe was most apologetic to the Episcopal priest whose second class cabin was no longer his.

Avram stood on the stem of the side-paddle steamer watching the crew weigh anchor. As the sails unfurled, the wind caught them in a series of cracking whip-snap sounds. He could hear the creak of boards and metal grinding as the ship sailed on the ebb tide. He remained there until the coal-stained horizon over Liverpool gave way to the Atlantic Ocean and his past disappeared over the curve of the earth. Leaving the deck, he searched out the steward and, by lewd gestures, communicated his need. Avram Ringelblum had three weeks before the ship would arrive in Boston. He had much to do.

Avram found what he was looking for deep in the ship, near the quarters of the sailors. When he opened the door, he was greeted by a flood of memories. The overpowering stench of sweet perfume, sweat, and cheap liquor. Sonja on Chabot Street.

"Are you here to look?" High pitched laughter taunted him from all corners of the room. Half-naked girls sidled up to him, amused by his awkward new clothing and the foreign manner,

"He's just a baby."

"Sonny, I think you've made a mistake.

"Come back at the end of the trip. Maybe you'll be bigger by then."

He could not understand the language, but by their gestures, he could guess what they were thinking. For an instant, Avram considered turning back. Before he could decide, a strong hand with practiced fingers slid down the front of his trousers into his crotch and hefted the heavy contents. Before he could stop, a tall blond-haired girl was unbuttoning his trousers.

Whether it was the erotic surroundings or memories of Chabot Street, he could not help himself. He grew excited. His penis rose quickly from his groin.

"Well, he is <u>not</u> a baby." She showed off her prize, her fist clenched tight around the shaft engorging the head. "Look," she stood up, almost towering over Avram. "Our little visitor is a Jew." She smiled, "Well, my little man, Jew or not, I think we can make you happy. But first," her voice hard, " you must pay."

Avram did not understand her words.

She repeated, "Money....Gold.."

It was no good. She picked out a man drinking champagne in the corner, his fingers working deep into the pubic hair of the naked girl on his lap. He translated into Polish. Avram took out several coins. The blonde woman reached out. He was too quick. His hand closed over the money and dropped to his side. He asked the man to translate a special request. He wished the unusual services of one of them in his cabin for the crossing and would pay well. His expression contained no humor or lust. The whore must possess a certain talent. He could see them laughing at his request. He did not care. He knew what he wanted.

His bargain consummated, Avram found it was the tall blonde whore who accompanied him back to his cabin. Except for an occasional walk on the deck and meals, the two never left the cabin. There were the few hours, after his labors, when Avram surrendered to her time-honed artifice.

The night before docking, Avram was satisfied with the success of his task. He fell upon the whore for one last time. Her hands gripped his buttocks, nails digging in deeper with every thrust. Her fingers penetrated, massaging the prostate. He exploded in one wild ejaculation.

When he was asleep, she crept quietly out of the cabin. She returned with three sailors. One was obese and bald with black hair curling over his chest, his arms and fingers. The other two were thin and covered with tattoos and scars. They held him down while the girl searched for his money. Avram wrenched free. The fat one cracked his fist across the Pole's face, crushing his nose and ripping his right cheek with his brass ring. Avram fell back with pain, as he tried to stop the blood streaming down his face. They left, laughing loudly, already in the process of dividing the money.

Avram would always carry on his face the marks of that assault, the broken nose bending to one side. The laceration healed and left a jagged scar across the top of the cheek, ending his handsome features.   It was a face which strangers would pity.

Avram accepted the disfigurement. He could not know of a more lethal gift from the Old World. It started with a sore on the end of his penis near the opening. It did not hurt and vanished within a week. The blonde whore may have stolen his money and his looks and seeded him with syphilis. The Jewish boy had been a quick and clever student. He was <u>not</u> penniless. The prostitute had taught him the English language.

Rich with that currency, Adam Ring stepped ashore into the land of milk and honey.

CHAPTER FIVE

Part Three

The Boston waterfront was that unique marriage of business and adventure at the interface of sea and land. It was a grey fall day, filled with the chill of approaching winter. Layers of fog and coal smoke hung over the crowded docks. Miles of hemp rigging dripped black drops of water. When a cool breeze wove its way through the dense tangle of masts, reefed sails would buckle and dump the wet contents collecting in the canvas folds on the young refugee. Adam Ring turned his collar against the damp. He left the disembarkation pier where the tender had deposited his group after their internment on Deer Island.

Boston, in 1862, was prospering from the War in the south. Europe needed supplies of timber and grain, The Harbor was cluttered by ships with unfurled sails or massive revolving side paddles. There were even a few ships without masts or wheels. The newly invented screw propeller sped them out of sight, as if by magic. Adam stared transfixed by the excitement. Suddenly a huge dray cart pulled by oxen, drenched him with a puddle of murky rainwater filled with dead rats, decaying garbage and horse feces. Cursing, he sought refuge out of the path of lumbering traffic.

At the junction of the streets leading away from the piers, Adam Ring saw groups of people waiting for the new arrivals. Families from his ship walked around him, almost cowering from the strangeness. When a family recognized a relative, it would break away and joyfully seize the small link with the past.

Adam Ring envied their happiness. His cheek still throbbed under the blood-soaked plaster. When he walked, sharp pains stabbed through his rectum. His penis burned when he urinated. A gonorrheal discharge stained his single article of underclothing.

He had no money. He had not eaten since leaving the ship the day before. He wished he, too, had a family to greet him. A tide of people passed by, uncaring. He choked back his helplessness and loneliness and hurried on. By nightfall, Adam had located the industrial slums by the stream of workers, tired, walking fast, shoulders stooped, too exhausted to talk.

The shadows were lengthening in the streets, bathing the crooked alleys in hazy darkness. The sky was a narrow band framed by roofs. One two early stars were visible. His search was almost at an end.

His nostrils caught the aromatic scent of raw wood. He entered the small shop of Jacob Kowalski, Cabinetmaker. For an instant, Adam imagined he was back in Biala-Poliaska. The tall elderly Jew with the long greybeard and black *yarmulka* was his father. The shuffle of dried sawdust on the floor. The familiar piles of fresh wood chips and shavings.

The three workers glanced suspiciously at the stranger. The owner put down the lead pot of boiling hide glue and waved the boy towards him. He stroked his frayed whiskers already weighing the dilemma. Another one, he thought. Just off the boat. But his clothes? Rich materials. Good cut. He saw the bloody bandage. A thief? He moved back, cautious. A *schnorer?* What else? Enough is enough. Every day another beggar..

Why don't they stay over there? He grew angry at being forced to decide between charity and greed.

"What do you want?"

"A job." Adam looked the man full in the face.

"Hah," he laughed. "A job? What do you think this is? The work house? A job?" He waved his hands towards his workers who suddenly started working again. "I go hungry. I starve just to feed those ingrates. What do I need you? A *pischer.*"

He had not missed that this young immigrant could speak to him in English. True his accent was pronounced, his grammar awkward, but somehow this injured boy with *chutzpah* had managed to learn something it had taken him three years to do.

"Here," he reached into his trouser pocket and brought out a small coin. "Take it. Go away. Enough."

Adam returned the coin.

" No charity. Work." He inventoried the room. Before anybody could stop him, he walked over to the youngest worker, a tow-haired bull of a youth two or three years older than himself. He scooped up a handful of shavings. He repeated the process, collecting samples from the other work tables. He brought the specimens over to Kowalski. Adam closed his eyes.

"Pine. Spruce. Hardwood, probably birch." One by one, his fingers isolated a shaving, a crude chip of wood. The tips caressed the grain, parting fibers. "Too much moisture. Unseasoned. Probably fir. And, this...," His fingernail indented the hard surface, "Close grain," He raised the wood to his nose and smelled the resin. "Mahogany. Very nice wood."

Kowalski watched the pantomime, nodding with each answer. The three workers had stopped working. The old man broke the spell, shaking his head violently,

"No. No." he insisted. "I don't need anybody else."

Adam did not say a word. He walked over again to the Swede and threw his saw on the ground. He said in Yiddish,

"That is a rip saw. It should be used only for cutting <u>with </u>the grain. Never across the rings to splinter the surface. No. The *schmuck* should be using,,..." his eyes darted around the room until he found a crosscut saw with tiny off-set teeth, "this!" He thrust the tool at the acne-scarred boy who stood there with a vacuous expression.

"Mr. Kowalski, I will work for nothing. Just a corner to sleep and food. One week. At the end of that time, if I am no good, I will take your charity and leave."

He could see the old man waver, start to shake his head, but stop and examine the ruined plank of wood. The Pole waited, feet planted firmly apart, his fists clenched tightly at his sides, his eyes hungry.

The next morning, the blonde-haired boy was gone. The other two men said nothing, but Adam thought they trembled a little whenever the street door opened.

CHAPTER SIX

B y the spring of 1865, the Confederacy was gutted and flayed by the armies of Grant and Sherman. The fall of Richmond was the *coup de grace* for the long struggle. After the surrender at Appomattox, John Spencer accompanied the Massachusetts Regiment to Washington where he was decommissioned. By now the agonies of war were seared into his memory for a lifetime. Why had he joined the Union cause? A Canadian by birth, the Battle of the North was not his. Perhaps it was the moral issue of slave emancipation, the reverence for all life, which he inherited from his father.

The July sun baked the cinder covered roofs of the train. The cars had been well-used during the war. The *New York, New Haven and Hartford* gilding the sides were tarnished with grime. John managed to force open the stubborn ratchets of the window. The moving car sucked in the searing heat. The wind sent dried tobacco dust twisting in the air. The filth stuck in his throat, choking him. He quickly lowered the window and leaned back, crushing his sweat soaked army jacket against the mohair.

As the miles and hours slipped by, Spencer sank into a pleasant half-slumber. The car gently rocked him from side to side. He felt an almost erotic excitement as his thoughts drifted. Without his knowing, the body started the long process of repair.

His thoughts were dilute. His eyes closed. His head fell forward, nodding with each bounce. He slept as the train drove north skirting the Connecticut River. It crossed into Massachusetts where the fast-flowing river was joined with streams rising in the north. As the locomotive crossed the iron trestle to the west bank of the Quabbin, it let out a shrill whistle awakening the physician. He looked out through the window. It was an eerie sensation. He could see nothing but empty space on both sides. The whine of the wheels rose in pitch as the girders tensed under the weight. It was a relief when the tracks touched earth.

The conductor entered the crowded car. His black suit and stiff round cap defied the heat. His body lurched from side to side, with feet wide spaced for balance. In one hand, he held a limp handkerchief, black with sweat and coal dust.

"Cromwell, Cromwell," he called out.

"How long?" Spencer asked.

"Twenty minutes."

The conductor looked at the dark blue Union uniform, the tall gaunt frame. Without realizing it, he counted four limbs. He thought of his own son, discharged home after Chancellorsville, without his right arm or leg, at the age of eighteen,

"You are...one of the lucky ones," His voice was sad and held a hint of bitterness. His eyes watered. Giving Spencer a guilty pat on his shoulder, he hurried on.

Spencer guessed the man's personal sorrow. It had been like this everywhere on the trip. Families waiting patiently until the steam locomotive quivered to a stop witha screech of scraping steel and billows of steam. At the head of the platform, the soldiers awkwardly descending the steps, most with bandages, crutches and supported by comrades or by the conductor. The few like him, walking with two feet, two hands.

Always with eyes averted from stares, moving swiftly to leave the scene, ashamed to be intact. At the other end of the train, the freight wagons, packed with long wooden coffins. The weeping. The anger. The bewildered children.

From his window, John saw the scene replayed over and over. He reached under the seat and brought out his case of surgical instruments. The black leather was scuffed from years of field duty. The rongeurs, the scalpels, bistouries, all lay cushioned in their worn velvet depressions. Cleansed of blood, but dull with a patina of use. The precious metal tools and fifty dollars were all that he had to show for his labors. He had sent most of his salary to his father. John cradled the case on his lap to keep the contents from spilling out as he removed the letters kept within. In solitude he reread the private words.

.Department of Materia Medica

McGill Medical School
Montreal
February 11, 1865

My dear Spencer,

May God speed your safe return from the debacle on our continent.
Each day, the newspapers tell of the exploits of Sherman and Sheridan, generals whose names, I am certain, are more immediate to you. We hear of miles of destruction, families made homeless and fatherless, as if every cold statistic was a sacrifice to some Baal. Even our own good citizens partake vicariously in the senseless carnage.
We heard rumors that, early in the War, the President of the United States, Abraham Lincoln, and his Secretary Seward, re-

ceived three Commissioners from the Confederate States aboard a Union steamer at Hampton Roads, Virginia. The London Times states that the South was offered peace with re-union or, at the least, an armistice, along with funds to reimburse the slave-owners for freeing their chattels. Allegedly, the Confederacy rejected the terms with umbrage. Yet, recently, in the Southern Congress, the same rebellious states voted to allow slaves for military conscription <u>with emancipation</u>.

I am afraid, Spencer, that my ancient brain cannot comprehend the Byzantine politics of our warring American neighbors. Pray to God that our own country, united and one under the Crown, with Anglican Saxons and Papist Sons of France co-existing in harmony, will never resort to such barbarism.

I treasure your letters. I have taken the liberty, nay in truth, a privilege, of reading selected portions to your former mentors. We think that we here are in the vanguard of man's fight against disease with our few patients. But our petty efforts seem just that when we hear of the incomprehensible scale of slaughter which you picture for us so graphically. Our satisfaction is knowing the skills you acquired in our midst are alleviating some small mite of suffering.

Spencer, chastise me if I am wrong in detecting over the past year, an unfamiliar note of bitterness in your letters. Your emotions seem trapped in the pathos you are witnessing. My heart, too, weeps at the senseless slaughter. That is why I fear for you. As a physician, you must never lose your sensitivity to the wounded about you. A good physician must always feel the pain of his patients. Yet, never allow such feelings to influence your task of healing, even if the perversity of man in decimating his neighbor is repugnant,.

Recall your first year studies in the foundation of modern medicine. We instructed that life is a combination of humors, each sustained in perfect balance. When the composite harmony is disturbed, illness presents. That is the bedrock of our faith, dating from Aesculapius and Hippocrates. Our task is to re-balance the scale, to purge the excess, to fund the deficit, until all elements are restored in equal proportions. That is the process of healing.

The health of the mind partakes of this process, as does the physical corpus. To illustrate. Grief after loss of a loved one is acceptable. But, only to a point. Then, it must shrink back into the self to allow resumption of normal existence.

Hostility is plumbing your conscience at this very moment. Cynicism has possessed your soul. This reaction to what you have been through is normal, salutary, perhaps even laudatory. But, only to a limited degree! It must not be allowed to consume you or to paralyze your future ambition as a doctor.

Hate your fellow man for what evil he hath wrought. Berate your limited abilities to correct such insults. Curse at your God, if you must. Then, when it is all over, reduce such resentment to an imprint which you will treasure only as a faded memory, not a fresh pain. I pray that you can decipher this old man's concern for the precious gift which lies within your head and heart and hands.

It is with this tedious preamble that I approach your request of December 29th. I have deliberately delayed the response. I feel it would be unwise for you to enter an academic sinecure. I see you shake the page in protest. Please hear my reasoning even though you may disagree. Rushing from the bloody fields of battle to the sterile seclusion of a classroom would be a tragic error at this point in your life.

Oblige an aging doctor who, childless before the day Bishop McCallum and your father brought you to Trinity College, has looked upon you as the flesh and blood God has denied me. Do not retreat from the world. Your life is not a life destined for quiet contemplation. I know that all you crave now is the peaceful halls of erudition._ For my sake, resist the temptation to bury the hateful memories at the cost of artificial entombment.

Take six months. A year. Enter a community. Practice within the surroundings of those of your class and circumstance. Repair the abraded sinews of your conscience. Drink once again from the fount of optimism and faith in your fellow man. Do not turn your face away because they did not live up to your expectations. Relax. Preen. Get fat (I still see your scrawny frame). Seek companionship. Fall in love, even if only for a while (vain advice from one who has never). Drain your cup of bitterness so that it will be empty to receive a fresh draught of life.

Please, John. I beg you to rejoin this wonderful species of upright animals created in the reflection of their Lord. Then if you still desire to cloister yourself from the world as I have done, I will do everything within my power to help you achieve a station commensurate with your talents.

I have inquired of a position for you in Massachusetts. The town is rich and prosperous. It is close enough to Boston so that the inspiration of the Harvard Medical School and the new Massachusetts General Hospital (built, if you can imagine, upon the proceeds of lottery) will insure you of the stimulation you require.

Go there before deciding what you want for the future. I promise to abide by your choice.

May God vouchsafe you home.

Your affectionate servant,

Professor Elias Guthrie

The second letter was from his father.

Britton Spencer was a missionary clergyman who had emigrated to Kingston, Ontario to tend to the Anglican needs of the new settlers. In 1837, he departed with his bride of six months from his home in Falmouth, England. The harsh amenities of the rural settlement proved fatal to his frail wife. She died of pleurisy, her short life destroyed by tuberculosis.

Britton never remarried. From the age of one, John grew up cared for by the spinsters of the parish. He had an easy relationship with his father who watched his only child mature into a solitary lad. Even early, the boy possessed a restless curiosity which challenged everything until proven in the crucible of his reason. He never laughed at his fathers explanations about the physical world. The boy simply disregarded them.

Britton knew John would search endlessly to understand the mysteries of nature. He feared the quest unblessed. The true riches of faith….. contentment and peace of mind….would forever elude his son.

The Vicerage
Kingston, Ontario
March 1, 1865

My dearest son,

John, my prayers, that you will return safely from the holocaust which visits our American friends, are so diligent that I shame my-self in disregard of others who suffer more grievously than I. I know that you will have concern when you receive this letter, for the hand is not mine own. Mistress Abigail Craig, who has been attending me these past months, has insisted in taking down these words to spare my energies.

Do not be alarmed. The long harsh winter has exacerbated the touch of pleurisy inhabiting this poor mortal frame (though I would scarcely know why it would pick such a pallid host). Your kind friend, Doctor Elias Guthrie, has made the arduous trip this winter past through the snow-driven roads to attend me. He has ordered me to bed and has laid down strict orders which I must obey. When I am tempted to rebel,(as he anticipated), he has perversely ensnared my long-time friend, Bishop McCollum, to acquiesce in his nefarious scheme. So I am confined to lying under my feather-down coverpane, trapped at the end of my life between linen boundaries just as I entered this world fifty one years ago.

I know that when the spring is upon us and the thaws ignite the pent-up life hibernating in the field, then, I, too, shall share in the annual rebirth and return to good health. Such time is not far off. Closer to my heart, I have good cheer to hear that the horrible War is drawing to a close. May God protect you these last perilous moments.

Professor Guthrie has told me of your request. I wish that I could assist in your struggle to find your true calling, but, as during those years that I shared with you, I have always been reluctant to influence your choice. Medicine was your vocation, as the Ministry was mine. Who can predict in what manner the Almighty assembles the cells and humours which make up man and breathes the spirit of life, and then sends His creation down the path of His divine choosing. We must not question our destination, but only serve to the utmost of our ability. In that pursuit does one find the greatest personal satisfaction.

I have never regretted the tracks of my life, though now, at the end of my mortal thread, I have companionship of neither wife nor son. Instead, I have the memories of those I loved and who loved me in return. I have the affection of the Parish. Most of all, I possess the knowledge, that by some totally incomprehensible magic, my immortality walks the face of the earth playing his role in alleviating the ills of mankind, albeit of the flesh, rather than of the spirit.

If ever in your life the slightest vestige of guilt has risen that you did not follow in my path, cast out that unworthy thought. We are what God has made of us. All I ask is that you always carry compassion in your heart.

I blush at my inadequacy to convey my thoughts. I must resort to the words of another who, like me, once saw his son off on a perilous journey, uncertain as to what would befall him. (You can see that confinement has rekindled my love for the literature of my youth.)

"This above all. To thy own self be true. And it must follow, as night the day, thou canst not then be false to any man."

One final admission of guilt on my part. I know you may be offended by my act. I have scrupulously sent to Bishop McCallum each of your monthly stipends. Though such reciprocity was not conditional when the Episcopal Diocesan Office in Toronto provided you with scholarship to Trinity and then to McGill, I feel it may help his Grace to provide such generosity for another like yourself.

Do not fear for my needs. The good neighbors of Kingston have kept me well-provided and comfortable. I want for nothing except to caress the sight and sound of my only son.

Your loving father,

Britton Spencer

John never knew why he had kept Zebadiah Harcross's letter to his son.

Perhaps to accompany Matthew's reply.

**Harcross Water power Company
Cromwell, Massachusetts
September 19, 1862**

Dear Matthew,

It grieves me to write this letter. Circumstances, however, compell me to the distasteful task. It is an unfortunate but undeniable fact that your behavior has been a continual source of consternation. I can no longer countenance such a flagrant disrespect for the duties which are your's by inheritance.

I have watched you flout your contempt for what I have wrought in Cromwell. I fault myself for not exerting stricter control at an earlier, more formative time in your development. If I am guilty, my alibi is preoccupation with affairs, an activity I have pursued solely for your eventual aggrandizement.

However, this short letter is not meant to be a mea culpa. Regardless of the flaws which have produced the unhappy situation, I have taken definitive steps to correct, once and for all, the calamitous set of affairs.

In this undertaking, my resolve is firm. Nothing you may say or do will shake me from my purpose.

I said nothing when, in a fit of spite, you fled to the Union Army. A rash and stupid act! I stood by when you refused a Commission in Washington which would have protected your life and limbs from harm. Now I have received word from Surgeon-General Letterman that you were wounded in the battle at Antietam Creek in Virginia. Unfortunately, neither the War Department nor you have seen fit to appraise me fully of your condition. That oversight is of no importance. I have set in motion the final means to extricate you from your past and to set you resolutely on the path I have chosen for you. The path which is your's by right of blood.

You may comfort yourself that the wealth and power of the Harcrosses are confined to one insignificant valley, the ' fly-dropping on a map ', as you once so profoundly castigated it. Be forewarned. I have this day consummated arrangements by which you are to be discharged from the Army. Secretary of War, Edwin Stanton, with whom I have transacted commerce, assures me by telegraph this morning, that you will be evacuated immediately to the Army

Hospital in Arlington. I have arranged for a private train to transport you back here.

Once in Cromwell, you will recover from your injury. After an appropriate interval, you will start your formal ascension to the position which awaits my heir.

I will brook no further argument on this point. Do not contemplate any action to dissuade me. You will find that my influence is great. There is no place where you can escape my will.

The dam at Pulpit Rock has been started to trap the spring rains for release in the summer and fall. Soon, the river will run at full power.... for us. The dream will be complete! You will take your place by my side and share that dream as your inheritance.

I am still in my prime, but your mother, whom I honor, can have no other children. Someday, your sister Elizabeth, will pass from the Harcrosses to submerge not only her flesh but her name, to that of an alien family. You are my single fragile link with posterity, albeit tarnished. You will walk beside me on the hills overlooking the valley. Your head will be held high with pride, as my own. The fruit of your loins will issue forth.

I will live to see my future. My vision fulfilled. My river. My valley. My immortality.

I shall not appeal to you out of love for me. Nor out of charity.

I do not plead!
You will obey me in this thing I have determined.

Your father,

Zebadiah Harcross.

The physician's expression turned sad as he replaced the letter back into the worn envelope. He took out the last letter, his son's reply. The missal written, but never sent. The plea from the victim, one which would never pierce the fahers deafened ears.

September 18, 1862

Dear Father,

Forgive me,

Matthew,

John wondered whether Zebadiah Harcross had cried once in his entire life.

CHAPTER SEVEN

That Adam Ring was a prize which the good Lord had dropped into his lap was evident. The young man did the work of two, ate little and said nothing. It was Adam who picked out the warped lumber at bargain prices. It was Adam who showed the other workers how to build seaman's chests out of left-over pieces, but cut on the bias, to disguise the boards. It was Adam who filled a wagon with wood and went to warehouses along the waterfront, offering to build shipping crates on the spot, to any size. Within a month, Adam's wages were raised, but less than the other men. Jacob explained they families to support. Adam took the money and said nothing. By this time, he had moved upstairs and joined the Kowalski household.

Try as he could, the proprietor could not learn anything of his past.

Jacob never asked what Adam did with his meager wages. Some mornings he could smell stale whiskey and the stink of cheap perfume. He saw the scratches on his back when the Pole worked stripped to the waist. Whatever he did at night, Adam was still the first one up, washed and at work, long before the others arrived.

Jacob closed his eyes to what he did not want to see. What lay heaviest on his heart were his two daughters, twenty-six and twenty-nine. The aging spinsters shared their fathers hooked nose and thick lips. Tall, ungainly, and hunched over, they were silent reflections of their sire.

Adam remembered the tactics of his own father to marry off his dowry-poor sister back in Biala-Poliaska. He smiled inwardly as the Kowalskis fatted him like a golden calf. He smiled outwardly as they extolled the virtues of their homely daughters.

He did not smile at all when he seduced them both. One after the other, he stripped them naked, aroused their hopes and forced them to perform acts which consumed them with shame and a craving for more. Soon they were competing for his favors. Many nights, with the room dark, he lay back in the attic, legs spread apart, as the two women made him forget the hours of sweat in their fathers shop, the impoverished wages, the charity of a bed, and hardest of all, the scarred face which stared back each morning in the broken mirror. At those times, he could purge the bitter memory of Casmir Landsteiner, the Ukrainian log rafter, the girl on the steamer, and the sailors who ravaged his face. When he ejaculated, for those brief seconds, he was finally at peace with himself. The pleasure never lasted long.

The Kowalskis alternated between their growing affection for him as a surrogate son, and interest as a potential son-in-law. He never joined in the religious activities of the Jewish ghetto. He refused to make friends with the workers whose tenure was short when Adam felt they were not working hard enough

Some nights, he would take the tramway out of the South End and roam the unfamiliar streets, observing, listening. He saw the marshland south of Beacon Street drained and subdivided for the high bay-windowed townhouses of the affluent. He marveled at

Trinity Church supported on wooden piles in a lake of water under the building.

He visited the new Boston City Hospital. They told him nothing could correct the scar on his face. The good doctors gave him laudanum for his recurring headaches How could they know of the spirochetes infesting his brain?

Adam did not dare enter the elegant Parker House lobby, only stared. He paid twenty-five cents to watch from the orchestra John Wilkes Booth perform *Hamlet* in the Boston Theater. He spent the two hours inspecting the mighty, clothed in jewels and furs, hovering above him in velvet-lined boxes.

Adam Ring hungered as an alien in a strange land, picking at the fringes of vast rich society. He would return to the shabby shop and tip-toe up the stairs to his garret bed. He could see out of the top slit of the shutter a sliver of sky and moon. He refused to cry. Instead, he investigated the fabric of his small world, thread by thread, always looking some magic to escape.

The harbor was his favorite retreat. He stared for hours at the ships going in and out. He felt he could reach out and pull the ocean towards him like a rope, and, at the other end would be a treasure.

It was not to be.

He would enter a saloon and drink with the dock-workers. The next day, he was more withdrawn than ever, angry at his failures. Seeing his expression, Jacob Kowalski would defer his matchmaking.

When opportunity came to Adam Ring, it was from an unexpected source. The winter of 1863 was a cruel one. The poor huddled together for warmth in the packed slums. The harbor froze over. Water and sewer lines cracked. Cesspools backed up. Hygiene ceased to have any practical meaning.

For a hundred years, familiar diseases had scourged the slums. Malaria, yellow-fever, typhus, dysentery, typhoid. This time it was different. The diphtheria liked children! A chance cough, a sneeze, was all it needed.

Ten. Fifty. One hundred. One thousand a day! The parents watched and wept and could do nothing

The first month, 11,000 children died.

Adam Ring acted.

"Coffins! Coffins!'* he shouted at Jacob.

"Coffins?" Kowalski echoed back.

He could not stop the boy. Adam was possessed. The funeral parlors could not keep up. The casket companies were busy selling coffins to the Union Army.

Adam moved fast. What was a coffin anyway? A fancy chest. Some stain and shellac. A piece of cloth glued inside, something Kowalski's brother-in-law could make cheap in his sweat shop. Adam did not know how long the epidemic would last, but he intended to profit from this gift from God.

He made the rounds of the waterfront, seeking out the crew bosses. At the *Turk's Head* on *Tea Wharf,* Liam Flaherty laughed at him.

"You're telling me you want to <u>buy</u> from us the lumber we steal off the wharfs?" The burly stevedore emptied his whiskey in one gulp, then wiped his mouth with his forearm. He looked half quizzically, half suspiciously at the young Jew.

"Hah," he laughed, "who do you think you are?" He winked at the pock-marked barmaid who grinned back a toothless smile, "Listen, little *kike.* Come back when you've grown a foreskin."

"So I can send it back to Ireland to make another dumb Mick like you?"

Flaherty's face turned angry and he started to get up from his chair. Adam did not move. He remained calm. Liam could see the young boy seize hold of the empty whiskey bottle by the neck, ready to crack off the head. The kid had guts! Flaherty smiled,

"Alright," he drawled, his greed aroused by the Jew's offer. "Not promising that I can get my hands on any lumber," he nodded to his friends seated at the other tables. The short husky men had stopped talking and were listening to the strange conversation between the dock boss and the wiry dark-haired Jew-boy with the scarred face. "What would you be wanting with the goods, anyway?"

"Just tell me the price," Adam replied, "What I do with it is none of your affair."

Flaherty tilted back in his chair, calculating prices and profit. "How much will you be buying?"

"How much can you supply?"

"A thousand board feet a week." There was a hint of pride.

"A day," Adam shot back,

"A day? What in hell do you think we are?",

"The best damn thieves on *Tea Wharf*," Adam smiled.

Flaherty laughed, "A thousand board feet a day. What about it?" he asked his comrades. The men were excited at the prospect of more money.

Liam's voice broke through the chatter, "It will cost you,"

"How much?"

" Ten dollars a thousand, and that's half what its worth," He squinted at the lad, holding the top of the empty glass in front of his face like a mask.

"Two fifty," Adam countered, knowing the rules of bargaining. He was aware that each minute more and more bodies were piling up, frozen stiff in empty lots, waiting.

" Four.....and not a penny less." Flaherty's grin vanished. This was no joke.

"Agreed, but only if half comes from the new shipment sitting over in Warehouse Nine."

Flaherty looked at him in amazement. How did the little kike know what the Bangor Lumber Company just got in? The thief stood there as brazen as a wet bantam cock. Jew or not, Liam admired brains.

"Adam Ring, there is one condition," he warned. "Cash......<u>in</u> <u>advance</u>."

Adam started to object. Liam shook his head. "No money, no deal. You take my goods and I will never see your money. I can find you and slit your throat, but the lumber? It's not as if I can complain to the police. No, little man. The money in advance."

Adam struck the same deal over and over, as he traveled up and down the waterfront. In some cases, he was forced to pay a higher price, as news spread. By the time he returned to Jacob*s shop, he had committed himself for $500.

Kowalski listened as Adam went over the deal.

"The coffins will cost us, at the most, 75 cents for the wood. Maybe 50 cents for labor. Add another 25 cents for the stain and shellac. 50 cents for the lining if your brother-in-law is only half a *gonif.* For 2 dollars we can make a coffin. This noon the undertakers were offering $5 and even $10 and begging for them. The parents see their children lying on the ground. The wild dogs roaming the streets for a meal. They don't think of money."

" I talked to Selig to use his wagon shop for extra workers. You stay here and I will oversee next door Take a chance, Mr. Kowalski. Buy the lumber. Rent Selig's space. Hire more workers. I will train them myself. This is what I've been waiting for. Please. Act now. There isn't much time. Please! Please!'

Jacob could see the starving boy, fresh off the boat. Adam was talking more than in all the months he had arrived. Perhaps the figures were right. Maybe the boy was telling the truth. What if there was thousands of dollars to be made? He had been in America thirty years and never found the promised gold.

Adam had never been wrong. Still, he was just a child. A *pischer.....* but a bright one. Jacob examined the figures under the dim light. He nodded as he confirmed the totals. If Adam was right, the profit would be enormous.

The risk! All the money he had saved. A dollar here. Fifty cents there. Carefully, painfully, since he opened his shop. What if he should lose his eyesight or his fingers? It was all he had in the world.

How did the boy know he had the money to begin with? His daughters! They probably told him everything he wanted to know. His daughters......? He looked up at the impatient boy. If Adam could have seen under the beard, he would seen a smile.

"Adam," Jacob began slowly. "These figures.....These figures......" He shook his head* "I don't know. I just don't know."

"Mr. Kowalski," Adam begged, "you do agree? We can make money and lots of it."

The old man allowed a reluctant nod. "Yes, if you are right. I am not saying that you aren't. He paused for effect. "It will take at least a thousand dollars before the buyers pay us back. While we wait.....the lumber... the salaries.... the rent...?

He stabbed his fingers into his chest.." Where am I going to get the money?" His expression was guileless as he waited for the boy to answer.

"Mr. Kowalski. I would not have brought the deal to you if I didn't know that you could finance it. I don't only go by see here," pointing around the shop. "You can afford the investment. It will make you many times what you risk."

"Ah," Kowalski agreed. "Risk. Yes, it is that. A risk. Adam, I do have the money, but it is not <u>mine</u> to spend."

Adam was confused.

"It is a trust."

"A trust?"

"Yes, for my daughters. A dowry. $500 for each one, to be given to their husband on their wedding day. If I give you the money what will happen to them? Should I sacrifice their chances so you can get rich? You tell me. If you were a father, what would you do?"

Adam saw the father now as someone to truly admire. The black numbers danced on the white paper in front of him. Money. One chance for the gold to escape. He thought of the two Kowalski girls. In the light of day, lust was replaced by revulsion.

Adam locked eyes with the old man.

"Alright. The younger one."

"Five hundred for the younger. The full thousand for the older."

Adam hesitated for a minute. He laughed.

"The older, with half the profits."

"Agreed. But only <u>after</u> I earn back the thousand dollars. <u>Then</u> we share as partners."

The boy started to object.

"Adam, I must think of the younger, too. A father does not discriminate between his children. She must have a dowry equal of her older sister, to win <u>her</u> Adam Ring."

The epidemic lasted four and a half months. To Adam's joy, the death rate climbed each day. By the April thaw, Adam had sold 7200 coffins and had made $8000. He now slept in Rebecca's bedroom, her younger sister displaced to his former room in the attic. He continued to do the work of two, still ate little, and resumed saying nothing.

It broke the father's heart mornings when the new groom's skin would mock with fresh scratches. The old man cried. He knew Rebecca to be a gentle child.

CHAPTER EIGHT

"Come in! Come in!" The boisterous greeting boomed across the bedroom.

Two short dark-haired maids flashed Spencer shy smiles as they curtsied and stood back.

"That's it. Come closer. Don't be afraid. I won't bite you." There was a roll of laughter ending in a series of gasps. "Though I can't say as much for those imps."

The room was dimly lit by two kerosene lamps. Maroon drapes hung over the windows giving the room a seductive mauve glow. A fire was burning in the grate, although the day was warm. Spencer made out the broad bed in the center of the room. Naked nymphs and angels climbed up the mahogany posts. The bed was piled high with a sea of pillows propping up a short elderly man, his round face red and glistening with perspiration. He was bald except for a few wisps of grey hair which stuck in all directions.

He peered at John through half-lens eyeglasses which perched on a small nose. His smile creased deep folds into the heavy cheeks and jowls. When he laughed, the entire bedframe heaved like a ship at sea. He waved his short pudgy arms in the air.

"Well? What do you say?"

John came closer, unsure what to answer.

Shaw Billings laughed again. He pointed to the two young girls. " Well, which one would you like?" he teased. "They both bite about the same."

There was a yell as he slapped them on the buttocks and shoved them towards Spencer who retreated towards the door.

"Alright. Alright. <u>You</u> won't come to me. I will go to you." He started to raise himself out of bed. "Here...here....girIs....help me.". He struggled to maneuver himself off the mattress.

The servants were twins, about sixteen or seventeen years old. They wore a thin cotton chemise with a loose-laced bodice over full breasts. As they knelt on the sides of the bed, John could see attractive legs and buttocks.

Billings teetered on the edge of the bed like a humpty dumpty about to fall. One girl inserted his feet into emerald green slippers. The other wrapped him in a long velvet dressing gown with quilted lapels and tied the sash. Billings was not the least embarrassed by the stranger. Reaching around their waists, he shoved himself upright. He stood there, trying to catch his breath while the girls adjusted his robe.

"Shaw Billings. <u>Doctor</u> Shaw Billings," he announced heartily.

He pumped John's hand. "You must be Spencer. If not," he winked mischievously, "you are invading a gentleman's private bedroom without reason."

Was this the partner professor Guthrie had selected for him? For six months? A year? It must be a joke! Did his mentor known anything at all about Shaw Billings? <u>Doctor</u> Shaw Billings?

The older man came close and started sniffing. His nose wrinkled in disgust.

"Il sent mauvais," Billings said to the girls.

John blinked in anger. Billings looked surprised. "Of course, you are Canadian. You understand French. Oh, well," he shrugged, "I guess the girls will not be able to keep <u>anything</u> from you. I should have remembered from Elias' letter." He sniffed again. "Seriously, Doctor Spencer. In French, or in King George's English, you really do stink. My bath. Is it ready?" he asked.

One girl nodded.

"Then let our pungent guest have first turn. Remember," he chuckled, "when he has finished, scrub it well before drawing mine. One must be pure of body as well as of mind and spirit. Am I not right, Spencer?" He gave the young doctor a leer. "Before I forget, Spencer, this is Yvette. And, this is Suzette. They are identical except for one delicate part which I leave to your discovery."

"Now," pushing the two girls towards John, "please take him before I lament that Montreal has sent me a Yahoo."

⊱✦⊰

The high cast-iron claw-footed bathtub was strange to him. His washing was usually a cloth and water from a basin. The tank was filled to the brim with steaming water from pitchers heating on a stove in the corner. Before he could stop them, the two girls started to undress him. He brushed them away, but they persisted, unbuttoning his jacket, unbuckling his shoes. They dodged his hands leaving only his long one-piece woolen underwear. He clung to this last remaining vestige of decency. They left the room with wistful glances.

John Owen Spencer's attempts at sex had usually been the products of too much alcohol and left the realization that he was naive in the ways of love. The few memories evoked a sort of cringing embarrassment.

At this particular point of time, seduced into a job with a licentious physician, trapped in a tropic-like room in worn underwear, surrounded by teasing maidens, John felt a rising prurience. Naked, he climbed up the three steps and lowered himself.

He shrieked as the scalding water burned his foot. He pulled his leg back, rubbing his toes. The door opened and the two giggling girls entered with pitchers of cold water. He shied back and forth, one foot still poised in the air, the other teetering on the rim in a ridiculous pose. The two maids chattered to each other with approving gestures. John blushed and plunged his erection into the boiling water.

By the time he emerged, his skin was a bright pink and tingled from the air. His clothes were gone. In their place was one of Billings' dressing gowns. His arms and legs stuck out like a scarecrow as he scuffled into the hall in a pair of his host's slippers.

"Ah, much better. See. Now, that didn't hurt a bit now, did it?"

Billings was seated in a large wing chair facing the fire.

"What do you think of it? The tub ! The tub! I had it shipped from London. I don't think that there is another in Cromwell. Even Zebadiah doesn't have one, or, if he did, would spend time away from his immortal Quabbin to sit in it. No, John, you have just been baptized in the latest product of the Commonwealth Hydropathic Society of which I, Shaw Billings, am a founding member."

"What happened to my clothes?" John was angry. He had been treated shabbily since arriving, ordered about, even stripped naked and bathed like a foundling baby.

"Well, at first we considered washing them," Billings was pure innocence. "Yvette and Suzette agreed the result was not worth the effort. So.... we burned them."

Spencer protested.

"Don't worry. After dinner, the girls will show you to your room. It was my son's. Malcolm's. You can find something until we have you fitted up. Malcolm was about your size. Tall and thin, like his mother, though God knows how fat he has gotten in Boston, skinning the poor people in his father-in-law's bank."

As he talked, his words came out in short puffs, interrupted by rasping wheezes. The doctor was now a dusky hue as he strained to breathe. The veins in his neck stood out. His ankles were grossly swollen. John took Shaw's hand. The pulse was irregular with skipped beats.

"Dropsy. Overweight. Right?" Shaw asked.

John laid the hand lightly back on the man's lap.

" Sarah, before she died, would nag how fat I was. Someday it would kill me. She made my life a living hell. She was scrawny, Spencer, like a plucked chicken. Ate like a bird, too. And pecked. Always clawing and screeching like a gaggle over parched corn." He smirked. "I lasted her out. She died four years ago. You know something, Spencer. I never was a religious person. Now, when I think of the Lord plagued with her sharp tongue, berating <u>His</u> belly, I pray for Him. He is the one who needs saving."

"Oh....! Oh....!." he pressed his hand over his bladder. "Over there, on the mantle. Bring it to me. There....there...." he pointed at the long silver tube.

The catheter was hollow and bent at one end in a gentle curve. Shaw opened his dressing gown John could see the shriveled genitalia under the folds of fat. Billings spit on the catheter and inserted it into his penis. Spencer held a porcelain basin between the old man's legs to catch the drip. Finished, he took the tube out.

"Ah....much better. You forgot to include enlargement of the prostate, Doctor Spencer. God's gift to men who live too long." He gave a good-humored laugh.

"Tis a shame. 'Tis a shame. The only time my poor member is stiff is with the silver rod.   The years wasted with Sarah receiving my nocturnal emissions as if they were fleas from a pet hound. Oh, to be young again....and....without Sarah!"

Billings suddenly broke out coughing, as fluid in his lungs from heart failure choked him. His head was thrown back to capture air. John hesitated for only a second. He rushed down the dark oak stairway for surgical instruments.

"Yvette! Suzette!" The house rung with his cries for help. "Quick, A basin."

He opened his case and selected a lancet. He wiped it carefully on his sleeve. He stretched Billings' left arm out and searched for a vein. The spurt of blood changed into a steady stream. The wheezing subsided. The color lost the dark hue. John bled three pints of blood He pulled up a chair and sat next to the patient, checking his pulse.

Billings said nothing. He had not missed Spencer's calm command of the crisis and soothing confidence. Elias was right. This was a rare physician. Skillful, yet, if Guthrie were to be believed, tainted with innocence.

Shaw had been surprised to receive a letter from his old classmate. Why was he urging him to hire the young Canadian into his home after his discharge? What could an aging small city doctor offer a graduate of one of the British Empire's greatest medical institutions ? He agreed, though unsure of Guthrie's intentions.

Shaw, Spencer has learned all that we can teach him. He possesses the skills of our age as well as a great personal modesty. However, this young man, whom I love as a son, is a flawed physician. He cannot tolerate the failings of his fellow mortals, any more than separate himself from the sufferings of his patients. Like Cassandra's gift, this curse will either destroy him or, at the least, void his future happiness. We healers are not holy priests with a divine calling. We are not angels. All of us were cast from the Garden, for our arrogance is a sin of hypocrisy, You must teach my acolyte that we physicians live and breath like other men and share their failures. We make mistakes. We bleed. Spencer must realize that imperfection is the natural lot of humankind. God recognizes this. That is why he sent His son to redeem our sins. Spencer must learn the same charity towards his fellow man that we attribute to our Maker. That, my dearest friend, is your task.

Guthrie's words swam through his consciousness.' *We live and breath like other men'*. What Elias really meant was, 'shit, piss and fornicate like other men.' Billings opened his eyes to see John's fingers still pressed on his pulse. Shaw gave him a large grin.

'Shit piss and fornicate'. With three catheterizations a day and two phlebotomies a week, it was a sign he was not going to last forever. If he did not wish to disappoint his classmate, it would be wise to start the lessons soon.

"Thank you, my good friend. I am impressed," He caught the girls eyes looking where John's gown had fallen open. "So are these young maidens," he teased.

John blushed and tied the sash tighter.

"Spencer," Shaw continued, "do not fear. You have nothing to be ashamed of." Before John could stammer some inane reply, Doctor Shaw Billings, escorted him to dinner. There was much work to be done.

John Spencer's first day in Cromwell had begun.

CHAPTER NINE

S haw Billings wasted no time in starting John's education. He introduced him to the elderly and ailing of Cromwell as the new physician whose training was acquired from abroad, his pedigree and heritage lauded until John would shy away.

"Pay no mind," Billings explained. "You are a better doctor than me. All I learned has leaked away like sand. A cup of wisdom, from which I have drunk without replenishing. You, John are newly hatched, with knowledge of the century. I wonder whether Elias sent you to stir me from my sloth." He shook his head. " Like the dinosaurs, I will perish fat and be content in my swamp. Remember, though, if the people do not trust you, your talents are for naught. I have been here forty five years. Perhaps outliving most of my patients has convinced the rest of my skills.

Shaw approved his companion's appearance. The suit of grey cheviot, the high collared shirt, the blue silk cravat. John resisted the moonstone stickpin, only to find it in place when the girls brushed his jacket and the new sprouting muttonchops of fiery red.

" Yes, John, you should do well........for as long as you are here."

Professor Guthrie had advised ' time.' It would be dishonest to force a decision until the year was over. He would keep his options open, and hope.

Slowly the scars of the War faded. John enjoyed the monotony of the daily routine. There were the house calls each morning to the Highlands where the mill-owners lived. High on the bluffs overlooking the Quabbin, their mansions were protected by spike-topped fences of wrought iron. In the afternoon, to the Flats.... crowded, disease ridden blocks where whole families sweated for the Harcrosses.

The Dispensary was in the small building owned by the Sisters of Mercy who had come from St. Joseph's in Worcester. First catering to the French Catholics down from Canada, later to the Irish fleeing the famine, the nuns assisted Billings in a make-shift clinic on the Lower Canal.

At night, the elaborate dinners, as the matrons of Cromwell decided their doctor's protégé a worthy consort for their daughters.

" Bed them, my boy," Billings encouraged. "Tell me, man to man, you know how to fornicate, don't you?"

John could never decide how to answer. Instead, he stammered and protested, perhaps too clumsily, that he damn well knew how to fornicate, and, even if he didn't, which wasn't to say that he didn't, it wasn't any of Doctor Shaw Billings damn business !

"Aha, Johnnie," seeing his bluster, "finally got you roused up. Look at the choler going to your head. Wasted! That is what I mean. It is the wrong place for the blood to be going. Below the umbilicus, my friend. To the nether regions! That is the route for a man! Suzette and Yvette find you exceedingly attractive. Both of them would be insulted if you didn't bed them. You can fornicate each separately, but together…..ahhh… …..they could be a double delight."

He chuckled as John stalked out of the room, slamming the door. There should be no problem. The blood was there. Just redirect the flow.

He <u>had</u> promised Elias.

⪫⪥⪦

Shaw was right. It did not take long. Billings had accepted a dinner invitation. John sat by himself in the large dining room. The drapes were drawn against the dangerous night air. The two sisters hovered about him, silently serving, but always refilling his glass with rich Bordeaux claret. Without the usual bawdy jokes, John drifted into a fatigued reverie. The flames danced and his vision grew hazy. With a loud belch, he started from the table.

The two girls helped him up the stairs. His gait was unsteady. They removed his outer clothes and, ever so gently, his underwear. They maneuvered him, naked under the quilt, fluffing up the pillow for his head. The fire kept the room warm. They undressed and let down their hair.

They eased their way into the four-poster. He could feel their skin, cool and smooth, against his hairy legs and chest. Their hands traveled up and down his body, pausing here, touching there. Twenty finger tips teasing in the curly hair below. His penis responded to the erotic stroking. John uttered half-cries as his body twisted, his head still heavy from the alcohol. His thighs opened to trap whichever one was making him shiver with excitement. His eyes were not focused, as he held out his arms for each in turn.

When Shaw Billings returned home a little unsteady after too much brandy, he was surprised that no one was there to help him. Then, he remembered. He cautiously opened the door to John's bedroom. The trio were buried in the down mattress, the two girls pressed up against the snoring naked male. It had been torture to stretch out the evening at Widow Pratt's home, but the girls had insisted on his absence. Before retiring, Billings decided, first thing in the morning, to write to Elias. Guthrie need have no fear. His young protégé was an apt pupil.

Over breakfast, the young man was quieter than normal. Whenever he looked up, Billings averted his eyes. Finally, John pushed back from the table,

"Alright, Shaw. Say it and get it out of your system."

The doctor peered over the top of his glasses.

"I should say Johnnie boy, that it was you who got purged. Judging by the food Yvette and Suzette are piling in front of you, they must have an interest in keeping your strength up. You know as well as me that the loss of one ounce of semen deprives the male of more vital ichor than a phlebotomy of forty."

He waited until the two girls left the room.

"Johnnie, I would recommend French letters. A thin pouch of the finest lamb intestine to scabbard your instrument....... unless you prefer the consequences."

"What consequences?"

"You must be joking. Babies! Babies! Even Canadians recognize the facts of life. Did you think you could deposit your seed and not procreate?

John glanced nervously at the door. Shaw could not resist teasing.

"If it is too late, I can get Isaac Hollis down at the City Clerk's Office to give the girls a marriage license. I will provide death certificates for their departed husbands, from an accident down at the mills. You, Johnnie, will provide each with a gold wedding ring, twenty five dollars, and a one-way ticket to Quebec. They should have no trouble getting husbands for that dowry."

"Just think, Spencer! Someday there could be dozens, maybe hundreds, of red-headed little bastards, all named John Owen

Charpentier, or John Owen Langelier, or what you will," He dissolved into laughter made all the more delightful by his listener's dismay.

Suddenly, Shaw stopped. He had a mischievous grin. He took a coin from his pocket and spun it between his fingers.

"Quick now. Tell me Johnnie lad, pride of McGill College. No dissembling.   One gold piece if you can remember. Yvette and Suzette. Which one has the three nipples?"

It was one wager he had no doubt that John Owen Spencer, visiting diagnostician par excellence, in the cold light of day, was sure to lose.

CHAPTER TEN

"Well, Doctor Spencer, what is your opinion?" Billings stepped back from the bed. The young patient looked at John with the age-old expression of hope and fear. The man was slight of build, no more than twenty-two or three years. The skin was drawn over the bones of his face. The black stubble of whiskers could not hide the sallow complexion. His eyes were closed in dark-ringed sockets. He was lying on his side, legs drawn up in a fetal position, afraid to move.

John felt at the wrist for the artery. He was shocked by the weak rapid pulse, signs of dehydration and fever. With Billings' help, John rolled the man over onto his back. Gently, he straightened the legs until the patient was flat. The man bit his lips from even the slightest motion. John pulled up the soiled bed shirt.

"Do not be afraid, Thomas. I will not hurt you."

The lungs were clear. The abdomen was grossly swollen. The slightest pressure produced an agonized scream. The abdominal wall was rigid, the muscles locked in spasm. In the corner of the room, Shaw Billings investigated the chamber pots which he had asked the wife to save. The urine was scant, dark amber. The bowel movement was only shreds of mucous despite the daily purges.

Two weeks before, Spencer and Billings had been called when fever, cramps and vomiting kept him from work. At first his abdomen was soft. Only the right lower quadrant was tender. Shaw prescribed rum with magnesium nitrate in rosewater. This was changed to calomel and enemas.

The symptoms got worse. Two pints of blood were removed on alternative days, along administrations of quinine. Blistering plasters of mustard and cantharides of Spanish Fly were placed on the skin to draw out the inflammation.

The patient's fever climbed. The vomiting was unrelenting.

They comforted the thin pregnant wife, frightened for the death of her husband, the loss of his income, two young children, and a third due in four months. They left laudanum to keep her husband comfortable until he died.

"What do you think?" Shaw asked as he climbed back into the carriage for the rest of the house calls.

"Abdominal pain of two weeks. Starting in the center and then localizing in the to the right lower quadrant. Accompanied first by nausea; then vomiting. First diarrhea; then constipation. The lungs clear," The fatal words, "perityphlitis."

Billings agreed. "The prognosis?"

"Death, in two or three days."

Billings agreed. "You know, Johnnie, I have seen two cases survive, In both, the inflammation was confined to the right corner and had not spread throughout the abdominal cavity to cause peritonitis."

"What happened?" Spencer was curious.

"In the first patient, it seemed as if the inflammation at the start of the large bowel had turned upon itself and drained back into the intestine, and was discharged as a normal movement. In the second patient, I opened into the abdomen."

Spencer was shocked at what his friend was telling him. To open even a healthy cavity was forbidden. Peritonitis would always follow, killing the patient. "The patient started very much like Thomas with fever, nausea. Purgatives only made him worse. I gave him opium to comfort his last days. To my amazement, the patient got better. His fever disappeared. His appetite returned. Within a week, he was make at work."

"Then, he returned with a new complaint. A dull ache over the cecum. I felt a firm mass, very tender, which grew larger each day. I increased the blisters hoping to draw the underlying purulence to the surface, even as Nature seemed to be doing. One day, the mass was visible. I lanced it as one would a carbuncle, removing the laudable pus. I changed the dressings myself, every day. Within weeks, the wound closed. The patient has been completely well for five years We can visit him and you can seethe healed scar where the perityphlitis was expelled from the body ".

John could not believe the story. Not even the foremost surgeons in Canada had ever cut into the body's big cavity. Limbs... yes. But the abdomen was sacred and not to violated. Yet, he wondered, if Nature had managed to wall off the foulness and direct it to the skin to be discharged, could not the physician aid her? On the other hand, if the patient had a disease which only mimicked perityphlitis, It was not a true test.

Shaw had never been brave enough ever to try again the surgical cure of perityphlitis, even though, God knows, he had dozens of patients a year die from the disease.

Two days later, the widow refused permission for an autopsy. Despite their entreaties, she sat in the bedroom where her husband's body waited for the undertaker. John started to plead with her when he saw Billings motion him to desist.

That evening, Shaw rose from the dinner table after consuming raw oysters, baked grouse, a lamb roast, vegetables and potatoes, two bottles of wine, and half of a deep dish apple pie. John, who was a Spartan eater, could only watch with alarm.

"Come, Johnnie boy," Shaw pointed to the front hall, "We have great deeds to accomplish this night "

John was not told where they were going. Billings just waved him out to the stable where the horse and carriage were waiting. Billings hoisted himself onto his seat and motioned John to join him.

The two kerosene lanterns on the sides of the jolting carriage did little to pierce the darkness. The air was cold and foul mists rose from the canals as they travelled deep into the slums.

After much coaxing, Billings allowed, "You Britons may have your Burke and Hare, but Cromwell has its own Resurrectionist….. me!" He beat his chest with pride. "Shaw Billings, Grave Robber Extraordinaire. The equal of those Edinburgh thugs any day!" He refused to say another word until the carriage stopped in front of Patrick O'Connell's funeral parlor.

How Shaw Billings persuaded the Irishman, John never found out. The man, racked with persistent coughing, greeted Billings more like a close friend, rather than what one would have expected between two of such different classes. They clasped each other on the back and huddled in the corner in conversation for several minutes before Shaw introduced John to the Irish immigrant. There were things John had yet to learn about Billings.

"Johnnie, this here is O'Connell. The best damn undertaker and tenement owner and money lender in Cromwell. Do not be put off by his shabby appearance. He is a deceiver. He still thinks the troops of King George are about to steal his money for taxes." He poked the father in the ribs. "Where do you keep it, you old faker? Under your mattress?" O'Connell smiled, his toothless mouth creasing along the empty gum lines.

"Let me tell you, it is what he did, on <u>top</u> of the mattress that is his true treasure. Where is she, Patrick? Where is she?"

O'Connell shrugged his shoulders, pretending he did not know what the corpulent doctor was about.

"Kathleen! Kathleen! That's what I mean. Johnnie, you must see her. How this old derelict ever managed to produce such a heavenly treasure, only the angels above know. Where is your daughter? I want her to meet this Adonis of the north." He pulled John forward.

O'Connell spit out the plug of tobacco. It missed the cuspidor, and settled in a spreading stain on the floor. He wiped his hands affectedly on his soiled trousers before shaking. "Welcome, Doctor Spencer, though I can't for the life of me understand why you would associate with this fat old blow-hard up in the Highlands."

Billings laughed at the insult "Where is she, O'Connell? You probably keep her hidden like your gold."

The parlor contained a worn maroon horse-hair covered sofa, Two carved wooden arm chairs, and a stone mantle holding an assortment of framed papyrotamia. He spied Kathleen standing in the doorway. She ran into his arms with delight. He gave her a strong hug which almost crushed the young girl. He pointed to Spencer,

"Here is someone even more handsome in face and calf than am I. May I introduce you to Doctor John Owen Spencer. Still a bit wet behind the ears. I suspect a few months more in our Garden of earthly pleasures will make him more of a man."

John blushed at the private joke.

The diminutive figure was dressed in a soft pink dress, high waisted, with the belt pulled tightly under small breasts. To Spencer, she appeared so tiny, so fragile, so incredibly beautiful. When she moved, the faint light clung to her pearly skin. When John shook her hand, he imagined that he had taken hold of a child's. He thought she held his an instant longer than usual. Or, was it he who held on to the touch?

She lowered her eyes to the floor, then flashed a shy smile "We have heard much of you, Doctor Spencer. Welcome to our city." She

81

curtsied and moved back, but not fast enough to escape Billings. He grabbed her waist and pulled her to his side. He gave an affectionate pat upon her rear.

"Well, what do you think of her, Johnnie boy?" He beamed in delight, as if showing off his own daughter. "Hard to imagine I delivered her seventeen years ago. She was a beautiful baby even then. Just like her moth...." He stopped short. Patrick stiffened. Shaw quickly recovered his aplomb. "What a loud yell," he laughed. "Seventeen years ago, I slapped her bottom. Now, my boy, admit it. The blow did no harm. Look here. "He spun Kathleen around in a circle, ignoring her protests. "No, not at all."

"Patrick, if I were you, I would be careful about her. It won't be long before some one with less honorable intentions and certainly more capability than me, will be after her. Maybe even our foreigner here. What do you say, my boy? Isn't that a derrière for the gods? Look at the rest of her, <u>too</u>." He dissolved into a gale of ribald gestures during which time Kathleen managed to escape his clutch and flee from the room and John succeeded in recovering his dignity.

Patrick led the two physicians to the embalming shed. His lantern made weak circles of light on the pitted ground. The two men picked their way between the roofed outhouse, the dug well next to it and the small barn with chickens and pigs.

The naked body was stretched out on a stone slab, finally free of pain, his legs straightened. John smelled the decomposing flesh. O'Connell hung the lantern over the table. But, before Billings could pick up a knife, Patrick stopped him,

"Not the head, or the face," O'Connell warned,

"Have no fear, Patrick," he promised, "we only want to examine the lower abdomen. We will be clean and neat and sew everything up afterwards," His voice lowered, "I thank you, Patrick, as I have for years. We both thank you,"

Scarcely had the blade penetrated the peritoneum, when thick yellow pus spurted up.

"Ah, Johnnie," Billings exclaimed with delight. "The bowel must be perforated. Smell that! Smell that!"

Billings fingers moved faster. His ungloved hands were buried up to the cuffs. They both identified the hallmarks of peritonitis, but where had it started from? Was perityphlitis the source?

Billings withdrew from the incision.

"Feel for yourself."

John inspected the organs to find the guilty one. The kidneys, the gall bladder, the liver, the spleen, the pancreas…. they were all normal. Why did he even suspect them? They did not reside where the pain was strongest… he right lower quadrant. Billings stole a furtive glance at O'Connell who had shrunk back into the corner of the room and was dozing peacefully against the wall. Without saying a word, Billings took the knife and extended the incision into the right lower quadrant, directly over the cecum. With patient dissection, Shaw maneuvered the cecum into view. With one last poke he entered the abscess which had formed around the bowel.

"There it is, Johnnie," Billings boasted. "You were right. Perityphlitis. The corruption started here. The body tried to block it off it off from the rest of the belly. It didn't succeed. The pus escaped. Peritonitis. Death!"

John held the gangrenous cecum. Shaw was right. This is where the disease started. But why here? The cecum was no different from the rest of the eight feet of large bowel which ended at the rectum. Why were these few inches so deadly? He inspected it from all sides. It looked no different ….except of course, for the funny little worm-like tube which stuck out from one side, Normally pink and healthy, here eroded and ruptured by the same putrefaction.

Elias had once asked his class at McGill, what was in God's mind when he created the appendix. It didn't seem to do anything! John flicked at the end of the stubby tissue. He replaced it without a second glance. He had made the correct diagnosis. Perityphlitis. He had predicted the prognosis …. death.

The question still nagged, long after he helped Billings sew up the incision. Why did the corruption erupt at the end of the cecum? Not even Shaw's joshing about man's larger appendage, the cock, could erase the perplexing thought. What if one was to drain the cecal corruption before the pus spread and killed from peritonitis? He was being foolish. To open the virgin abdomen would murder the patient as surely as did perityphlitis. That was a medical catechism!

There, too, he wondered half out-loud, Why? Why should the abdomen be so sacred? Why does opening into a normal abdomen always produce peritonitis? Could it be the air ?

He turned and tossed for hours before sleep. Brief glimpses of people. Billings. Guthrie. His father. Faces that faded before he could question why they appeared. In the early hours of the morning, he conjured up the beauty he had met that evening. It was an unsettling dream. The vision fled beyond reach, tantalizing him. When he caught up with the teasing figure, his hands passed through empty air. They were bloody.

Even in the sunlight of the new day, the premonition frightened him.

CHAPTER ELEVEN

Part One

Adam Ring's arrival into the valley was different from John
Spencer's. For this Polish immigrant, there was no solicitous
preceptor to prepare his way. He did not carry memories of a happy
childhood. He had no valued skills as a healer. His heritage was a
liability. He was not tall or commanding or even fair of appearance.
Worst of all, after two and a half years of back breaking work, he
was a bankrupt.

Adam wore a suit of soiled white linen with the jacket cut away
from the neck button to expose a vest of dark grey. Deep creases
were set in the limp fabric from the cramped trip from Boston.
A flat straw bowler with crimson ribbon topped his head of wavy
black hair. High buttoned shoes completed the dapper *au mode*
look.

The three years since his landing had changed the stunted
youth to a man. He had not grown in height, but, instead, muscles
strained the striped ticking shirt and the tight stove-pipe trousers.

His blue cravat was tied low. A detachable white paper collar framed the beard which now partially hid his scar. The broken nose could not be disguised. When he talked, or worse, when he smiled, the corner of his lip was tugged up into a scowl.

As the train hit a sharp curve, sun caught him full in the face. The blinding flash triggered off another of the fierce headaches which he accepted as part of daily life. Staccato beats pounded his head. He squeezed his skull between his hands to drive out the demons. He took out a bottle and choked down the bitter opium extract, gagging from the taste. He waited the minutes of hell until the white pain dissolved. The attack over, he opened his eyes to see the watery wasteland flooded by the new dam at Pulpit Rock.

The last years of the War had been a time of opportunity for Adam Ring. The large Maine timber mills were busy working for the Union army. The casket companies, happily selling coffins at rigged prices to bribed Army purchasing agents, neglected their home territories.

Adam drove his workers mercilessly, expanding Jacob's shop to the entire street. He borrowed heavily for wood-working machinery. He bought a curtain factory and converted it to sewing linings for coffins. He still bought stolen lumber from the docks. For the rest, he used damaged wood, green boards, mill ends which he painted somber colors to hide the defects. He could never see profit building caskets out of prime material. Who would know if they rotted earlier than guaranteed?

By Appomattox, he owned Jacob's half of the business, at a fraction of its worth, by threatening to leave and set up in competition. Adam considered divorce a waste of time and money. He merely moved out of the Kowalski household for good.

The end of hostilities was the death knell for his fringe operation. Deprived of the huge war-time markets, the casket companies resumed their competitive strides. Within six months, fueled by rivers of cheap timber pouring out of the north with no place to go, the large mills had recaptured their traditional markets. The factory was shutdown except for one small corner where Jacob and several workers continued to make boxes for the waterfront.

Adam walked through the deserted space, touching the silent tools, kicking the piles of sawdust, counting the varnished coffins, now as worthless as the raw lumber rotting in the courtyard. He knew that Jacob and the workers took a malevolent delight in seeing him humbled. He said not a word. What he needed was not self-pity, but a market for his inventory. To convert those hollow boxes to cash, before his creditors called in his promissory notes.

Adam gave a jolt as the train suddenly braked. The sun was blotted out by the brick buildings lining the sides of the tracks. He thought back to that first night in Boston, hungry and cold, without a penny. Through the window, the mills stretched as far as the eye could see, their saw-toothed roofs cross-ripping the sky. The passengers were collecting their belongings to leave. He carried no possessions. He waited until they left before making his way out.

The fear was now gone. In its place, a shiver of excitement. The challenge! He thought of the empty coffins back in Boston. The debts he owed. He pulled his watch out and checked the time. He searched the crowd. Where was Patrick O'Connell?

Part Two

The War between the States furnished a kind of leavening throughout the North. The prosperity, the inflation fueled by printings of government bonds and cheap paper currency, enriched not only the industrialists, but also the small business class. Like Adam Ring, Patrick Francis O'Connell, used the four and a half years to change coffins into gold.

Patrick's funeral parlor was the most profitable of his endeavors. In death, the poor immigrant was buried in a new suit with yards of satin and velvet, encased in a box of varnished wood, and surrounded with flowers, liquor and food. For the family, the cost was a deadly weight. All too often, the debts were ignored after the grief had cooled. Collection was futile. Families in the flats had no assets to attach, and, when the husband had been the wage-earner, no income. Unpaid accounts threatened this lucrative business.

In a flash of insight Patrick conceived of the idea of selling burial expense protection. For a fee of a few cents per month, paid in advance, the family would be guaranteed a proper burial with no further cost to his family. But, how to attract people to the plan? The answer was at hand.

Each immigrant group had its own ethnic association to help arrivals get a job, lodging, even a spouse. The Germans their Bund. The Irish their social clubs. All contracted with local funeral parlors for burials. Poorly managed, the associations usually floundered, only to be taken over by a successor until it too went broke. Seeing an opportunity, Patrick sold all of his businesses except for the funeral parlor. He converted his tenements into cash which he used to buy up the lists of members. He bribed their officers, usually volunteer laborers, to direct all burials to the O'Connell Company. The local parlors could not compete with this strangle-hold on large blocks of population. Patrick bought them out cheaply.

Success followed success as he invaded from town to town. By the end of the War, O'Connell dominated the central heartland of the Commonwealth. He then merged all the groups into the Quabbin Valley Mutual Burial Association which immediately signed an iron-clad arrangement with the O'Connell Company for its services.

At Kathleen's urging, Patrick dressed in a suit, but no amount of tailoring could disguise his rickets-twisted shape. He ate better, but no amount of food could check the parasites in his cells. Each night, he tallied up his wealth, but no amount of gold could satisfy his greed. Some nights, he travelled to the high bluffs outside Cromwell where the moon whitened the flooded fields behind Pulpit Rock. He felt the cleansing wind on his face, a wind which never dropped into the valley. He snapped at the horse on his way back Flats, impatient of his dream.

Patrick O'Connell's prosperity did not go unheeded by his competitors alarmed by their eroding profits. They watched the Quabbin Valley Association, in an incestuous alliance with the O'Connell Company, subvert, absorb and expand. They fought back and quickly. The Bay State Funeral Undertakers Society was formed. These good Protestants had political connections and money. They hired a firm of Milk Street lawyers in Boston. Within weeks, they struck.

In Superior Court in Boston, the Bay State Undertakers Society sought an injunction against the Quabbin Valley Burial Association, claiming that it was violating state insurance laws. The Quabbin Valley fought back. O'Connell hired his own firm of Milk Street lawyers. The trial was short and swift. The decision went against the Cromwell business man. The Court ruled that the Quabbin Valley Association was in fact, a form of insurance business, thereby subject to the authority of the State Commissioner of Insurance and in violation of its regulations. The Court ordered the Quabbin Valley to *cease and desist* immediately from such illegal business.

The decision was catastrophic. All financial arrangements between the Quabbin Valley and the O'Connell Company were ruled null and void. No monthly payments could be collected. Within days, the monopoly began to disintegrate, to the delight of the Bay State Society who predicted Patrick's bankruptcy.

Part Three

Patrick's fight had not gone unnoticed by Adam Ring. The O'Connell Company had been one of Adam's best customers until the postwar casket firms underbid him. The Polish immigrant studied the court's decision. He thought of a bold plan, which had long intrigued him, linking the survival of the Quabbin Valley Association to his own. He agreed to come to Cromwell to discuss a way out of their mutual dilemma. An untried idea, conceived in desperation, it was to prove the salvation of two immigrants, similar only in their ambition and faith in human death as a source of profit.

"It can work," Adam pointed to the papers spread out on Patrick's desk. For several hours, Patrick watched the young man's absorption as he checked columns of figures and shuffled the pages. Finally, he rose to stretch his legs. Patrick O'Connell disliked making snap decisions, especially about people. Ring seemed almost too bright and quick. Yet, he felt an identity with the young man. They both had come to America for survival. Both were hungry for success.

Patrick had no illusion that this stranger was trustworthy. Ring was a scavenger..... just like him. However, as long as their goals depended upon mutual support, he would accept him. If circumstances changed, well then, he would cross that bridge later.

"Anything that has even the slightest hint of insurance is no damn good," O'Connell said. "Those sons of bitches in Boston took care of that."

"I know that. I have gone over your accounts. Your funeral parlor was never very profitable until you organized the Quabbin Valley Association." Patrick started to protest the brutal appraisal. "Listen, I am not here to judge you. The figures do not lie. As long as you had to compete with the other mortuaries, your margin was low. Why else were you so happy to buy my cheap caskets? As soon as you set up the Quabbin Valley, your profits quadrupled. That was a clever gimmick, selling a funeral in advance, at so much a month."

"Now.....what are your alternatives? You could then go back to competing for work." He could see Patrick stir uneasily. "But that 's not kind of profit you have been accustomed to. Or.... you could keep Quabbin Valley with their members, at your prices. The problem is that the 'honey', the insurance plan, is illegal." Adam leaned closer, "What if I could tell you how to feed your suckers another kind of sweet?"

O'Connell clutched Ring's arm.

"Listen to my plan." Adam leaned back, confident. It was simplicity itself. Neither the Quabbin Valley Association nor the O'Connell Company would sell burial insurance. The Quabbin Valley would still contract with the O'Connell Company for all members' funerals as before. The O'Connell Company would provide the burial at <u>no</u> charge. The funeral would be <u>free</u> for each member of the Quabbin Valley Association who had purchased a coffin on the installment plan. The monthly charge was the same as before. The funeral service was the same. If the deceased died after he had paid for the casket, there was no further obligation. If he died before the casket was paid for, his family would pay off the balance with a small monthly fee.

Adam had done his homework well. There were no restrictions on selling caskets on the installment plan any more than on furniture or ice boxes. Adam anticipated little difficulty converting the members to the new installment plan. The newly formed O'Connell-Ring Corporation agreed to apply all monies paid up to that time towards the coffin purchase.

If Patrick had any reservations, he kept silent. He could see Ring's wiry body tense even while resting. The boy had brains, and, judging from the scar, guts. Patrick remembered another immigrant boy. He thought of Kathleen's future. What was there to lose? He walked over to Ring and shook his hand.

"Adam, you and I are either the worst bunch of crooks or the smartest thieves in Cromwell."

Adam Ring travelled back to Boston that night. He transferred his Company's assets to the joint corporation with Patrick. Two days later, he returned to Cromwell for good, leaving Jacob in charge of the factory. Over the next weeks, he drove up and down the Quabbin Valley, familiarizing himself with the territory. With him was Fredrick Dearing, a new young lawyer who had moved into Cromwell and was still starving.

The two men pleaded, connived, and lied, and managed to convert almost all of the members of the Quabbin Valley Association to the new agreement. Adam lost a few, but most signed, taken in by his smooth patter and the officious high-collared, black-suited young lawyer with him. Who could resist the promise that money paid over the years thought lost was now miraculously restored with full credit?

The job completed, the three men plotted their next moves into virgin territories. They drank to the defeat of the Bay State Society.

Adam cautioned, "We may have won the battle, Patrick, but not the war. I don't think that our Boston friends are going to give up."

O'Connell's hand stopped in mid-air, spilling whiskey down his shirt-front. The joy drained from his face.

"No, Patrick," Adam warned, "those bastards still control the State just like your Zebadiah Harcross owns the Valley. They will strike back. How and when I do not know." He clasped the father on the shoulder. "To fight them, we need money. If....only....."

"If only, what?" Patrick asked.

Adam saw crying children, choking to death from diphtheria. "You know what we need?" He did not give Patrick a chance to answer, "A little sickness to frighten the people . One epidemic, just a small one, and we can dam our own river of gold."

CHAPTER TWELVE

The days were growing shorter. Since the end of June, the north pole was tilting further and further away from the sun. When it set in the west, the valley was buried in heavy shadow, and the air grew cool. The creature's brain could measure this infinitesimal change. In response, as it had done for millions of years, the animal prepared to ensure the survival of the race. The odds against success were astronomical. It required two things: water and blood.

No one knew for certain how long mosquitoes had inhabited the Quabbin valley. Their existence must have been a fragile one. The river was fast flowing and dashed the egg rafts against the sharp rocks. Fish consumed the rest. In the hot fall sun, pools and ponds would dry up. The early colonists drained the marshes for farms. Buzzing, swarming, irritating, their bites were harmless and the numbers decreased each year. Then, a determined white man decided to subdue the river. For one mortal struggle, the Aedes and the Anopheles rose in the air to challenge Zebadiah Harcross for title to the valley.

For two years, the waters had climbed behind Pulpit Rock. Each spring, the dam was closed and the rains collected in the meadows. Beginning in late summer, the gates were opened each day, leaving pock marked land with stagnant pools and puddles, without currents or predators. Spreading over hundreds of sodden miles, the two species exploded in numbers. Gathering strength, they waited to attack. Only they needed a weapon.

The female mosquito had an unusual need. It had to suck up a drop of blood from mammals to nourish her eggs. Up to now, wildlife animals were sufficient for its needs.

The virus of yellow fever and the plasmodia or malaria are invisible to the eye. They live in the mosquito. They leak into wound when the insect bites, infecting. Neither the mosquitoes nor the settlers knew this.

The early pioneers brought with them the usual diseases of the big city, the tuberculosis, measles, and diphtheria. The out breaks of yellow fever and malaria were few and short lived. This was about to change!

As the War of the Rebellion raged, the migration of Negroes from the south swelled into a flood. They carried the virus and plasmodia from Africa and the West Indies. If the white people had noticed any increase in the 'shakes' or the 'ague', they could hardly blame the newcomers because these complaints had been around long before. By the fall of 1865, when Zebadiah and his daughter flooded the headlands and the Anopheles and the Aedes grew mighty in number, the dark skinned inhabitants of the shanties were there for feeding. The chance factors of fate clicked into place to create a critical density of blood and water poised to take back the valley from its spoilers.

It was too late!

The first frost came early.

The ground froze solid.

The waters iced over.

The aggressors prepared to sleep.

They were patient.

In six months the earth would shift as it had done for four billion years.

Then….. would come the summer of 1866.

CHAPTER THIRTEEN

Zebadiah Harcross' house stood like a medieval fortress on the windy ridge overlooking the valley. It tried to coerce the viewer into accepting the pile of stone as a home for a Medici of old. The attempt failed, through no fault of the riches which were poured into the uninspired design. Tall windows capped by arches and keystones, a gable jutting out over the front door, a three-story square tower, peaked with its own tile-covered roof, baroque brackets underpinning the impractical eaves, a high pillared *porte cochere*, all gave an odd appearance to this puritanical New England merchant's home. However, the thick stone walls and central stairwell drawing damp coolness from deep cellar ice storage made it pleasant even during the hottest months.

It was now November. The house cast a long shadow as the sun passed westward. Shaw Billings shivered at the finger of arctic air pointing at the valley. He drew his jacket collar high. The sky was cerulean blue with a few errant clouds resisting the push of the northwest wind. The air was crystalline, sharpening outlines. The river was a white scar branded into the crack of the valley.

The sunlight ignited the hills with splashes of orange and red and yellow.

The beauties of Nature were not Shaw Billings' concern. He and Spencer were worried over the rise of malaria and yellow fever cases. He licked his finger and held it in the breeze, thankful for the Canadian winds which purified the malevolent vapors from the wet bottom-lands.

"Well, Zebadiah, how are you feeling today?"

"You tell me," the patient slammed back. "That's what I'm paying you for, Shaw, and damn well. When can I get back to work?" He scowled as he reluctantly shook the physician's hand. Shaw ignored the hostility.

"Now....now...Zebadiah, just relax, he purred. "Your river can run without you. Do what I say, and let it be."

He picked out Harcross' daughter in the comer, unwilling to intrude."Elizabeth, come here. You are not too old that you can't give Shaw Billings a proper greeting. Remember, I'm the one who tied off your belly-button." He held out his arms. She hesitated, unwilling to display affection in front of her father who was looking on, with disgust on Shaw's good humor. Billings clasped her to him. She stiffened, gave him a peck on the cheek.

"Now, that's better. Don't mind your father here. Since when do I come to your house and you refuse to give me a proper greeting? A man who hungers for the touch of a beautiful woman ". His belly jiggled up and down as he laughed. He gave her another hug. "If only... if only... I was thirty years younger. With my looks and intelligence and your skin-flint fathers gold..." his eyes rolled upward in mock joy. "What a coupling! A union fit for the gods."

"I will be in the drawing room when you finish, Doctor Billings," Elizabeth said, embarrassed. "The water you requested is over there."

Billings palpated the patient's abdomen. There was still slight tenderness in the right lower quadrant, but the severe pain and rigidity had subsided.

"Any more vomiting?"

"No. The wine and broth have stayed down."

"The bowel evacuations?"

"Not a thing since you were here last two days ago."

"And the laudanum?"

"Haven't needed any the past day."

Billings opened his black leather bag and removed two long -stemmed silver goblets. He heated them in the flame of the kerosene lamp. When they were almost too hot to hold, he quickly flipped them over the tender area where burned rings of previous cuppings could be seen outlined. Zebadiah gave a stifled cry as the hot rims pressed into the skin. Tears of pain started and he looked away. When the bowls cooled, the skin retracted into the partial vacuum. Billings pulled the goblets off with a loud pop as the rims broke the seal. He repeated the process four times to draw out the evil humors.

"Alright, Zebadiah. Now, one good clyster and I will leave you alone."

The patient cursed under his breath, but rolled over on his side and drew his legs up close to his chest. Billings withdrew a large copper piston syringe from his satchel. He filled it with a pint of water from the pitcher. He attached a curved ivory tip and coated it with oil. He inserted the nozzle into the man's rectum and forced the plunger down. He pulled out the syringe and refilled the container for a second insertion.

Almost immediately Zebadiah was on his feet, looking for the chamber pot. With loud bursts of fluid and air, he emptied the contents of his lower bowel.

When Zebadiah had finished, Billings inspected the contents of the pot. Mixed with the water were several well-formed lumps, testifying to the bowel's recovery.

Billings was all smiles. He covered the chamber pot with a linen towel and sat down next to his patient. He tucked him in and smoothed out the cover pane. His slow movements were not appreciated.

"Well, damn it, Shaw. What's the verdict?"

Billings gave him an innocent grin and pulled the quilt higher.

"I would say that you are threatened with survival. Just keep on with the mustard plasters to draw out the inflammation. Take the laudanum when you have a spasm. I will see you tomorrow. I will inform Elizabeth that she will probably have you ranting and raving in your counting house next week.

"A week! A week!" Harcross argued.

"One week," Billings insisted. "Besides, from what I hear, Elizabeth can squeeze the river for gold as well as her father. Some say all she needs is a codpiece to be another Zebadiah."

Harcross seized Shaw's hand in an iron clasp. "Don't Shaw! Don't!"

"I'm sorry, Zebadiah. That was thoughtless. But Matthew has been dead for three years. Elizabeth is cleverer than he ever was. She is a true Harcross. She loves the river and the valley. He never did. Even you know that. Be thankful that you have another child. "

"I didn't mean to hurt you, Shaw," he apologized. "It still pains when I think of Matthew and what could have been."

"Be proud, instead, of Elizabeth."

"Elizabeth may be smarter and stronger than Matthew. I know she loves the Quabbin, whereas he despised it. But, Shaw, she is a woman. Someday she will no longer even be a Harcross, and the valley.......my valley, will pass to another." He turned away in sorrow. The doctor was unable to say anything to ease the private hurt. He left the room.

Elizabeth Harcross. It was time Zebadiah came to terms with the fact of his surviving heir. This latest attack was the third in less than a year. Perityphlitis had no awe of the Master of the Quabbin.

⇥⊹⊹⇤

Billings was preoccupied. His concern for Harcross was coupled with fear of a worse epidemic of malaria and yellow fever next summer. He barely greeted the nuns as he entered the two story brick which the Sisters of Mercy had converted from a warehouse into the only hospital in Cromwell.

Although both the French and the Irish obeyed the same God and Vicar, each group supported its own parish and Priests. Only in the Dispensary did they lie side by side. At first John identified with the French, as fellow expatriates. As time passed, his sympathies changed to the Irish. He admired their tenacious energy which had tamed the river and worked the mills. Much as he tried, both groups considered him an outsider.

John heard Shaw enter. He quickly finished the last patient. Billings was no more communicative to him as to the nurses. Spencer knew the summer's death toll had depressed him.

With Yvette and Suzette helping, John managed to change the older physician's life style. They limited his diet and alcohol. For a while, they succeeded. John adjusted the digitalis and foxglove for the dropsy. Billings' weight dropped. His gait was quicker. His breathing freer. Billings was privy to their tactics. The victim said nothing, except for an occasional lament when his favorite desserts were no longer served, or, an overdue supply of liquor failed to arrive. Though, at times, it was almost too much for his willpower, he tried to cooperate.

Then, as the deaths from yellow jack and the ague mounted, Billings withdrew as if blaming himself. After a long day at the Dispensary, he would sit silently at the table compulsively eating. He would decline John's offer of companionship and retire to his library with several bottles of brandy and a basket of confections. He would sit in his wing chair and stare into the flames. Those nights John would awaken to hear the obese physician start up the stairs, pausing every few steps to catch his breath and wheeze, as he made his way to bed.

Many mornings Shaw did not come down until after John had left. Spencer knew that the doctor was inflicting his own phlebotomies, ashamed to show John the recurrent signs of cardiac failure. His lips were the same dusky blue as when John first met him. The skin over his hands were mottled from the poor circulation.

Gradually, he turned over more clinical responsibilities to the young doctor. While John took the burden of the Clinic and Surgery, Billings would climb into his carriage and make house calls on his personal patients. John did not complain. This was his first private practice. He enjoyed the age-old chemistry between patient and healer.

"How was your prize patient this morning? John tried to break through Billings' mood.

"So far, so good, I don't know how many more of these attacks he will have before the perityphlitis spreads."

"Does he realize the threat?

"Zebadiah? He still believes that the River Styx is a small tributary of the Quabbin, and just as subservient. He wouldn't believe he was dead until O'Connell sent him the bill. Then he would rise up like Lazarus to complain." His mood softened. "I have been in Cromwell almost as many years as Zebadiah. I have seen him grow to master an empire. Zebadiah may be rich, but he is not beloved. He wasn't even by his son, Matthew."

The name was a ghost from the past. John had never discussed the Harcross son with anyone. It was ironic. He, a total stranger, was probably the only one in the valley who knew the true facts of Matthew's suicide.

Billings was curious why the mention of Zebadiah's son would have any effect on Spencer.

"Matthew was Zebadiah's only son. He died at Antietam. You were there, weren't you, Johnnie? Antietam. I remember your telling me one evening. Did you know Matthew Harcross?"

John pretended he was trying to remember. "It was possible. There were so many that died in those three days. But, how would I know? They weren't even faces, or human beings as God made them. Only pieces."

Billings continued to stare at Spencer, picking up the hesitancy. If young Canadian knew more, there was a reason for keeping privy.

" Johnnie, Zebadiah Harcross is not a loved man. Certainly not by his wife, Clara, who blames her husband for Matthew's decision to join the Army. Since his death, she has kept to her room, and emerges only on Sunday for Church. It is a strange house, Johnnie, dark and gloomy, with Clara Harcross haunting the upper floors. Zebadiah petulant and hostile as a beast in a cage. Thank God for Elizabeth. She is probably the only normal one there."

"Elizabeth Harcross?" John had heard often of Zebadiah's daughter.

She never invited comment of a neutral nature. There were those who crossed themselves when mentioning her name. Others praised her talents. John would have been hard pressed to make an intelligent portrait out of the scraps of conflicting hearsay.

"I feel sorry for her, Johnnie. I know that's an odd thing to say about Elizabeth Harcross," Billings insisted. "You have never met her." He surveyed his partner's lean handsome body. "She is one of the few people in Cromwell, perhaps the only one, who really loves Zebadiah. When Matthew rejected the valley, it was Elizabeth who cried for Zebadiah's broken heart. The father himself said nothing. His eyes were dry on that day, and ever since. She tried to become the surrogate son. What has she gotten in return? The contempt of both sexes. "

"Why do I feel sorry for her? Because of the cruelest blow of all. Her own father, will not accept her."

John did not understand.

"No, not as a daughter, but as a son!"

Despite John's entreaty, he would say nothing further. If his Canadian friend wished to learn more, it was his own task. As he entered the ward, Shaw Billings had the feeling he had already said too much.

CHAPTER FOURTEEN

The Dispensary had been a warehouse, with broad beams, and a pitted floor with deep ruts from heavy use. The walls were white washed to disguise the black blotches where the damp had lifted up the peeling paint. Although it was noon, windows were shuttered against the dangerous night air. Kerosene lamps hung from the high ceilings.

The male ward contained adults and children mixed together. The patients stirred and moaned. A novitiate was busy emptying chamber pots and filling water basins next to the metal cots. She stood back along the wall as the doctors entered.

John recognized the stench of urine and feces, the sweet scent of rotting flesh, the acrid odor of vinegar into which were plunged hot iron pokers for protective fumes. All mixed with the clean fragrance of tobacco and gunpowder smoke ignited through the night, to ward off the miasmas. Whatever was responsible, John was grateful no new cases of yellow fever were brought in.

John knew the first patient well. This was his fourth admission in as many months. The disease made him look older than twenty-three. His skin was stretched taut over his bones. His eyes blinked from the bottom of sunken sockets. His mouth expelled a foulness. When he spoke, bleeding lips barely moved.

John could see the dilated pupils. The pulse was weak. A foot long scar started at the left groin and wrapped around the thigh when his body had been flayed open at Gettysburg. The wound had healed. There was no bone fracture. The belly cavity was spared. No major artery cut. The man could walk without help, though with a slight limp. The man's eyes were glazed over, unfocussed. The body had healed...but not the soul!

Spencer could not count the numerous cases of drug addiction he had seen since the War ended? There had to be thousands across the States. How could it have been avoided? Could the men lie for months on iron cots, wounds festering and stumps draining, without the juice of the poppy for relief? If, in the years following, they kept their love affair with morphine, was the crime really theirs'? Neither the Surgeon General nor Congress ever recognized this affliction in the rush to bury memory of the War.

Billings agreed. There was nothing to do but feed and clothe him. Remove his lice and give him broth. Then release him with a new supply of cheap laudanum. Wait for the Constable to return him one night from the gutter, unresponsive and prey for the sewer rats.

Next, a young boy no older of eight or nine lay curled upon his side, legs drawn to his chest. His heart was racing too fast to count. His breaths alternated with long pauses. His lips were parched. Despite an insatiable appetite, he had extreme weight loss. He never seemed to get enough water to drink and would immediately void it out.

"What do you think?" Billings asked.

John tried to fit the clues. The boy had come in a week before. Despite efforts of the nuns to feed him, he grew thinner until John suspected one day he would be no more.

"Look there." Billings pointed to the chamber pot under the bed. The dish was full of a pale yellow liquid. A dense cloud of flies and mosquitoes were buzzing as if the pot contained honey instead urine. John shook his head at his stupidity. He inserted the tip of his finger. He smelled the sample and touched his tongue. It was sweet. The boy would be dead of the diabetes before sundown.

The next man was in his early thirties, medium height, stocky, with short muscular arms and legs. His round freckled face was topped with sandy hair.

"Any pain today, Timothy?" Shaw asked. His eyes watched the man's face closely as he probed deep into the four quarters of the abdomen. The man shook his head. Young, healthy, but uneducated, Timothy's only asset to support his wife and three children was the strong body God had given him. Now he would never work again.

Four years of lifting heavy rolls in the Pratt Paper Company print shop had crippled him. Billings had prescribed the only treatment, a heavy painful leather truss for the hernia. Nothing helped as the man lifted and lowered, bent down and straightened up, a thousand times a day, with sixty pounds of weight on his back.

Two days ago, a loop of small intestine had become stuck. Billings and Spencer tried everything. They hoisted his legs with a pulley. They mixed wheat bran and flaxseed and applied the hot paste to the skin. A blister of corrosive green beetle only eroded the skin over the swollen lump in the groin. The cramps worsened. He started to vomit as food could not pass through the trapped bowel.

In desperation, Shaw decided to operate. There was no surgical treatment for hernia disease itself without causing peritonitis. He could, however, cut the tissue pinching off the intestine and allow it to slip back into the cavity.

John gave the ether. Billings made a half inch incision in the groin and slowly moved the blade tip back and forth. With a 'pop', the stuck bowel slipped back into the abdominal cavity. Billings applied a linen plaster over the cut and sent the patient back to the ward ....to die.

Two days had passed and still they waited. They continued to greet Timothy with the false smile. They congratulated him on the relief from pain. The absence of vomiting. The clean healing of the incision. They did not tell him that the released bowel was damaged. The pinched wall would weaken and perforate, leaving a passageway for feces and peritonitis.

Timothy did not know his doctors' fears. Billings inspected the chamber pot, hoping for a formed stool to prove to prove him wrong. There was nothing. It was still too early. Maybe tomorrow would tell his fate.

The two physicians moved from bed to bed with cheer and optimism. If they could not heal, their mission was to comfort.... with smiles and opium.

Before entering the female ward, John stopped and asked, "Shaw, do you ever think the day will come when more patients live than die?"

What could he older man say? Physicians were men with just a little more schooling. John Spencer was entitled to his false hopes, as were his patients.

"Maybe, Johnnie, that day will come." He pointed to the Sisters, "but, if everything were perfect here on earth, there would be no need for Heaven. ...and, then, what would all these good ladies here do?" He took John's arm and hurried him on, lest Spencer ask another question.

Despite the same diseases, the female ward was the quieter. Were the patients embarrassed before the nuns or too proud to cry from their pain ? Whatever the reason, John was more at ease here.

The first patient had been on the Ward since John arrived in Cromwell. She was obese, in her late fifties. Her face was round with a dark moustache outlining her upper lip. Straggly hair escaped the hair ribbon. Her large jowls quivered as she tried to raise herself to sitting. Her color! The amber bile pigment stained her skin, even yellowing the whites of her eyes.

The woman was in agony from a violent itching. Night and day, she scratched her body with her nails, trying to relieve the irritating bile salts accumulating in her skin. The doctors had tried every known poultice. Even a plaster of mercury in oil only inflamed the bleeding skin. Only massive doses of laudanum would let her relax and the hands uncurl.

For twenty years, this mother of four had recurrent attacks of gall bladder 'colic'. The cramping pain would start followed by vomiting and shaking chills with fevers. There was no treatment if the stone did not pass. One month ago, this happened. The stone remained stuck in place. The backed up bile spilled over into the blood stream and was carried to every part of the body. Soon she would die of hepatitis. Until that time, her life was a living Hell.

"How much longer?" she pleaded.

"The stone will pass. It will pass."

"When?" Her hands ripped over her body.

"Soon." He patted her on the shoulder and moved quickly to the next patient, afraid to say more.

The next woman, too, was marked for quick death. Stones blocked both kidneys. Uremic poisons were building up in her blood street. She, too, had nausea, vomiting, chills and fever. But, her urine was red with blood. She had born each attack with screams, dampened by laudanum. For three days, she had voided only an occasional drop. "Is this all?" Billings asked the nun.

"That is all since yesterday, Doctor Billings."

The patient sensed his alarm. He forced a cheerful smile as he clasped her hands in his.

"Be patient, Martha. we are going to give you a different medicine to help the kidneys."

What more could he do? The purgatives and cathartics had not worked. Calomel, rhubarb, castor oil, Epsom salts and camphor. Cupping and blisters of Spanish fly over the kidneys. There was one medicine left. There always was. Shaw whispered to the nun. At least, she could have her laudanum, now hidden in the exotic fragrance of oil of cinnamon and steeped in the magic of rosewater.

The last patient was a child. A thin scared girl of nine, flushed with fever. Her hands were gripped around her throat. The nuns propped her against the pillow. John sat down on the side of the bed and gently stroked the young girl's hair. He kept up a soothing patter as he pried her hands away. He could feel the swollen lymph glands under the jaw. She whimpered when he pressed too hard. John held her close to quiet the tears.

He motioned for the nun to move the lamp closer. He coaxed the child to open her mouth. Both tonsils were covered with pus. When John finished, Billings examined her.

"I agree, Johnnie," he whispered. "It is the quinsy. The boil behind the left tonsil has grown. The abscess is at the surface." He pursed his lips. "I think the time has come."

The child heard the words and shrunk back. His hand lingered softly on the side of her cheek. "Do not be afraid, Emily. You are going to be alright. Trust me."

The nuns scurried from the room. By the time they returned with his surgical kit, Billings and Spencer had taken their places on opposite sides of the child. The patient clawed the doctors' hands away, terrified.

"Now... Emily..." Billings purred, "please open your mouth again. I would just like another look." He held his empty hands out in front of her. "See...... I am not going to hurt you."

Two nuns stationed themselves at the foot of the bed ready to immobilize the legs. Two nuns stood ready to hold the arms. A fifth nun was at the head of the bed. She was holding, concealed from the child's sight, a curved scalpel. Billings nodded. John seized the child's head. His fingers crunched in the angle of the jaw forcing it open. The child struggled. Upon command, her arms and legs were immobilized. Shaw probed the child's mouth, locating the tip of the boil. He plunged the scalpel deep. The thick creamy fluid poured out, gagging the child and spraying the doctors.

Billings did not give her a chance to scream. He stuck his right index deep into the cavity, milking out remaining pus. Satisfied, he motioned to release the child. She sprang back into the arms of the nuns. They wiped off her tears and blood. They gave her warm water to drink. She swirled it around, cleaning her mouth.

"Laudable! Laudable!" Billings boasted. "There it is, Johnnie boy, "Laudable pus. Find and drain it and the patient will be cured. Wonderful! Wonderful! "He nodded happily at the child who was casting hateful scowls at her benefactor, "Yes, Johnnie, a week and the little one will be home safe and sound."

John had followed the signs of a hidden infection. The fever, the chills. He knew the corruption was in her neck. Had it not pointed outward, but spread inward where the knife could not lance, the child would have died. Death had let one victim escape. Yes, laudable pus. Emily was lucky.

There was a sudden scuffle in the corridor outside. The patient could not have been more than sixteen or seventeen, pale complexion, long brown hair gathered in a cheap cotton bonnet. She was pregnant. Her feet were widely spaced, her shoulders flung back to support the swelling. The nuns were forcing her to enter the ward. She was dragging her feet, trying to escape their grasp.

"What's the trouble?" John ordered the nuns to release the woman.

"Please," she begged. "Please. Please."

What was the girl so frightened of?

" You will help me?" Her tear-streaked face turned up to his. "You won't make them put me in the Ward?"

"The Ward?" What did the girl mean? He looked for an explanation. The girl clung to him, tearing his jacket.

"Here. Here." he held her arms. "Tell me. I will help you, but I don't know what you want. What about the Ward?" He glanced at her abdomen. "You will be having your baby very soon, won't you?" He gave her a friendly smile. "I would think any day now. Isn't that right?"

"Please, doctor. Let me go. I will leave Cromwell. Go back to Boston. Just don't make me have my baby in there."

John stood confused while Billings and the nuns managed to put the patient in a bed. They moved cloth screens around the bed to give her some privacy. The patient continued her sobbing.

"I don't understand, Shaw. Why is she so frightened of the Ward?"

"Johnnie, that young girl doesn't want to have her baby here because she is afraid of dying*"

"Dying?" It made no sense.

" Yes, dying. She may be right."

Billings led Spencer from the Ward to an empty room. "Most of the deliveries in Cromwell are delivered at home by midwives. If there is a complication, a breech or pelvic contracture, then they know to call me. The midwives in the County are good, Johnnie. They know when to ask for help. I deliver my own private patients at home, too. Rarely at the Dispensary."

" The woman you just saw is a charge of the County. The child was probably conceived out of wedlock. She could be an inmate at the Work House or the jail. She has no home. She has to be delivered here at the Dispensary. The chances are great she will die here. The child birth fever, Johnnie. The child birth fever."

John sat down. No wonder the poor child was frightened. He and Billings must have looked like executioners. Childbirth fever. He had seen the victims in Montreal. The would enter, happy and expectant. The delivery itself usually successful. The child strong.

The mother healthy …. at first. Then the change. The discharge turning foul. The chills. The fever. The vomiting. The peritonitis. The child….motherless.

What was the secret of this disease? Why did it strike some and not others? The deliveries were the same. The physicians were the same. Yet, without explanation, waves of purulence would sweep through the Maternity Ward killing eighty percent of the mothers who entered.

Elias Guthrie's words came back, ' Gentlemen. You ask your'selves the cause of this virulent plague which attacks the young female at her most glorious moment, when she has created life. Puerperal fever exempts no one. No station in life is free from it. Some claim the disease resides in the child which is itself spared. I do not concur with this theory. Others claim that the afterbirth is at fault. I have examined countless placenta and never detected any difference. A few claim that a difficult labor causes an imbalance in the humors of the pelvis. Which of these I cannot be certain.'

' I do believe, however, that there is an imbalance. Unfortunately, it does not produce laudable pus which can be drained and the patient saved. Instead, the sepsis spreads internally.'

The nuns had prepared the trembling young mother. Her two legs were spread apart. Shaw Billings carefully pulled up the sheet not to embarrass her. With slow, gentle movements, he inserted his right hand far into the vagina. The labor was proceeding well. Everything was going to be fine. Then he withdrew his hand…… leaving behind the stain of Emily's laudable pus.

The last patient was at that wonderful age when the softness of youth was ripening to full womanhood. Except for the large linen turban around her head, she gave no evidence of being ill. Although her cot lay near the window, the patient edged way from the light. John knew the reason.

A month before, Spencer had been summoned to the Bell Alpaca Mill by a messenger. At the word 'emergency', the Sisters had packed his case with bandages, splints, tourniquets, and laudanum. The workroom was filled with strange whirring machinery tended by gnome-like creatures, bending, swaying, bobbing up and down like the arms and levers of the looms they served. As he adapted to the half-gloom, John could see a young girl propped against the wall. Above her, flapping in the air from a broken pulley, was a twisting leather strap. It had whipped across the girl's head tearing off her scalp.

John removed the bandage. The entire skull was exposed, hard and white. The left ear was missing. The right ear hung in crushed fragments. John measured out the opium. He washed the skull with rose-water and bound it with linen strips.

"Johnnie, she will die," Shaw said the next day. He was right. The bone would flake and crumble from the drying air. The brain, unprotected, would rot. "Johnnie," Billings insisted, *there is nothing you can do. Keep her comfortable. Give her faith and laudanum. Hope that the end will be swift." It was a harsh verdict. What else could they do?

"Shaw," Spencer asked, "have you ever seen anyone scalped by Indians?"

It was an odd question.

" Never, Johnnie."

'When I was in the army I treated a soldier from Kentucky. I forget what brought him to the Field Hospital. What I remember was that he had no scalp."

"No scalp! That can't be."

"This man was alive, Shaw, and very healthy. He had a strange story to tell. His family had been attacked by a band of Indians in the Western Reserve. He was hit with an arrow. He lost much blood and fainted. That is what saved his life. After the attack, the braves thought he was dead and took his scalp for a trophy. He did not know how he held back from screaming when the knife sliced a ring around his head and his scalp was wrenched off. The next day, settlers found him. "

" The man was lucky. There was an old white woman who had been captured by Indians when she was a child. She had seen young braves scalped like this soldier. They had been treated by their medicine man …and lived."

"Damn it, Spencer! Medicine man! Old woman! Or Luke the Healer himself ! Enough of the preamble! What is the secret?"

Over the next half-hour, John revealed what had saved the Kentucky man's life*

"What do you think?"

"I don't know, Johnnie boy. I just don't know."

"You know what will happen if we do nothing. "

It sounded far-fetched. Could something so simple, invented by a heathen medicine man, observed by a frightened captive child, practiced on an illiterate Kentucky farmer, work? There was no alternative.

"You will have to tell the patient that we cannot guarantee anything," he warned.

The next day, John explained to Mary Ann what he planned. "What we must do is to give the bone a new skin. "

Over the next week, John drilled hundreds of tiny holes into the skull surface. Blood immediately seeped up, covering the skull with a clinging scab. To John's delight, when the slough fell off, a thick scar remained shielding the bone. John proudly showed the happy result to Billings who vowed to write up the case for the annual County Medical Society Meeting.

When time came for discharge, the young girl became depressed. She avoided light, mirrors, shrinking away from people to hide her appearance. The young girl had no family. She lived in the factory dormitory owned by Marcus Bell. The sisters made arrangements for her to stay with a local family until she felt confident enough to go back to work.

One afternoon, John was surprised to see the girl talking to a stranger. John thought that he recognized the voice. The visitor stood up to let him examine the patient. The kerosene light caught her, backlighting the raven hair and heightening the white skin. The girl gave him a shy smile of recognition and curtsied.

John caught his breath. The funeral parlor late at night. The crippled father with the beautiful daughter. O'Connell. The child Billings had delivered. The girl he had dreamed about that very night.

"Kathleen O'Connell. Miss O'Connell," he got out.

"Mary Ann will be coming to live with us."

John was still staring at her. He had a rash desire to hold her and squeeze her and she would become him in a harsh sexual urge to possess. His heart raced. He felt so silly. He couldn't understand why he suddenly as like he did. So strange. So different from any feeling he had ever felt before in his life. A grown man who had seen a mere girl only twice for a total of less than ten minutes no more than a dozen words he shivered although he was not cold.

" Yes….. yes…, he stumbled. " Within a few days." A smile formed on his lips.

" Don't be worried, Mary Ann. I will come to visit you….. often." Then he stood erect, bowed, and said goodbye to the young girl whom he would make his wife.

CHAPTER FIFTEEN

The near epidemic of yellow fever was a mixed blessing to the O'Connell-Ring Corporation. The rising death rate in the valley made it easy to sign up new subscribers. However, it was this very success which threatened the company's survival.

Patrick rustled the papers at his new partner. "Adam, we are in trouble! We are three times larger than before, but, the new subscribers are dying faster than we can collect premiums from the rest. We must stop looking for new business until the winter kills the sickness or the numbers will bury us." The plea fell on deaf ears. There was no stopping Adam Ring. He drove himself as a man possessed, no sooner reporting back to Patrick than he would be on the road again, sizing up prospects for another branch, or urging managers to work harder. Somehow, Patrick managed to find the money to pay their legal commitments. By the time the ground froze solid, Patrick's fears were over and the profits climbed as Adam had predicted.

If Patrick O'Connell's worry was for fiscal stability, Adam Ring's concern lay elsewhere. He refused to believe that the Bay State

Undertakers Society would leave the fledgling Company alone. He feared they would try to throttle it once and for all.

Patrick could never understand why his partner chose the penniless young lawyer to represent them. The tall thin attorney was everything Adam wasn't. Light sandy hair, a flat expression which never changed. He spoke in drawn-out phrases, as if talking would deplete his verbal inventory and render him bankrupt. He had the annoying habit of pausing in between sentences, carefully weighing each word, and at times, each syllable, a practice which drove Patrick to distraction.

Adam saw in the somber third generation American a cleverness beyond his years. Even more, Frederick Dearing projected a counterpoint to his own frenetic personality. Adam Ring was quick to see how the deliberate mannerisms of the Harvard Law School graduate inspired confidence.

During the November recess of the State Legislature, Dearing reported back to Cromwell.

"Look at these legislative Bills, Adam." Dearing handed over a thick sheaf of legal documents. "I expected the Bay State lobbyists to come right out and get a law passed against the O'Connell-Ring Corporation. Never once did a single legislator on their payroll single out you or Patrick. That's what so suspicious."

Adam skimmed the papers. He could not see why the young lawyer had bothered to bring them. "As long as they leave us alone, who cares? What is so damn mysterious about these Bills anyway?"

"I'm not sure. Look, Adam. Here are four separate Bills, each passed without debate. Four laws designed for only one purpose, to strengthen existing laws already on the books regulating insurance companies."

Adam had stopped his reading and was listening intently.

"I still don't understand." Patrick looked at Adam. "Do you? You just read them."

Adam waited to hear what else the lawyer had to say.

"I didn't understand either, Patrick. Especially when I checked around Beacon Hill and found that nobody seemed to know anything about them. I met with Thaddeus Bigelow, the Commissioner of Insurance. He didn't know anything either."

"Was he telling you the truth?" Adam asked.

Dearing seemed a trifle offended. "Thaddeus is a distant relative of mine, on my mother's side. Why would he lie to me? The Bigelows haven't needed money since the slave trade. No, I believe him."

Patrick stood up, disturbed by the talk of a mysterious conspiracy. "Damn it, Dearing! Get to the point. There must be something in those damn Bills to get your dander up."

"I think I know what's troubling Frederick." Adam read the four statutes.

"House Bill No. 3750 forbids any insurance company within the Commonwealth from designating the undertaking parlor to conduct the funeral for an insured person."

" House Bill No. 3891 says that the proceeds of any insurance policy must be paid to the beneficiary in legal tender."

"House Bill No. 4006 states that an insurance company cannot enter into any type of legal contract with any funeral parlor or individual undertaker."

"Finally, House Bill No. 4065 makes it illegal for any insurance company to supply any funeral merchandise as repayment for insurance."

"So what, Adam? Those laws have no possible connection with us. They are only for insurance companies."

"That's just the point, Patrick. Why the four laws?" They both spoke at once.

Dearing continued, "There isn't an insurance company in the State with any financial connection to a funeral parlor. Not one! Yet, here are the laws."

Adam paced back and forth, his brow knotted in thought. The two men watched him. For several minutes, he said nothing. "You've done a good job, Frederick. I agree. Something smells bad here. I can't put my finger on it. The Bay State group is in on it. I just don't know how. These four Bills didn't get passed just to make work for the Legislature. The recess will be over soon. Keep your eyes and ears open in the next Session. I think we will see the missing piece."

Two weeks later, Frederick Dearing was back. Adam and Patrick were at the station in response to his urgent telegram. The lawyer had barely stepped off the train.

"Its bad, Adam. Worse than anything we could have expected. Here. Read for yourself."

Adam took the typescript of House Bill No. 7100 which was passed hours before. It did not take him long to see the threat.

A contract of life insurance is one whereby the insurer, for a consideration, assumes an obligation to be performed upon the death of the insured, or upon the death of another in the continuance of whose life the insured has an interest, whether such obligation be one to pay wares or merchandise, or to other things of value, and whether the cost or value of the undertaking on the part of the insurer be more or less than the consideration flowing to him. Every person, form or corporation writing or issuing contracts of life insurance, as defined in this section shall be deemed to be engaged in the business of life insurance and shall be subject to all the provisions of the laws of the Commonwealth of Massachusetts regulating life insurance companies.

The three men sat long hours that night. Several times Kathleen came in to see if there was anything they wanted* The platters of food remained untouched.

"Alright, Frederick," Adam broke the silence, "let's go over it again. What exactly does this law do?"

"The Bill, with the four previous statues, changes the definition of life insurance in the state. In your case, it defines an installment plan for a burial service as a type of 'insurance'. You and I know that there is only one company in the State to which the law applies. The law is now on the books and it prohibits you from functioning. Even worse, it provides legal sanctity for the Bay State Group."

"What does that mean?" Adam asked.

"Before today, it was the Bay State Society against you. One business against another. Now, it is different. The Commonwealth of Massachusetts is your adversary. The Attorney-General's Office is compelled to uphold the law."

"Only if the State elects to enforce the law. You know Bigelow. Have you any other family connections on Beacon Hill? Can we buy any?"

"I already thought of that. So did their lawyers. They are damn clever. They managed to get their Chief Counsel appointed as a Special Assistant to the Attorney General. The bastard is serving, without pay, as a public service. Within five minutes of the passage of the Bill, he served me with a writ, bringing suit against the O'Connell-Ring Corporation." He threw a thin folded paper docket on the table. "There it is. Signed and sealed. The people of the Commonwealth claim that you are conducting an insurance business outside the regulations of the Department of Insurance. You are ordered to *cease and desist* forthwith'."

Neither Adam or Patrick bothered to pick up the writ.

"What is our next step?" Adam asked.

"Our legal position is obvious. We will claim that we are not conducting an insurance operation."

"When is the trial?"

"They didn't waste any time. In two months before the Third District Superior Court in Cambridge.

"What happens if we lose?"

"We appeal all the way up to the State Supreme Court. Remember, though, if we win, the other side will do the same."

"If we lose the appeal?"

Dearing looked at the young Pole whose face was without expression.

Then, at the old Irishman whose hands trembled as he raised the liquor to his lips. The lawyer stammered. For once words failed him. Much as he tried, he could not deliver the death sentence.

＝━ ━＝

Adam Ring noticed the change in his partner. The father seemed detached from the impending law suit. Much as he tried, Adam was unable to discover the reason. He concluded it must be a personal problem unrelated to their business. Not even wildest guess would have revealed the truth.

Since the injured patient took lodging with his daughter, Patrick had watched Kathleen's growing attachment to the young physician. If John Spencer thought the frequent house calls camouflaged his true purpose, the naïve ploy did not fool the father. The daily visits continued after Mary Ann had returned to the Bell dormitory.

For two years, Patrick O'Connell had watched young men pay court to Kathleen. By one excuse or another, he blocked them. The Canadian doctor was different. The man was mature, responsible, of a good social caste, intelligent and handsome. Someday he would inherit Shaw Billings' practice. Despite a prayer to deny it, he found John Spencer an eligible suitor.

There were nights when Kathleen returned from Spencer that a different emotion clung to her. She would enter his bedroom and lay her head on his hand. When she looked at him, there was a kind of love he had never seen before. He would lie awake the rest of the night, seeing another. He would cry out. His body would tremble, not from the ague, but from fear.

At the breakfast table, before she left for her job at the Cromwell Nursery, he would press her close. He knew the love she wanted would cost her her life.

━╪ ╪━

Shaw Billings was not surprised when Patrick called on him at home. The visitor was tense.

"I know why you are here, Patrick. Its Kathleen and my Spencer, isn't it?"

"Shaw, he can't marry her. He will kill her."

"Patrick, I may be wrong. Only God can know that for certain. Maybe with Kathleen, He will be merciful."

"Merciful! Damn Him and damn you! How merciful when Rachel was pregnant? When she was in labor? Tell me! How much mercy when He took one life to pay for another?"

Shaw remembered that terrible time eighteen years ago when Rachel came to him, her abdomen swollen with her first child. Nineteen and married one year. Her mother and father dead. Her brothers in Pittsburg. How proud the first day she felt movement. Her breasts got larger. The nipples deepened in color. How she laughed when she walked like a drunken sailor. Soon ....she would nurse the product of love between two human beings.

Shaw told the father his joy was premature. "She can never bring a baby through her pelvis. Rachel's pelvis is constricted. I measured the width. I measured the head. The child cannot be born as God willed."

The husband's objections were in vain.

"If we do nothing, the uterus will push the child's head against a door which cannot open."

The husband could hear his wife cry out in the bedroom. The pains were still far apart.

"What are the choices?"

"I can operate. Open the uterus. Take out the child. It is called a Cesarean Section. The child will live if the operation is done in time. But Rachel will die."

"Why?"

How wonderful, even if just for an instant, to recite a clinical abstraction and forget there were lives in the next room.

"Patrick, if we open the uterus, it will hemorrhage, or worse, risk peritonitis.

"What is there is a chance, even a single one, that she might survive?"

Billings' resolve crumbled. He could not help himself.

"Yes, there is a chance."

"Doctor Billings, I cannot take a life. Any life. I am a Catholic like Rachel. I cannot kill the child.......it is in God's hands."

Rachel had the Cesarean Section. Rachel hemorrhaged to death that night. Patrick took the child and held it above the blood-soaked sheets, shaking it until it cried in fear. Billings was in the room. He would never forget the scene.

"As God is my witness," Patrick swore. "Let the Lord preserve my soul for an eternity of torture, if I ever let you die as I let your mother."

Now, the father sat before him to save his daughter's life. Kathleen. With Rachel's black hair, her complexion, her soft gentle ways. Most of all, she shared the congenitally contracted pelvis of her mother.

CHAPTER SIXTEEN

For almost a week, the weather had introduced winter, skies lowered by a grey quilt of clouds, winds tingling the skin. Then, on this early November Sunday, Nature permitted one respite. Viewing the Quabbin Valley from the Summit House atop Mount Holyoke was an annual rite for Cromwell quality. After Thanksgiving, the rambling Tea House would be closed until the spring, windows boarded, awnings taken down, the white wicker furniture from the veranda piled in the common rooms where now people gathered in conversation.

John Spencer moved through the crowds with the young girl at his side. When Kathleen glanced up, she caught his pride. Her head barely came up to his shoulder. She was forced to walk with an extra half step to every one of his to keep up with his brisk pace.

"That damn bonnet!" John swore. He stopped and brushed away the ribbons which tickled his neck. "Either you grow another foot or take the silly thing off."

Kathleen removed the hat. The wind sent her tresses flying in all directions. John caught them and made a thick bundle which he lifted off her neck. Kathleen tied on a ribbon and let the black braid drop over her shoulder. John's hands lingered on her and bent down to kiss her. At the very last moment, she pulled away and ran down the narrow trail away from the Tea House.

"Damn!" he swore again. He picked up the hamper to follow. Since he had started courting Kathleen, she resisted every attempt at affection. John sensed an alarm which blocked him. He did not know the reason.

John Spencer had never been in love before. It was a strange unsettling feeling. There were the nights after returning from the O'Connell home when he slept fitfully. He would invite Yvette and Suzette into his bed. When he cried out, it was not their names the girls would hear. They accepted in their hearts what Spencer was testing in his.

It was more than the need for sex. For the first time in his life, John felt the need to protect another human being. When they were together, he was convinced he was her shield against anything bad in life. John had decided to remain in Cromwell. It must be a future with Kathleen as his wife. He knew she loved him. If only he could understand her fear.

The *Goat Trail* led away from the Summit House. At places, it came close to the edge of the cliff, then sauntered back into the evergreen woods where pine needles softened sound and the wind whistled in a low hush. When he caught up with her, Kathleen was talking with familiarity to a person he had never seen before. He heard the man's foreign accent and his awkward formal gestures.

"This is Adam Ring," Kathleen said. She saw Adam's embarrassment. She took his hand and tugged him gently towards Spencer.

John introduced himself. "Have we met?"

"Perhaps you saw me at the Dispensary. Doctor Billings has been giving me lauda..." He stopped, and started to leave.

"Adam, have lunch with us. There is more than enough."

It was a selfish thought, but John did not wish to share Kathleen. It was obvious from her concern, the man was lonely.

"Please do, Adam. She must have packed enough for the Union Army. If nothing else, there will be less to carry back."

Kathleen found a small patch of high grass sheltered from the wind.

Adam sat to one side, eating slowly. Kathleen rested against John who was lying propped up on one elbow. Whether it was the heat, the food, or the dark claret, but gradually a languor crept over the trio. The pale young virgin. The tall Canadian doctor. The scarred Polish immigrant. For the first time, their three lives probed through barriers of sex and background and touched one another.

"Do you come here often?" Kathleen asked.

"Many times," Adam replied. "In Poland, where I come from, the land is flat. We have rivers and fields and farms. Hills, mountains, there are none." His gaze swept beyond his sight. "When you stand here, you are different and higher than everyone else. One can never have such feeling back where I was born."

John was intrigued by comment. "Is that what you want ?"

Adam walked over to the cliff's edge. He stood there, searching the valley below. He answered the question by thrusting out his arms to encircle the land. "<u>This</u> is what I want."

"Why?"

"Everyone wants to possess something." He pointed back at Kathleen. "That is what <u>you</u> want, isn't it?" Adam's fingers touched his scar. "Do you think she or any other like her would be mine for the wanting?" Adam continued, "I can have those who are beautiful like Patrick's daughter. But, I must pay for them. Then, for those few hours I can pretend that I am tall and handsome. What is the memory ? Love? No. Only a business transaction. "

"Don't you believe that for every person there is someone to love them," John protested.

Adam turned away, angry. "There, Doctor Spencer, is the only reality. Look at it. What do you see?" he demanded.

"Beauty." The two men were not aware that Kathleen had silently joined them. She placed one arm around John's waist. "Beauty," she repeated.

"She's right, Adam. It is beautiful."

The three stood there. The valley floor was burnished with fall. Wherever a cloud passed before the sun, a black shadow would follow. Through it all, the river meandered like a painted line of blue,

"Beauty?" Adam's scorned, "What I see is the personal property of one man. There is only power and greed and gold,"

"Adam," Kathleen argued, "does the fact that the valley is owned by Zebadiah make it less beautiful?"

"It does to me. Where ever I look, everything is owned by someone who came before me. Back in Biala-Poliska, it was the Landsteiners who owned the land and took the taxes. In Boston, those who lived on Beacon Hill and prayed at St. Paul's owned the docks and the factories. Here, it is the same thing all over again. The Harcrosses possess what you and I must look at from a distance to call beautiful. Is there any place on earth where some person has not already gotten to first?"

The two young people standing together were so obviously in love, Adam was jealous. A familiar pain throbbed across his temples. He felt in his jacket for the reassuring shape of the glass bottle,

"You asked me, John Spencer, what I wanted. Someday I want to be able to stand somewhere and see <u>my</u> valley. It does not matter what color it will be, or whether it has a river, or even if it is a valley. Just as long as what I see is mine."

"Not all of us are given that privilege," Kathleen said..

"It is <u>not</u> a privilege. Power is not given. It must won by the strong. "

"Does that make it right?" John asked. The Pole had a disquieting effect on him. Ring made him feel that he had never wanted anything hard enough in his whole life.

"Right? Right?" How many years ago since he had been that naive? "Tell me, Doctor Spencer. Why is it right for you to make money from disease and to be respected ? When I profit from the same death, I am despised. We profit equally from pestilence. Yet, you gain gold and honor. I gain gold and dishonor. Where is the righteousness?"

"I don't understand."

"I make coffins. I bury the dead. I am the scavenger. Yet, take away the ills which feed my company and where would you be? In the workhouse, with no skills of value to society"

"Adam, I did not become a physician to seize a piece of the earth. "

"Whatever your reason, you benefit like me."

There was an unpleasant logic to his words. "The gold is of no importance," he insisted.

Adam gave a wry laugh.

"Comfort yourself in that belief. Someday, you will stand up here and look down into the valley and feel the need to have power, for whatever purpose. Only then, my friend of this afternoon, will you realize that the only beauty of the valley is in its possession. Zebadiah Harcross knows that. Elizabeth Harcross knows that. Patrick O'Connell knows that. You still think that you can remain pure because you have two magic letters after your name? There comes a time when each man gives up his innocence. He is then a harlot, selling himself for profit."

Adam stared at John, wondering, testing. " You have never had to trade something you love for something you want. Someday that time will come for you. What will you do then?"

Kathleen and John watched Adam make his way back to the Summit House.

"I have seen him spend much time with my father. Patrick says he is a clever businessman. I have the feeling he has been hurt badly. Scarred not only on his face, but deep inside. He must make peace with himself. Life is too short to be angry forever."

John knew Kathleen was right. However, Adam's question remained unanswered. "Do you still think that you can remain pure ?"

It was late by the time the horse-drawn carriage entered the Flats. The only sounds were the horse's hoofs on the cobblestones and the water softly rushing in the canals. With the sun's setting, the late fall chill had returned to the earth. Every breath of beast and passenger gave off a white haze which hovered in the air like smoke before fading. The horse whinnied and gave a shiver as the cold touched its sweat-covered flanks. John transferred the reins to his left hand and carefully tucked the woolen folds of the blanket around his companion.

The O'Connell house was silent. A small light was shining in the second story window. John waited in the parlor while Kathleen went upstairs to her father's room.

He stirred when she pulled the quilt up. He opened his eyes but his look passed by her. She kissed his forehead without arousing him, put out the light and closed the door behind her.

Patrick had banked the fire before retiring. John shook the grate to quicken the embers. The dried coals crackled and blazed into incandescent showers which swirled in the dark hearth. Quickly, he added wood. The fire caught the logs and darted streamers of heat into the room.

Kathleen paused in the doorway watching him. Why had she rejected his advances? Her thoughts were all confused. Terribly mixed up. For years her father tried to persuade her to take the veil. A novitiate, then a nun in the Mother House of the Precious Blood. Why this urging when he had rejected the Church after her mother's death? Patrick's answers were always evasive.

She loved John with whatever that new word meant. She had noticed him on his rounds at the Orphanage long before he came to call at her house. He was a kind and gentle person, devoid of guile or deceit or envy. As she watched John stoke the fire, she knew she would marry him, and bear his children and learn whatever love meant between a man and a woman, no matter what secrets her father feared.

John could not tell how long she had been standing there. The fire sparkled on her taffeta dress when the fabric moved. She seemed so small, so weak, so helpless. His heart beat faster as he held out his hands.

"Kathleen," his voice was soft and low, "come closer. The room is cold and it is warm here by the fire."

His arms enveloped her like blossom pedals closing in the twilight. She did not resist. His hands encircled her tiny waist, then moved higher to mold her bosom. His fingers cupped each breast. The nipples hardened under the teasing touch. Her hands reached around his neck and tangled in the curls around his ears. She bent his head down. Her lips grazed his brow leaving a faint moistness to mark the spot. His lips sought hers.

Kathleen could feel John's muscles tightened. A strange hard swelling pressed against her. She tried to shift away, but John held her, crushing his groin against her body to squeeze out the frustration. His hands moved in swirling patterns. An unaccustomed emotion stirred inside her. An ill-defined feeling which replaced everything else. She could no longer think of Patrick or his warnings. She could not think of the future or even the past. Her whole being just was in the moment. Her body quivered, but not from anything that had ever made her quiver before. A single thought. To satisfy the strange man caressing her as she had never been touched before. To satisfy him in some way she could not be certain about.

Kathleen did not object when John started to unbutton the back of her gown. The buttons were sewn close together and his fingers were almost too large. She removed her chemise and underclothes. Naked, she stood before him in shy modesty. The light flowed up and down the hollows and curves of her body, trading places with melting shadows. She reached undid the ribbon around her hair.

John dropped his clothing in a pile at his feet. He knelt down and held his hands out for the girl to join him. He could tell the hesitation. Kathleen wrapped and unwrapped her arms around her, unsure what else to do. She was frightened of the naked male in front of her. Her eyes kept finding the dense thicket of red hair between legs where his organ rose arched and rigid. She shook in fear of trying to understand what going to happen.

"Don't be afraid, Kathleen. All I want in the world is to love you as my wife. I will not hurt you. Trust me."

She stood there, undecided, her fingers twisting at her waist, pleading......What did he want? She started to cry. She did not know why.

"What is it? Tell me," he implored. "How can I remove your fear if you keep it hidden?"

She was unable to speak. Her eyes wandered over his body, stopping each time at his erection. She stood there, tremulous, hesitant, bewildered, confused, tingling, nervous, afraid, determined...... waiting.

"Don't be afraid. God made men and women to love each other," He made no attempt to conceal his nakedness. "Is it me, Kathleen? Are you scared of what I will do?"

"Oh, Johnnie. It isn't you." She knelt down sculpted the gaunt lines of his face, then traced a path down the front of his body. The testicles, so heavy and solid, retracted at her touch to escape into the groin. John shivered as she possessed his manhood in a firm clasp.

"I am not afraid of making love although I have never been naked before a man as I am now, nor seen one like you, so eager. But, Johnnie, what if we have a child? Patrick warned me. My mother died when I was born. I know others who died."

He started to speak. She touched his lips with her fingers to silence him until she finished.

"It is true, Johnnie. There was a girl. Several weeks ago. We have her baby at the Orphanage. The mother never came out of the Dispensary alive."

How could John ever forget the patient? The young girl struggling and screaming as the nuns held her. The mother who was afraid to die at the hands of the two doctors. They reassured her nothing bad would happen to her. Trust us, they promised. The child? Perfect. A baby girl. The mother? Dead of puerperal sepsis within the week. Why? John had no more answer now than when he and Billings carried out the autopsy. The abdomen was distended with pus. The intestines gangrenous. Again.....the question.....why?

Spencer wiped the tears. "Kathleen. I remember that girl. She was not alone. The sickness was in the Dispensary. The yellow jack and the ague. The malaria. The pestilence. Many died in the Ward. Not just that mother. We closed the Ward and burnt sulfur candles to purify the air and kill the miasma. "When you have our child, you will deliver at home. Shaw and I will take good care of you. Nothing bad will happen to you, Kathleen. I promise. I will protect you. Trust me."

His hands slid to her groin. The fingertips stroked the silken skin between her thighs. She lay back, her legs separated as he parted the moist lips. Her body began to twist as he cleverly caressed the tender bud hidden in the black curly hair. She moaned funny sounds. He kissed her face and nipples with teasing bites of pain and pleasure.

She stroked his penis. It was smooth and warm and hard. Her touch made him quiver. She lay back. Her arms encircled his neck.

He knelt between her thighs. John ignored the warm body under him. He needed somehow to get rid of the tension forcing him on. He moved back and forth, his penis up against the hymenal ring, straining to rip the fragile membrane if it did not give way. He could see Kathleen's pain. Her face was drawn. She bit her lower lip to prevent crying out. Her fingers and nails dug deeper into his back, trying to resist the urge to pull away.

Faster and faster he rocked. His movements were automatic, beyond his control. His mouth was open, head thrown back. "Please," he begged. "I'm sorry! I'm sorry!"

His arms now locked Kathleen in place, crushing her so she could not escape. With one harsh thrust, he tore her virginity. Over and over he came, the ejaculations ending in a rigid convulsion. Kathleen screamed as he discharged into the frayed chamber. There had been no pleasure for her. Only pain where she had never in her life felt any before. Even at that moment, when she looked up at the stranger for some sign of love, some affection, all she could see was the self-serving male relieving himself inside her, not caring about her at all.

Spencer's breathing slowed. The spasms which had driven his sperm deep ceased with one final tremor. He looked at the girl. He could find there no joy, but only the pain he had given her. He felt shame, disappointment.

John lay back on the carpet and watched Kathleen put on her clothes. He buried his head deep into her pubic hair, softly kissing as he caressed her buttocks. Carnal desire was now replaced by desired contentment. His hands ran over her body. Around her waist. Her pelvis. The caressing suddenly changed. Now, it was no longer a lover expressing thanks. It was the firm deliberate touch of the physician.

If God blessed the act of love, a life would grow inside her belly. Trust me, he had sworn. How could he? In his selfish joy, he had just murdered one of them.

CHAPTER SEVENTEEN

"Damn it, Elizabeth," Zebadiah scowled. "When will the work be finished? Tom Kennedy told me they had ice up at Pulpit Rock." The room was cold. The bedroom fire had gone out during the night and the servants had not yet rekindled the hearth. The room was heavy with the odor of dead smoke and fumes from the full chamber pot. Zebadiah sat in the hard wooden chair in front of his writing table. The pale morning light etched deep lines of age and chronic illness on his sallow complexion.

Zebadiah did not glance up at his daughter once as his orders, laments, and curses poured out. He would pause only to jot some cryptic notation on the bottom of a document, sprinkle sand over the wet ink and place it on the growing pile of finished work. Elizabeth watched her fathers grimace as he denied his pain. He would not give up. Zebadiah Harcross was still the Master of the Quabbin.

Since the recurrence of his perityphlitis, she had taken care of his financial interests. Maintaining a pace which exhausted Tom Kennedy, Zebadiah's Superintendent, she explored the complexities of his empire. It seemed that everything that lived in the valley, in some way or other, paid tribute to the owner of the river. Each morning, like a penitent, Elizabeth stood to receive the commands for the day. Late at night, she would report to him. Despite her diligence, never had he thanked her or acknowledged her labors.

Elizabeth tried to alibi away Zebadiah's callous behavior. She knew it pained him to be a prisoner in his own home. She felt the ache he still bore for Matthew, the immortality denied him. She sensed the silent anger always lurking beneath the surface, asking why God had played such a cruel jest on him.

A tear fell on the table. Zebadiah stopped. Elizabeth? A tear? He leaned back to examine his daughter. Was she ill, too? "Elizabeth," he pointed to the tears on her cheeks. "What is the matter?"

"Nothing, father." Her emotions were now under control. "I was just worried for your health. That is all," she lied.

Zebadiah was touched by her concern. He suddenly grabbed her arm, excited. "We are almost there, Elizabeth. The second dam at Pulpit Rock has succeeded as we planned. Finish at Cromwell and we will have finally tamed the river." Just as quickly, embarrassed by his emotion, he released his hold and retreated back into his shell of indifference.

It was too late. Elizabeth touched her arm where it still smarted. It had been the kind of gesture Zebadiah would have given to Matthew. She remembered Billings' grave prognosis. The peritonitis which could come with the next attack. That she would inherit was no longer the issue. Her father had no alternative. Would he die, though, without leaving her a treasure she craved more than thirty thousand horsepower? A father's love ? Would she ever receive his blessing as her birthright?

⟞⟝ ⟞⟝

The great dam which Zebadiah Harcross had thrown across the Quabbin River at Cromwell was one of the engineering marvels of the Commonwealth. Visitors would travel to see for themselves what the might of a single man could wreak upon Nature. The dam was a massive construction planted into the solid rock of the river bottom. A plank walk was suspended by iron rods below the crest. Young boys would show their bravado or win bets by scampering from one side to the other with scarcely a glance.

Elizabeth could feel the carriage clatter on the cobblestone along the first canal. It was seven thirty in the morning. The men had been working for an hour and a half at the mills. The streets were empty except for women drawing water from iron pumps. The road soon changed to a dirt path with well-worn ruts. By now the dam could be heard and felt by the two occupants on the carriage. Even the horse sensed the coarse vibrations which shook the earth underfoot. To Elizabeth Harcross, the dam was a captive Gulliver, anchored to the earth by the Lilliputians.

As they drew closer to the river, Elizabeth felt the thundering of thousands of tons of water falling perpendicularly over the crest. Her pulse raced faster. She heard the violent bellowing of the river as it thrashed against its man-made mountain of stone. Her eyes narrowed in anticipation.

Tom Kennedy glanced back at his passenger from his awkward perch. He was middle-aged, short, stocky of frame. His face, reddened by years of exposure, was noisily chewing. Dribbles of amber-stained liquid dripped from his chin as he shifted the plug of tobacco from one side of his toothless mouth to the other. He didn't care that the habit disgusted Elizabeth. He resented being nursemaid to the daughter during her father's illness. Every few minutes, he would lean over the side and expel a mouthful of the tobacco to provoke her.

"That damn woman," he cursed in the pub after work "If you gave her a pair of trousers, she could piss standing up. Knowing that bitch, she could probably hit the wall from ten paces." This never failed to win a round of laughter and commiseration for Kennedy's role as a lackey to the young girl.

"You know what she needs, Tom," would come the usual leer followed with obscene gestures.

"I do, but who here's the man to do it, even saying that the likes of Elizabeth Harcross would let one of you close enough to smell her? I've been with her for almost two months now. It will take a man with a bigger cock that's here in Cromwell to lay her upon her back."

Tom could see Elizabeth leaning forward as she caught the first glimpse of white spray. She did not see him watching her. He shook his head solemnly and spit once again. Any cock to tame Elizabeth Harcross would have to be a damn lot bigger than the river which one day would be hers to own.

⟞⟝

Elizabeth Harcross was out of the carriage and on the path to the gatehouse before Tom Kennedy had reined in the horse. The air was alive with spray from the waterfall. The ground was covered with puddles of water. Skirt tucked high, she picked her way to the red brick building. Built six stories tall, it towered above everything else in Cromwell. Elizabeth imagined her father had deliberately designed the beacon-like Gatehouse to satisfy his ego, although he steadfastly maintained that the looming height was necessary to monitor the reservoir behind the dam.

The Gatehouse base was built on top of the sluicegates controlling the river. Waves arched and plunged like dolphins as the river was split into three tongues of white foam and led, docilely, into the three canals. Elizabeth leaned far over the iron railing, her body suspended like a bird paused for flight. The spray saturated her cloak and condensed on her face. She closed her eyes and drank in the power flowing below her.

With the Irishman puffing at her heels, she rapidly climbed the six flights of stairs. Half-way up, she stopped to wait for Kennedy to regain his breath. He clung to the banister, his face florid, panting and choking from the exertion. Elizabeth could not resist, "Come on now, Mister Kennedy. One big disgusting spit over the side and you will be as good as new." With a chuckle, she hoisted up her hem, exposing a more than decent length of calf, and scampered to the top. Kennedy raised his head to see her disappear from sight. "Bitch! Bitch!" he swore before some tobacco juice dripped back into his throat and forced him to stop in a bout of coughing.

Her cheeks were flushed and perspiration stood out on her forehead by the time Elizabeth reached the top floor. The men and women working at their desks immediately rose to their feet as she pushed through the swinging gate into the inner office. Slightly out of breath, but delighted by the vision of her tormentor gasping on the stairs below, she nodded a brief, but friendly greeting and entered her father's private office.

The walls were the same raw brick of the tower itself. The ceiling rose two stories high to peak in the center. A wrought iron chandelier hung down with cups of melted wax frozen in bizarre shapes. But, above all, were the windows! No other room in Cromwell was like it. Ten feet high they enclosed the room in all directions. It was a breath-taking view. As one circled the space, the entire valley unrolled like a diorama. One felt the thrill of being a bird, soaring in space above the land.

If nothing else, Elizabeth loved her father for the display of power and pride which had decreed this architectural triumph. It was the eerie levitation of being suspended between earth and sky. A knock at the door, and Tom Kennedy burst in. There was a smirk on her face. "How nice of you to join us, Mister Kennedy." She moved to the table covered with papers and blueprints. "If you are quite prepared, perhaps we can start the business of the day."

Despite their overt hostility, Tom Kennedy and Elizabeth Harcross had earned a grudging respect from each other. The bond was their mutual concern for the safety of the dam. For several years, Zebadiah had suspected that the constant pounding of the water over the top of the dam was wearing away the river bottom below, threatening its stability. His illness hit Harcross before he could follow up his fears.

Tom Kennedy had been boss of the construction crew which originally designed the dam. At his suggestion, Elizabeth had hired divers to inspect the damage. Wearing with heavy suits connected by long cables to hand-powered air pumps, they probed the river bed. They reported deep gouges extended under the footing of the dam itself. Elizabeth was equal to the challenge. The answer was to fill the hollows and to let the water fall down a gentle slope to break the force at the base.

Elizabeth and Kennedy had driven themselves to finish before the cold weather set in. Large crates of stones were floated into the river and sunk in place. Many a farmer took advantage of the unprecedented market in boulders to load up his cart and bring them to the dam for a quick profit. Slowly, steadily, the work progressed. Only one small depression remained to fill. To the west, a mass of grey clouds paraded across the hills. A shrill whistle of wind rattled the panes in the tall windows. She shivered. Zebadiah was right. The cold season had arrived. He would be pleased with what she had done. The dam was safe.

As the pair gazed through the window, they saw the small human figures who had been scattered, stop to congregate at the river bank just below the base of the Gate house. Tom's face turned white. "There's been an accident, Miss Elizabeth," he whispered in a fearful tone.

If Tom Kennedy's climbing up the six flights of stairs had been labored, there was no hesitation going down. Elizabeth was at his heels. By the time they reached the accident, they saw that one of the divers had been severely injured. A stone 'crib ' had shifted its position in the raging current, swung towards him and tipped. By the time his fellow divers had rescued him, his air tubes were ripped and his suit filled with water.

The diver was no more than eighteen or nineteen, medium height. His face was pale with a soft blonde moustache. His breathing was erratic as he choked to clear his lungs. Miraculously, he had survived. Workers had stripped off his diving suit. He was naked. His body was thin and muscular. A triangle of curly blonde hair cushioned his genitalia and rose to touch his umbilicus. The skin was covered with bleeding lacerations and abrasions. As she came close, Elizabeth gave an involuntary gasp. His hands! Both wrists had been crushed. The bones stuck out through the skin like broken sticks. When he tried to raise one arm or the other, the hands dangled and flailed in all directions. He screamed in agony each time he lifted an arm to touch his face.

Tom Kennedy covered the youth's nakedness with his jacket. "They've already sent for the doctor, Miss Elizabeth. There's nothing else we can do 'till he comes." He took her arm to lead her back. Her eyes remained on the young man whose life had been saved and lay there mutilated

"Thank you, Tom," She knew that he wished to spare her. "I will wait. That's the least I can do."

Tom Kennedy brusquely ordered the crowd back to work. Elizabeth knelt down alongside the injured man. She cradled his head in her lap and whispered words of comfort. The man opened his eyes wide at the unexpected female voice. He recognized Zebadiah Harcross' daughter and tried to get up with the aid of his hands, but fell back screaming. For the first time he saw what had happened. Tears rushed from his eyes. His body shook in fear. "No! No!" he thrashed about in her arms.

Elizabeth saw his terror. Why was he so frightened? What about his hands? The doctor would here any minute. Tom bent close so that the boy could not hear. "He has fractured his wrists, Miss Elizabeth. Look. The bone is through the skin." He could see she was still puzzled. Damn women! "His hands! His hands! They will have to be amputated.

Elizabeth continued to shake her head in disbelief as John Spencer entered her life.

CHAPTER EIGHTEEN

"Damn that woman!" John Spencer watched Shaw escort Elizabeth Harcross out of the Dispensary and into the carriage Tom Kennedy had sent. He could barely contain himself until his partner returned. "Damn her!"

"Damn who?" Shaw's face was all innocence as he watched Spencer's smoldering anger.

"Elizabeth Harcross." He saw Billings was teasing him. "Christ, Shaw. You are as bad as she is." He could still hear the hoof-beats as the carriage disappeared out of sight. "I would rather have the devil himself around than that woman. Damn it, Shaw, why did you allow her to stay? You've never done that before."

Billings did not bother to answer. Despite what his young partner thought, Shaw considered the encounter highly amusing.

When John arrived earlier at the Gatehouse, his attention was directed to discovering the extent of the injuries. He dismissed the young girl kneeling alongside the patient as a relative or even his wife.

"What happened?"

"One of the stone 'cribs' shifted as he was monitoring the placement," Elizabeth quickly answered in an authoritative manner.

Even if John Spencer could have understood the technical terms, he had not asked her. Ignoring the answer, he repeated the question to Tom Kennedy. Elizabeth's embarrassment lasted for only an instant and was replaced by anger. This doctor was like all the other men in her father's world. No one would acknowledge her as an equal. She slowly rose to her feet. She smoothed the creases of her mud-soiled velvet dress which flowed down from the tightly laced waist. Her cheeks peaked with red, as she fought back.

"I apologize for language beyond your comprehension," the tone was cold and formal. "I forget that you are a stranger to the valley. However, even in Cromwell, ignorance is no excuse for rudeness." She pointed to the boulder-laden rafts floating in the river. "We were sinking barges of stones to fill the hollows in the river bottom when one tipped over from the current and trapped the diver. The other divers saved him. What I do not understand is why <u>you</u> are here. I expected Shaw Billings who is familiar with these injuries."

John realized that he had committed a terrible faux pas. This thin-skinned woman was no one to be trifled with. However, stranger or not, he was fully capable of treating the patient. He could accept the rebuke for his abruptness. But, to demean his clinical skills was uncalled for.

"Doctor Billings was occupied in Surgery when the message arrived. I came in his place because of the urgency of the call, Miss....."

Elizabeth let the question dangle for a moment before answering. "Harcross, Doctor Spencer. Elizabeth Harcross. Now, perhaps, you will be kind enough to take care of your patient." She stepped back to end the conversation.

John resented her condescension. He did not understand why he had allowed her to provoke him. With difficulty, he repressed the urge to continue the sparring. He bit his lip in silence and bent to his task.

The boy's body was covered with blooding cuts and areas where the skin was slashed. John knew these injuries were not critical.

"What is your name, son?" he asked.

"Martin, sir," the boy whispered, grimacing in pain. The act of breathing was agonizing. His chest moved in shallow excursions because of cracked ribs.

Spencer gave the patient a reassuring smile. " During the War, my assistant was named Martin. He was a good man. And damned smart. If he were here, he would tell you what I am going to tell you. You will live and be fine. Do not be afraid. I am going to examine you. First, I will give you laudanum to take away the pain. Yes, Martin was a good man. Just like you. Trust me."

John's words pattered up and down the patient even as his fingers percussed carefully over every square inch of injured tissue. He kept up the innocuous monologue, waiting for any pain which would have indicated hidden internal damage. All the ribs were intact except for two. The boy could move his limbs and turn his head, although with discomfort. John applied the stethoscope. The lungs were not harmed. The abdomen was soft. The pulse was rapid, but strong.

Satisfied there were no hidden injuries, John turned his attention to the shattered arms. Every time the boy shifted position, he jostled the dangling wrists, provoking a heart-rending cry. John gave the boy two ounces of laudanum. John asked if anyone had brandy. A bottle of whiskey was produced. The doctor held the boy's head up and let him swallow the spirits. While waiting for the opium to take effect, John washed off the wounds. He worked carefully, avoiding the arms which the boy held out away from his body. John smoothed the boy's hair away from his eyes, then removed the river slime off his face. Finally, with Tom Kennedy's help, he lifted the legs and pulled on a pair of trousers. A jacket was thrown over the chest to counter the shivers from the pain and shock.

The opium gradually did its job. The moans grew less and finally subsided. The head fell back, lax. The boy's breathing was slower and more even. His eyes glazed over and closed. Watching the boy's face for any reaction, John picked up one arm. He cushioned the flailed hand. The boy's cried out, forcing John to stop. He did not release the arm, but continued to hold it immobile for another few minutes while waiting for the narcotic to deepen. John inspected the mangled wrists, trying to picture the accident. The sharp edge of a boulder had fallen across both wrists, perhaps as the boy stretched out his arms to ward off the blow. The fingers dangled helplessly, twisted inward like claws.

John asked for two short lengths of board to make a splint. He could not handle the arm and planks at the same time. He was suddenly aware of Elizabeth Harcross at his side. Without asking, she reached under his arms and supported the limb while he strapped on the board. Together they slowly lowered the secured arm to the ground and repeated the splinting with the other arm.

"Thank you," John said. The words were not hard to speak.

"You are welcome, Doctor Spencer." There was no rancor in her tone. Whatever his faults, the physician was sensitive to the patient. Even Shaw Billings had a brusque manner which, on occasions, resulted in more pain than was necessary. John Spencer was different. He cleaned the patient himself, instead of waiting for the nuns to do it later. He clothed the boy's nakedness. He waited patiently for the laudanum to take effect before he touched the injured areas. He splinted the limbs to avoid discomfort before transporting him.

Elizabeth Harcross may have had a lofty sense of her own importance, yet, John admitted, she gave assistance without being asked. If their first encounter was less than cordial, the penalty lay with him. She stayed close to the diver as if his welfare was important to her. She did not flinch at his injuries. If she was dissembling, at least her presence comforted the patient. Spencer knew the boy would soon need all the comfort he could get, no matter from what quarter.

—◄— —►—

The patient was brought directly into the Surgery. The boy's eyes darted about him, taking in the nuns waiting by his side. He twisted his head and saw the steel instruments on the tray by his side. He could smell the odd scent coming the glass jar held by one of the nuns. The enameled iron surface under him was cold and hard. He tried to rise up, but a cluster of hard hands held him down. He cursed at his helpless arms still immobilized in the splints.

"No! No!", fear breaking through the narcotic cloud. "Doctor..,, please!" His words tore at the walls as if to shatter them and gain his freedom. He could see Spencer talking in hushed tones to an elderly fat man. He raised his head to see Elizabeth Harcross leaving the room. "Miss Elizabeth. Please. Do not leave me."

She paused in the doorway. The two doctors waved her in.

"Do not be afraid, Martin, This is Doctor Shaw Billings. He has taken care of my family for years. He would like to examine you." She rested her hand on his cheek, and lightly stroked the skin. The youth looked up with a drawn expression, savoring the gentle touch.

It did not take Billings long to confirm the diagnosis. "Compound fractures. Bilateral," he concurred with John. You were right to bring him directly to the Surgery."

"If there were only some other way? To amputate both hands! The boy is no more than a child, What will he do? How will he live? Who will want him?"

Billings saw his partner's anguish. "Spencer. There is no other alternative. The skin, Johnnie boy! The skin! It is broken through. You must amputate unless you want the patient to die."

Shaw was right. There was no alternative. When the bone is exposed to air, putrefaction of the mangled flesh will set in at the mangled fractured site. Poisons will spread from to the rest of the body and kill. The treatment was the same for a thousand years, except the stump was not plunged into molten lead. Make a clean amputation above the trauma and new tissue will seal over the fresh cut and protect. The young boy could guess from their expressions what they had to tell him. He cringed back.

"Martin," Shaw began, "I have examined your injuries," He smiled pleasantly at the patient. " Fortunately, they are not too severe. You will live to be a wise old man with many children. Don't be afraid on that account. " He could see the boy relax.

Maybe these devils were not as bad as he feared, Hope stirred.

Billings' manner was slow and reassuring, "In order for you to be well, we must treat the injuries. You can see the damage as well as we can. The bones have broken through the skin." His words flowed in a bland disarming fashion. He hesitated before continuing. "We must remove the damaged tissue so gangrene will not set in."

It was evident that the patient did not understand what was being said.

"Martin," Billings' words were now soft, but firm. "We must dissever the wrists, to leave clean ends of the arms."He could see the horror recoil before him. "Martin, we must amputate both hands."

The patient let out an unearthly shriek which fought for an exit. "No! No! Miss Elizabeth!" he implored. "You won't let them do that, will you? Please! Please!" he beseeched each of the nuns in turn.

"Isn't there some other way?"

The two doctors would have known her question even if she had not opened her mouth. They shook their heads in silent agreement. There was none. Elizabeth bent down so that her head was close to the boy's. Her lips grazed his ear.

"Martin, the doctors wish to do what is best for you. My father and I will help you after you have healed. We will not forget you. The important thing now is to live and get well. You must trust Doctor Billings and Doctor Spencer. They know what they are doing. We must believe them, Martin. Trust them."

The last words were a deliberate challenge to the two men. The patient lay back, eyes closed, resigned to what had to be done. With a barely audible 'Yes ', he agreed to the double amputation.

Elizabeth was as good as her word. Even when Billings told her that the patient was unconscious from anesthesia, she stayed in the room. Dense fumes of ether evaporated off the cloth cone and filled the air. The two men tied on gutta percha aprons over their suits. They moved to opposite sides of the table, each taking an arm. Working swiftly to minimize shock from blood loss, they circumscribed through the muscles of the lower arm, about two inches above the fracture. The saws rasped fast. Within seconds, two detached hands fell to the floor. Twenty blood-smeared fingers quickly tied off the blood vessels which were pulsing crimson. The loose ends of the silk dangled over the sides of the table, brushing up against the trouser legs of the two men. Finally, a packing of coarse lint covered the stumps.

When the mask was lifted, Elizabeth realized how hard it was to remember a boy was on the table. Take away a face and hands, and what made a body a human being? How easy it was to forget.

The severed hands lay under the table like a pair of white spiders .... lifeless... thick and fleshy and blood-cloaked. She felt at any minute they would twitch and scurry towards her. A wave of nausea overtook her. She felt lightheaded. The room brightened and faded and brightened again. Voices grew indistinct. Her heart stopped, then skipped erratically. She felt weak, unable to stand upright. She thrust out her hands to hold back the floor which was rising fast to hit her.

"Quickly!" John called to Shaw for help. He caught her in a tight embrace. He could feel the full breasts under the bodice. The skin of her neck was cold and wet from shock. He carried her to a bed in the ward. He wafted a small vial of aromatic salts under her nostrils until she regained consciousness. When her eyes opened, Elizabeth Harcross searched the faces above her without recognition. Slowly, memory cleared. When her pulse was steady, John allowed her up. He expected her to leave the Dispensary. Instead, she asked to see the patient.

Elizabeth waited until Martin woke up. When he twisted in pain, she gave him laudanum, raising his head so he could sip from the spoon she held. She sat with him until he fell into a sleep compounded of opium and blood loss. Only then did she give her vigil to the Sisters of Mercy.

John watched her make ready to leave. " I am sorry if I offended you earlier," he offered lamely. "All of us, especially Martin, owe you a debt of gratitude."

Elizabeth rose to her full height. Perhaps the mutilation had made no impression on the doctor. That was his price for being a physician. For her, the tragedy would never be forgotten. "Doctor Spencer, what passed between us is of little consequence. I appreciate that but for my cooperation, it might have been difficult to persuade Martin to lose both his hands. I carried out your bidding without question. I also remember what I told Martin, ' they know what they are doing '. Tell me, did I tell that young boy the truth?"

She paused on the threshold. John started to answer, when she cut him short. "Because if I did not, Doctor Spencer, may God have mercy on your soul."

CHAPTER NINETEEN

S haw Billings knew that it was only a question of time before John spoke to him of Kathleen. Many times, the older physician had been tempted to broach the topic. Something always made him stop. If their relationship was not to be permanent, nothing would be gained. If, on the other hand, O'Connell's fears of the alliance were true, what could be said? Shaw knew that in matters of the heart, reason was a docile hand-maiden to love. He waited.

"Shaw, are you going out this evening?" During dinner, John ate little, toying with his food, his facial muscles twisting as if carrying out a conversation with himself.

"No, Johnnie, why do you ask?"

"I think it is time we have a careful conversation."

Billings chuckled, 'Careful conversation.' The man was so damned serious. Did he think his behavior was a mystery to those around him?

"Sure, Johnnie," he said with mock seriousness, "although I can tell you right now the answer is a dozen sessions inside a hot sweat box with your naked skin well-larded with camphorated mercury.

You may lose your hair. Your teeth will drop out. Your balls will shrivel and your pego will droop. But the French pox is sure to leave."

John was not in the mood to discuss the current treatment for syphilis. "Damn it, Shaw. Be serious."

" I will. I will." He screwed his eyebrows together making his round face look utterly ridiculous, "Is that better?"

John could not help laughing.

Shaw's face took its ease. He grinned benevolently. "Alright, Johnnie boy. Let's go to the Library. Then you can tell me all about your wanting to marry Kathleen O'Connell and your sudden interest in the financial fortunes of Cromwell's most prominent physician."

"You old faker," Spencer sputtered. "You know everything, don't you?"

"Well, it wasn't hard to guess. Your carrying on around the girl like a milk-fed calf sucking up to the big mother tit. You're not the first to feast at the altar of Aphrodite." His eyes twinkled over the top of his half-lenses. "You have supped there?"

John blushed crimson. Any reply was superfluous.

Billings poked at the hearth to bring the fire back. He poured a brandy for John, another for himself and settled back in his favorite wing-chair. He sent up puffs of smoke which circled above his head like mares' tails. He had waited for a long time for John to decide to stay in Cromwell. It was not the lure of a lucrative practice which was making it possible, but the sacrifice of a young girl scarcely out of her teens.

"Up until now, you received a monthly stipend in addition to room and board as agreed with Elias Guthrie. It is not much, but adequate. John interrupted that he was not complaining. Billings waved him down, "It is adequate for a <u>single</u> man. Soon things will be different. You will be moving to your own home. You will have responsibility for a wife.... and family." He stressed the last word.

Did Spencer know ? The man gave no indication. Not a flicker. Shaw let out a long sigh. This was going to be a difficult evening.

"First, Johnnie. The Dispensary. It is owned by the Sisters of Mercy from Worcester. The County Commissioners pay the Sisters an annual subsidy. The endowment is small. The Catholics in Cromwell are for the most part laborers and poor. The good Protestants, though they use the facility, have never seen fit to repay their debt other than by prayers."

"Now, Johnnie, the part that concerns you." He drew a long breath on the cigar, savoring the aromatic, slightly resinous taste. "Ah, Johnnie boy. Take away these heavenly creations of the devil and life would not be worth the struggle." He peered intently at his listener, trying to remember his train of thought. "Ah, yes. My income. Your income. It arrives from two sources. From those who labor for Zebadiah, he deducts a monthly fee from each man's wages which I receive. In return I provide all the medical care the family needs. You can see that it is profitable for me to keep the men healthy which is exactly what Harcross wants. He is a very clever man." He saw John's surprise. " I did not think you knew that the Lord of the Quabbin was responsible for a goodly percentage of our daily bread."

"Most of the other mill owners follow Zebadiah's example and contract with me for similar care. Everyone else pays privately whether they have real needs or just clysters every morning from over-eating." He beamed from ear to ear. "Yes, Johnnie, those constipated matrons in the highlands are the benefactors of all that I have come to love and cherish." He patted his abdomen, fingered the crystal goblet of swirling amber and exhaled another lungful of the pungent smoke. "Johnnie. Learn to give a good clyster, and you, too, can grow old and fat and content like me."

"But, never forget those in the Flats. Zebadiah does not pay when the men are sick or crippled. They have families to support.

Heal them and heal them fast. Keep them healthy, and collect your unconscionable fees from the enemas and phlebotomies from the rich. Do both with equal dedication, and you will have both a body and a conscience well satisfied."

"One final word. On your nuptial day, I shall give you as my wedding gift, a contract, pretty and legal with sealing wax and fancy words. You shall be my partner. An equal for as many years as I will have that privilege. " He stumbled over the last words and lowered his head. John had never seen tears in the old man's eyes before. Billings had always shielded emotion with banter and clowning humor. John had expected a long term of tenure before full partnership.

"Shaw, It is too much. It is not fair,"

"Johnnie. Let me talk of fairness. It is not too much. Where else could an old reprobate like me, at ten times the price, obtain such a vessel of virtue and innocence. Since you entered my house, I have the pleasures of starting out in practice again. The enthusiasm. It is almost as if I was young again." He put down the cigar and placed both hands on his crotch, well-hidden under the folds of fat, "I will tell you, Johnnie, Make this poor worn-out member young again." He gave a loud laugh. "And, I will be happy to give you the other half of my fortune."

Billings' levity evaporated as he knew the evening's preamble was over. "Its Kathleen you really wanted to talk about, isn't it?"

"It is, Shaw. You delivered her mother. You know the history."

"It should not be a secret to you, Rachel has a constricted pelvis. Kathleen was born by Cesarean delivery. The womb hemorrhaged. Rachel died post-partum."

"Patrick?"

"He fears the same for his daughter,"

"Why?"

Billings was certain the young physician knew the answer. Did he want to hear the death sentence from someone else? Did he hope that his diagnosis was wrong? John was too good a doctor for that. "You know the answer as well as I do. You felt her contracted pelvis?" It was more a statement than a question, "You have made love to her, haven't you? Johnnie?"

When Spencer raised his eyes to the old man's, there were tears. "I have loved her, Shaw. More than once. I needed to hear it from you. That is all." His hands fell limply to his sides.

"What will you do? A Cesarean section has been fatal for over a thousand years,"

"What can I do? I love her, Shaw. She loves me." The words emerged in a half-whisper. "She <u>trusts</u> me. I told her I would take care of her. I pledged no harm would come to her. She has faith in me, Shaw. What <u>can</u> I do?"

Billings stared into the fire somberly. Trust me. How many human beings have died believing those words? What else could the physician offer when his skills and nostrums failed? Wasn't it better to sell hope than nothing?

"There are....ways...." Billings finally offered.

"No, Shaw, if I use the prophylactics, or even withdraw, Kathleen will suspect. The old fear will come back. I cannot do that ... for her sake."

"Only... for <u>her</u> sake?" Billings challenged. "What about you? Don't you want a child? A son? At those moments when your excitement is at a peak, don't you want to <u>believe</u>, to trust that somehow all will be well? Tell me, John. Be honest. Be true to yourself."

Where had he heard those words before? What did his father caution?

This above all, to thy own self be true, and it must follow as night the day, thou canst not then be false to any man.

Shaw was right. He loved Kathleen. He also loved the thrill, the pleasure, the passion, the accepting womb into which he plunged his need and seed. Shaw was right. He did want a child......but.... he also wanted Kathleen.

He had never felt so burned up inside. Why must <u>he</u> make a choice? He was the healer. Conjurer of miracles. Choices were for others, not <u>him</u>. He felt ashamed for the sin of pride. 'Trust me' he had promised.

Shaw pulled a chair close to his friend. "Do not scourge yourself for that feeling. You are no different than any other man who wants a women for his pleasure, but also to give him an heir." He placed his hand on Spencer's shoulder. "You were a boy when you entered here. You became a man. Now you wish to become a father. That is the natural path. The crime is not in the wanting, but that we, as physicians, cannot guarantee the giving."

John squeezed the older man's hand. "You asked me, 'What will I do?' I can't stop loving her. Tell me, can your words keep her alive?"

Billings ignored the bitterness. The man was entitled to his anger. "Johnnie, let me tell you a story my father told me. It takes place in Persia many years ago. A Caliph was about to sentence a thief to death by the sword, when the man pleaded for his life. Asked why he should be spared, the man replied he was working on a marvelous invention that would make animals speak. The Caliph was astonished. He consented to let the man live one more year to teach his favorite horse to talk. If at the end of that time he failed, he would be put to a particularly painful death. The man agreed and left. When his friends questioned the bargain, he replied, "First, you forget that I will have another year of life. Maybe by then, the Caliph will have died. Or, I will have died. Or.... maybe., maybe... the horse will speak.""

Billings could see John listening. "The only advice is to take Kathleen's love. Return it. Make her happier than she could ever imagine in her life. Who knows," he shrugged his shoulders, "maybe you will not be able to have any children. Maybe, she will deliver normally, and maybe....maybe....though some miracle yet untested, we will be able to extract one life without taking the other."

Billings saw John take up the last creature from Pandora's Box and clutch it to his bosom. HOPE. He smiled to himself. It was a secret he would never reveal. The trust that he held out was nothing more than a fairy tale. For John Spencer, at this moment it was sufficient. The two men sat together without speaking long hours through the night. In truth there was nothing more to be said. They watched the brandy slowly fuse the dying flames into another new day.

CHAPTER TWENTY

S haw Billings would not tell John the reason for the unexpected dinner invitation from the Harcrosses. ' It is not purely a social occasion' was the only clue he gave. John knew of other nights the elderly doctor would go in the other direction with his attorney to review his real estate holdings in the Flats. John concluded that his partner had many irons in the fire, the nature of which would not be revealed until Shaw Billings was damned ready.

The streets were dark at six o'clock, the early December sun having set over two hours before. The air was full of falling snowflakes. There was no wind, and the white specks lingered a while before the gravity gently floated them down. The carriage moved slowly, the hoofs clattering on the snow dusted pavement. Cromwell was quiet. The new gas-mantle street lanterns installed on the thorough fares leading up to the Highlands shone with pale halos through the screen of swirling white dots. Here and there, yellow house lights framed shutters and drapes.

By the time the Morgan made the difficult climb to the Harcross mansion, it was snorting dense puffs of moisture which froze into icicles and dripped from its nostrils. Upon reaching the broad front portico, a servant emerged to help them out and then took the carriage and horse into the stables.

The change from the cold black night into the warmth and light of Zebadiah's home dazzled John. He had seen the new gas mantles used in the mills to allow laborers to work long into the winter twilight. Never had he seen such a profusion installed in a private home. Dozens of ornate iron brackets projected from the walls, each with a frosted glass chimney. Most striking was the amazing absence of shadows as the newly invented lights blazed with a radiance never before created by man. In each corner, strange cast iron structures with fluted ribs stood on claw legs pouring out invisible rivers of heat. Billings had told John of the recent craze towards central heating. He deplored the modern advance as destroying the moral fiber of the American. Whatever might be the devil's hand in the invention, John was selfishly delighted with the heat which drove the night chill out of his limbs and clothes.

"Welcome, gentlemen." Zebadiah advanced with hesitant movements. He had recovered sufficiently to leave the house each day. However, the long siege had weakened him. The slightest physical effort left him light headed. He had lost weight. He walked in a slightly hunched-over position, still fearful of the abdominal pain which no longer was present. John felt the tremor when he shook his hand.

Zebadiah was amused to see the young physician still staring with child-like awe at the gas lights and radiators.

"Damn lot of foolery, if you ask me." He waved his hand towards the objects with a scornful gesture. " Elizabeth had them installed while your friend had me confined to bed. Next thing I know, those useless toys will be paraded up to the second floor some day when I am down at the Tower."

"They are not useless toys, father."

All heads turned to see Elizabeth descending the dark curved staircase into the central foyer. John caught his breath. Zebadiah stood dumb-struck. Even Billings gave an involuntary gasp. She stood there at mid-landing, head thrown back with a mischievous smile. She wore a long gown of pale blue watered moiré which fell from the shoulder, pinched in at the waist, and then flared into a long train which trailed several steps higher behind her like a wake. When she moved, ripples of color spread out in ever-changing hues. Her bosom was pushed up, almost overflowing the severely corseted design. Her hair lay loose about her shoulders, spilling over the naked skin. Her color was high with a definite flush of red on both cheeks, put there by an artifice which would have provoked her father had he known.

She moved down the stairs slowly, the crisp material ruffling around her. She gave her father a kiss on the forehead. Then another, discreetly on Shaw's cheek. She held out her hand to John. He did not know what to say. This was not the same female all discipline and purpose, who had challenged him at the Gatehouse. Nor the compassionate girl who had fainted in the Surgery. This was a woman, ripe, enticing, confident of her feminine strengths. This was Elizabeth, the unveiled temptress.

Zebadiah had never seen his daughter display herself in this manner before. Why? The young doctor? It could not be. To him, the Canadian was only a foreigner whom his long-term friend had taken in. Handsome, but unsophisticated and poor. Elizabeth? A Harcross who someday would control one of the largest fortunes in the Commonwealth. Impossible!

Only Shaw instantly saw what was happening. If Elizabeth was Diana, it was evident who was the prey. He looked at Spencer and then at Zebadiah's daughter. He thought of Kathleen. He put out of his mind a particularly naughty thought which excited his imagination. *Quelle domage*! If only he was younger.

"I still don't know why you talked me into putting those damn things in the house," Zebadiah continued to complain. "I have lived for fifty four years perfectly well with kerosene lamps and fireplaces. I am satisfied." He swept his arm around the solid affluence of his home with pride.

"But father, it is important that Zebadiah Harcross have such 'toys' in his home. Everyone in Cromwell will want the same in their houses?" She gave him a secret grin.

Zebadiah explained. "You gentlemen know of the Coal Gas Works up at Smith's Ferry?" The doctors nodded at mention of this newest of the Harcross enterprises. How could anyone in Cromwell not know of that ugly square building after only one year staining its neighbors black from the foul smoke belching out of the chimney. When the wind came down from the north, the Flats were blanketed with the sour stink of hydrogen sulfide. "We bring in coal and heat it without air to make coke," Zebadiah continued. "The gases are drawn off and sold for illuminating gas. The coke is used in our smelters which cast not only our water turbines, but now at Elizabeth's insistence, a new product, radiators." He stopped and silently calculated. "You may be right, Elizabeth. We shall see. What do you think, Shaw?"

Billings laughed. "Elizabeth, my girl, get Zebadiah here to soak in one of my Hydrotherapy tubs. Think of all the cast iron you could sell. And the rest of Cromwell wouldn't stink so badly." He remembered John's first hours in Cromwell. "You should have been there the day this young scoundrel had his first bath at the hands of Yvette and. Oh, what a battle it was." His girth shook as he recalled the scene. "His clothes........we had to burn them. The lad himself came out as red as a lobster....all over. Especially his...." he pointed to his groin, convulsing with laughter.

Spencer turned scarlet. The wretched vision of himself, naked, poised on the tip of the bathtub trying to fight off the girls. An purulent twinge suddenly came over him and he turned quickly to conceal a growing erection.

But, not fast enough. Elizabeth caught him by the arm. "I should have liked to see that. You must have done a good job, Shaw. He really smells quite good now." Then before he could stop her, she hooked her arm into his and escorted the victim into the dining room.

John was furious. This was the second time he had encountered Elizabeth Harcross in less than one week. So far, the count was two to zero... in her favor. What disturbed him was why he was keeping score at all.

⊶ ⊷

Since her mother's nervous breakdown and confinement in the asylum outside of Waban, Elizabeth took her place at the end of the table opposite her father. Even to someone naïve to the wealth of the new industrial barons, John Spencer could see that Harcross possessed a prosperity beyond his reckoning.

The varnished umber mahogany table set off the delicate gold-embossed English china. Ornately chased silverware waited at each place setting. High goblets of leaded crystal cast shadows of yellow and crimson from their contents. Hanging above their heads were two chandeliers, each holding a pyramid of burning candles. The four walls were covered with a hand-painted Chinese garden scene. The servants moved quietly, bringing in dishes and refilling wine glasses.

Out of habit, Zebadiah ate little, still wary of the intestinal spasms. As usual, Shaw Billings more than compensated. Elizabeth merely sampled the courses. She was not so innocent with the wine, and to her father's dismay, enjoyed the claret. She grew more and more animated as the courses went on.

John could tell Zebadiah was carefully guiding the conversation.

"Elizabeth told me of the unfortunate accident with the young diver." Zebadiah invited John to comment.

"He is healing well. He owes his life to your daughter. It is strange how quickly I had forgotten such tragedies. In the War, it was the exception who escaped loss of a limb or two." John remembered Matthew." Perhaps knowing what misery those unfortunates would face, I wonder if some of them might have preferred not living."

"Never! " Zebadiah blurted out. His face was drained of blood. His knife clattered on the table. "Never," he repeated. "So what the loss of a leg or arm. My own son, Matthew," he stopped. "Did you know I had lost a son in the War? At Antietam?"

"I did. Shaw told me," John lied. How could he have forgotten? Matthew, the half man. The letters. One from Zebadiah to his son. Matthew's reply. The letters still secreted in the leather case under his bed. This sickly man was the father. So many painful things he wished to tell. How could he, as a guest in his home? "I am grieved at your loss," was all he offered to fill the silence.

"I accept your sympathy, as I have from all the rest. However, Doctor Spencer, never suggest, even for a moment, that a bodily injury is an excuse to give up life. Never. Never. What would I give for a son, scarred or maimed, just to be at my side,"

Elizabeth grew pale at her father's words. Then, just as quickly, she moved to deflect the conversation into calmer channels. "I believe that Doctor Spencer meant that when we see others afflicted, we compare them to ourselves. I imagine it is a question of degree."

Elizabeth was quick and resourceful. John admired the way she cooled her father's emotion. He wondered if, beneath the daughter's affection, there smoldered another emotion.

"Elizabeth is right. As a physician, I am embarrassed to accept anything less than the preservation of life. I apologize. What will happen to Martin after he leaves the Dispensary?"

"Elizabeth has arranged for him to have a job as a gate-keeper at the No. 2 mill. It will not pay as well as diving, but it is steady employment and compatible with his...." he groped for the proper word,"..... his disability. What I intended was to understand why the amputations? I have seen many fractures in my lifetime. Even one of my own." He raised his left arm. " I broke the bone when I was a child and it healed."

Shaw started to answer when John interrupted. Was Zebadiah challenging his clinical judgment? It was time to thrash the matter out once and for all.

"Mister Harcross. When you sustained your accident, was the skin broken, and the bone projecting through the wound?"

"No, Doctor Spencer. I had fallen from a horse. The skin was intact."

"In such a case, we splint the limb. Recently we started using the new Plaster of Paris strips to help. However, if the bone is exposed to air, we risk gangrene."

"I don't understand."

"It is as Spencer said," Billings interjected. "Exposure to the air, and the tissue will rot unless there is a sharp clean division."

"Accepted, Shaw. But, that is an observation. Not an explanation."

Zebadiah was not stupid. He possessed an executioner's instinct for the jugular. Like father, like daughter. Ready to pounce for the answer. What answer? There was none. The two physicians remained silent.

Elizabeth rose from her seat. "You mean to tell me that you amputated Martin's two hands without knowing why? That is a grotesque mockery if ever a Christian could see."

John refused to be baited any longer by Elizabeth Harcross,

"You are wrong. Because we do not know a reason, does not make a physical fact less true. Our failure to understand why speaks to the primitive state of our science. Neither you nor your father have the right to judge us. Rather hope that time will light the darkness."

Spencer walked around the room in long agitated strides. He suddenly stopped at Zebadiah. "You had the perityphlitis, Shaw treated you. We do not know what causes inflammation of the bowel. For the moment, your presence here tonight is proof of our skills. Do not demean the little we possess because of its poverty."

"True, Doctor Spencer," Zebadiah replied." We have railroads, steam engines, the telegraph, coal gas for illumination, even dynamos to generate a new power called electricity. What have you added to match those advances? Shaw has told me that in the thirteenth century, more people survived battle wounds than in the holocaust that consumed my son?"

"You have achieved wonders with the iron railroad and your gas light. However, you also have land mines and cannon shells that can kill twenty-four thousand men in twenty-four hours. In battles of old, it took one man to kill another. Now, a single artillery officer can kill dozens in the space of seconds. In the past, men used steel blades and knives. Many wounds were bloody, but sharp with intact bones. I saw the slaughter at Antietam. Explosions drove deep holes in flesh and then filled them with filth."

"I am not ashamed of my profession. It is not that medicine has not progressed. It is that killing has advanced faster. That observation is a fact. As for why, perhaps you tell me the reason....... you and the other men who profited by the slaughter."

There was a long silence in the room. John took his seat, embarrassed by his outburst. Self-consciously he resumed eating. He looked up to see that Shaw had an amused expression. Elizabeth was staring at him, with admiration. Zebadiah was scrutinizing him through half-closed lids. To John's relief, the Master of the Quabbin did not seem as angry as one would have expected. In a flash, it dawned on him that it was some kind of game they were playing at his expense. At least Shaw and Zebadiah.

"Very good, Doctor Spencer. Very good indeed." Zebadiah folded his napkin and placed it alongside his plate. He pushed his chair back and held his hand out to Billings.

"Come, Shaw. You were right. Your young whipper-snapper is a man of convictions, although I cannot say that I approve of them. I agree with you, though, I like his candor." He nodded at Billings, "I think he will do. Now let us retire to the Library. Some brandy for our hot-headed young Canadian. Some coffee. Cigars. When he has cooled down, I shall ask him."

The quartet moved from the room. The two older men led the way, whispering to each other like schoolboys. John and Elizabeth followed behind, ignorant of the mystery.

⚔

In contrast to the rest of the house, the Library was small and almost shabby. The room was an orphan, neglected. The dark walnut walls were unvarnished. There was no carpet, only wide planks of oak darkened from years use. The windows were covered with drapes of plain monks cloth which sagged in places. Hundreds of books were stacked on the shelves in disorder. There were no gas mantles or radiators. A strong fire took their place.

These were the surroundings John felt at home in. Well-used. Unpretentious. Above the mantle, he noticed a large oil painting. He moved closer for a better look. Before him stood the boy of Antietam.

"That is my son, Matthew." The father walked over to the portrait. The same square face, the thrusting chin, the thin piercing eyes. Then, the similarity ended. Antietam's Matthew had no legs unlike the perfect young man staring down at him from the painting. There were three male Harcrosses in the room. The father. The false son in oil. The real Matthew with half a body. It was eerie. He could swear the eyes stared at him. This was foolishness. He was a grown man. He was too old to be seeing ghosts or to be frightened by one.

"He was a handsome boy." John tore his eyes away from the portrait.

"He was, Doctor Spencer. This was his room. When you talk about Minnié bullets and land mines, do not think that such words do not cut deep into my heart? I control the river. My turbines extract power. I make paper and cloth and cast iron radiators. Others use my power to make bullets and mines. I do not. However, I am no hypocrite. I do not fool myself that I may not be responsible for another father in Richmond, or Atlanta, standing before an oil painting and hearing some doctor from Louisville or New Orleans say 'he was a handsome boy'. Don't imagine that I have not challenged my own conscience more than you or any stranger do."

165

"Father," Elizabeth said, "such things are past. Be proud. He died for a cause he believed in."

Elizabeth's sensitivity touched Zebadiah. He fought back the tears. Why did it have to be so? Elizabeth saw his eyes dart from her to the painting and back again. She knew what he was thinking.

"Doctor Spencer," Zebadiah said. "I have been in Cromwell for over a quarter of a century. The river has made me rich. I will not dispute whether it was a Divinity, chance, or my own labor which has been responsible." He stood with his back to the fireplace, his silhouette backlit by tongues of flame. " I wish to return to the valley part of what I have extracted. I accept my mortality. I have no wish to buy grace or ransom my soul. I do not traffic in dishonor. I have no fear of a hereafter. I honor my fellow beings as I do my contracts. My gift to Cromwell is not a sign of dotage or contrition for worldly success."

"I have decided to erect a hospital. It will incorporate all that is modern in medical care. It will care for old and young, men, and children of all faiths. It will stand as a gift of a single man who came to this valley in which five hundred people were starving and who left it giving life to fifty thousand." His emotion was naked. He did not care. "It will be the gift of Zebadiah Harcross, but it will bear the name of his son!"

Elizabeth heard her father's voice drift away. She struggled to stay calm. She could see the eyes of the three people focused on her. Her brother mocked her from across the room. Somehow, she managed to control her emotion. "Father, it is a beautiful surprise. I doubt a single soul in Cromwell would have guessed the nature of those clandestine meetings with Shaw."

John was dumbstruck. The city urgently needed to replace the converted warehouse. The near epidemic this past fall had shown the inadequacy. Moreover, since the discovery of anesthesia fifteen years ago, the Surgery was cramped and ill-equipped.

For the first time in his life John felt envy. He had rarely considered what power meant. Outside of the army officers, he had never met anyone who could control vast numbers of people. He knew the power of a cannon to destroy. Of a locomotive. Of a turbine to make water turn a thousand machines. Here was a man like himself, with two arms and two legs, a head and a cock and testicles. A man who shit and pissed and fornicated, and, yet, with a wave of his hand, could cause an edifice to be erected.

Adam Ring had once said to him, ' Every man wants something'. Before coming to Cromwell, he had desired very little. Now it was different. He wanted a woman to make love to. An heir from his loins. It was all new and frightening. His father had taught him desire is a corruption. Was he jealous of the sick man in front of him? The power of yellow coins which no amount of time would ever tarnish?

No, he argued. He was not a Zebadiah Harcross. He had no wish to issue commands which would make men tremble. To wave a hand and have a pyramid rise. He could not deny there was a morbid fascination about Zebadiah Harcross. Power did not seem to corrupt him. Perhaps his father was wrong. At that moment, John Spencer saw with a terrible clarity that his life had changed. He had witnessed the power of money.

"The people of Cromwell will be grateful," he said. Billings was beaming from ear to ear. How had the old reprobate managed to keep the secret? How many more secrets did his partner have?

"I have known Shaw since I came to the valley," Zebadiah continued. "As long as he lives, the Matthew Harcross Memorial Hospital will be guided as it should. Like me, he is mortal. A hospital, like a corporation, must transcend the life of its founder. Shaw's praise is boundless. I have made my own investigation. The reports are favorable, from my correspondent in Montreal, the Surgeon General's Office, and here in Cromwell."

"Shaw told me your wish to remain in our city as his partner. Your decision will provide the continuity for the hospital."

Billings could see Elizabeth's pleasure in Spencer's decision. Her eyes kept returning to the tall doctor. He had to move swiftly!

The best incision is a quick and sharp one. "There is more, Zebadiah," Shaw interrupted. " Our young friend is to be married. I, for one, am delighted."

Elizabeth had no sooner sustained one blow, when the second fell. The room was hot and she wished desperately to flee upstairs. Her corset was an iron press squeezing her lungs. She swore Shaw leaned over and whispered 'I'm sorry', but that would have been impossible. It must have been her imagination. She did hear him say, "You may have seen the girl, Zebadiah, Patrick 0'Connell's daughter. The undertaker. Down in the Flats."

Zebadiah wrinkled his forehead, " I remember seeing the girl once when the Board of Overseers met at the Orphanage. A pretty young thing, if I recall. Yes," he smiled. "A very pretty little thing. Doctor Spencer, we all wish you well, both with the new hospital and your wife to be." He called across the room, "don't we, Elizabeth?"

It was a silent boring pain she had felt many times before, but never to such a degree. A slow tearing of her flesh. An ache which spread until she wanted to scream out the anguish. The library, preserved as a shrine. Matthew's portrait denying his death. Now, a monument to his resurrection. John Spencer. A rare man who did not faun at the Harcrosses as the others in Cromwell. Betrothed to a Catholic undertaker's daughter. A girl who spent her day cleaning up after other children in the Flats. Her mouth hardened. The light caught the strong outline of her face. Her fingers clenched and unclenched at her sides.

"Don't we, Elizabeth?" her father repeated.

The words broke through her private Calvary. She forced a smile. "Of course, Doctor Spencer. Like my father, I wish you well. We must have you here one evening, with your bride. And now, I shall retire and leave you three gentlemen in contemplation of your great deed." John returned her handshake in an automatic fashion, still troubled by contrary feelings, Elizabeth gave her father a kiss on the cheek. Shaw reached out for her. He could feel her heart beating rapidly. She pressed close. When she raised her head to say 'goodbye', the tears were there. "Oh Shaw, Shaw....." she cried in a muffled half-whisper. "Why?" Then she tore herself from his arms and fled before anyone in the room could witness her tears.

Billings watched her leave. He wondered at that moment how much gold Elizabeth would have gladly exchanged if, only once in her life, someone had called her a 'pretty young thing'.

CHAPTER TWENTY-ONE

Those who had lived in Cromwell their whole lives could not remember a winter when the elements conspired with such a vengeance. The snows fell without mercy, month after month. The Quabbin iced over, cracking piers and wharfs. Frozen glass coated the three canals, forming a slippery bed upon which the snows accumulated as high as the land in between. Underneath the thick skin, the waters still rushed fast and free. The sluice gates remained opened. The chilled water hit the turbines which continued to spin with a terrible power of their own.

Cromwell was bleached of color. The sky persisted a monotonous milky grey. Occasionally it would host a black thundercloud. Always the snows fell. When the winds were driven from the northwest, the flakes sliced at a forty-five degree angle. Dry and crisp, they sculpted drifts which shifted like skittish white dunes. Tracks and footprints vanished within seconds as the whiteness lathered them over.

When the winds travelled from the south, the snow became fat and slovenly. It fell straight to the ground and adhered with a surprising tenacity. The particles clung to fabric and face.

Occasionally a sudden inversion of warm air would melt the embryonic flakes. Then, chilled by passage through the cold which shielded the land, each liquid drop would freeze and pelt flesh and window.

Whatever its texture and density, the whiteness was delivered out of colorless skies. It covered Cromwell. Roofs. Streets. Fields. Naked tree limbs were etched against a stark background. Evergreens became pyramids and spires. There was no sun, nor moon, nor stars. Daytime was marked by a diffuse light. Night was its absence. Only the kerosene lights marked the boundary between. There were no clouds nor planets, nor stars. There was only the earth and white.

The winter of 1866 was a silent season. People hurried in and out of shelters, wasting little heat on the passage. The streets were empty, except for wagons and trolleys. Even here, there was quiet. Wheels were replaced with sled runners which glided on the packed snow surfaces with a magical speed. The bitter cold sucked out any warmth. Few children played in the streets. Neighbors no longer gathered outdoors to chat. Clothe lines were retracted. Each family withdrew into itself, emerging only for work or food.

The winter of 1866 was a time to retrench, to husband energy, until spring. Under the blanket of white and quiet, Cromwell continued to live and labor and love. It remained a vast fabric upon which fifty thousand hands were weaving private tales. The winter of 1866 was many things to many people.

The winter of 1866 was a time of truth for Zebadiah Harcross. His ambition and drive continued but not the ability. He tired easily. His judgment was clouded by recurring spasms and the laudanum taken to dampen them. With deliberate haste, Zebadiah turned over more and more authority to Elizabeth. Though he would never admit it, he took a silent pride in her ability. The dam was repaired. The energy of the Quabbin was now trapped. Each day he received messengers from Vermont reporting the daily snow fall. Every eleven inches of winter snow would become one inch of spring water to flood downstream into his coffers.

There would be no Harcross to bear his name after he was gone. Descendants of another line would inherit his valley. The Hospital was all that was left to give him the immortality he craved.

For Elizabeth Harcross, the winter of 1866 was one of discontent. Unlike her father the river did not fill a hunger inside. She saw Zebadiah closeted with his lawyers at night drawing up plans for her brother's monument. As long as she lived, it would remind her of her father's sadness. John Spencer, a man whom she might have loved, if given the chance, married to a 'pretty young thing', now pregnant. Life continued for others. Elizabeth felt in a trap which she could never escape.

The winter of 1866 was a season of love for Kathleen. She had left her job at the Orphanage. It was a strange feeling to be mistress of her own home. She busied herself preparing for confinement. If it turned out to be girl, she would name it after her mother, Rachel. A boy, after John's father, who had passed away shortly before their wedding.

Kathleen could feel the life growing inside her body. It amazed her that from the act of love, another human being was created, like an unexpected prize. She never did understand how the child was the contribution of the male, when she felt so possessive. She and John continued to make love, although he warned that they would have to stop soon. The prospect was an unhappy one. With much tenderness and success, Kathleen discovered that sex tightened the bond between her and her red-haired husband. There were times when she could catch him looking at her swelling with a tense expression. When asked why, he would draw a sheepish grin over his face and mumble something silly. Those were the nights she made love with a passion she would have been ashamed of months before. The baby would be born in August. She crossed the days off on a calendar. Until then, her days and nights confirmed the wisdom to marry the young doctor and to surrender her fear of childbirth to his trust.

John Spencer watched the winter of 1866 with worry. He could see the same calendar rushing the days. He cajoled Kathleen into letting Shaw examine her, hoping for a miracle. Kathleen lay on her back, legs spread under the blanket for modesty. She blushed and pulled her legs in, but Shaw gently coaxed them apart. He kept up a light banter of how the area should be reserved strictly for the delights of Venus. He worked swiftly. There was to be no miracle.

Shaw left the room while Kathleen dressed. "Contracted. Every pelvic dimension foreshortened. She will never push the head through. Just like her mother. I am sorry, Johnnie. I am sorry."

The two men were all smiles when Kathleen came downstairs. Billings gave John a lascivious wink and clapped him on his back, lamenting that he now knew why his partner was in so much haste to hurry home each day. John reciprocated in kind, both conspiring to keep the truth from the mother. Each day, the fetus gained in size. Each day, Kathleen waited impatiently to be a mother.

The winter of 1866 was one of resignation for Patrick O'Connell. He had hoped Shaw could have prevented the marriage, but the wish was unrealistic. He was reliving the horrible nightmare. He wanted to wake up and frighten away the ghosts, but was unable. He could not explain to Kathleen his reluctance to visit, or, when he came, why he resorted to whiskey and pleaded to leave early. He watched her, radiant, in love, proud of her home and the family to come. He drowned his fear in alcohol.

To Shaw Billings, now entering his sixty-fourth year of life, the season was welcomed. He was no longer planning for the future. The phlebotomies, the catheterizations, the increasing number of pillows propping him up in bed so that he could breath.... all warned him that time was impatient. John had moved away with his bride, leaving the elderly physician alone once again. The dining table was quiet. The Library empty. Shaw did not mind. It was peaceful.

He had served the people of Cromwell for over forty years. He was leaving it with another every bit his equal, and with the enthusiasm of youth. In spring would come the dream of a new hospital. He trusted Zebadiah to follow through on his pledge. Whatever his failings, he was a man of honor.

Shaw smiled to himself. On the whole, he could not complain. Not even with the threat of seeing Sarah again, God forbid, for an eternity. Even with that, he was content.

Despite the shroud of white, life prevailed in the valley, not only for God's greatest creation, but for His lowliest creatures as well. Deep in the cracks and crevices of Cromwell, hidden in cellars and attics, tucked away in closets and carpets, trespassing in burrows of hibernating field rodents, in these and other insignificant places, the mosquito persisted. Looking at the sleeping insect, its wings folded primly by its side, one might have thought it dead. The Aedes and Anopheles lived. In its blood, lethal threats also slept. Lovers united. Waiting patiently.

Each day the earth gained ninety seconds more of warmth. Each week, ten minutes of sunlight. Each month, forty five more minutes.

The human beings may have been ignorant of this celestial maneuver as the earth silently approached the sun. The trees and birds sensed it with an instinctive wisdom. The two-legged refugees from the Garden may have thought winter's hold unbreakable. The Aedes and the Anopheles and the parasites knew differently.

Spring was coming, as it had for as long as life existed. When it arrived, the largest and the smallest of antagonists would clash in a final battle for possession of the valley.

CHAPTER TWENTY-TWO

"He looks like a bastard," Adam Ring whispered under his breath.

"Even worse," Frederick Dearing answered back. "He's High Episcopalian."

The case of the Commonwealth of Massachusetts against the O'Connell-Ring Corporation was held on February 17, 1866 in the chambers of Samuel Tatlock, presiding officer of the Seventh District Superior Court. The Judge, tall and distinguished, seemed the embodiment of JUSTICE who stared blindfolded from the wall over his head. His face was long and lean with pointing chin. Small eyes were set back under roofs of bristling eyebrows, the same color as the hair covering his head. His lips were thin and tightly compressed, as if keeping his inner thoughts privy was his most critical concern. Crossed flags of the United States and the Commonwealth flanked the dais on each side.

Every few moments Tatlock shifted in his seat. His piles were killing him. Despite the emollients liberally applied during the night, along with laudanum, the swollen blue veins pained whenever he sat too long in one spot. At least twice a minute, he looked up at the clock facing him. The brass pendulum swung back and forth, with agonizing slowness. He thought of the steaming tub of water his buttocks had left an hour before, and to which he would return as soon as he dispatched the case in front of him.

Tatlock signalled to the Court Clerk to begin. The sudden movement was a tragic mistake. A throbbing pain shot up his rectum like a searing hot poker. He gave an quick wince which made everyone in the room look about to see the cause. Tatlock slowly eased back against his high swivel chair.

The Commonwealth's case was simple. It contended that The O'Connell-Ring Company was selling insurance as defined by House Bills # 3750, # 3891, # 4006, and finally # 7100. Such activity was illegal unless authorized under existing laws governing the operation of insurance companies within the States. Frederick Dearing argued an equally simple point. Insurance, he claimed, was defined as an obligation to the beneficiary which terminated upon his or her death at the time the benefits were paid. This was not the case with his client. The promissory note was signed by the family and the owed balance <u>not</u> voided upon the death of the decedent. In fact, the estate had a continuing legal obligation until the debt was paid in full.

Tatlock listened patiently as documents and subpoenaed records were produced. He watched as one lawyer introduced affidavits to bolster his case. He nodded gravely as the other side introduced counter-affidavits arguing just the opposite. During a lull in the proceedings, Tatlock searched the notes in front of him. The newly appointed Assistant Attorney-General was a lawyer from Dedham, Paul Brewster, Jr. It was the first time he had seen him in his courtroom. He took better look at the man. No wonder the name seemed familiar. Many years ago, a Brewster had clerked for him. His son? There was a resemblance. He saw the young man peering up and gave him a benevolent smile.

The Defendants. Some scar-faced man. Ugly to look at. Dressed like an immigrant who had come into money, probably illegally. His lawyer, presentable. Not quite the type to associate with his client. Tatlock sighed. Things used to be so different before the War. It was Tatlock's life-long conviction that no attorney should ever have to take on a client he would not want to invite to his home for dinner. Dearing. A good name. The man should have known better.

When the two sides finished, Tatlock uttered a silent prayer of thanks. He had not been paying much attention to the case. What earthly difference did it make who was to bury people who were too dead to care very much one way or the other? All that mattered was that he would be damned if he would sit another minute on the tufted leather chair.

Two days later, Tatlock was flattered to receive a visit from his old clerk from Dedham who just happened to be passing through Boston. One week later, Tatlock assembled the parties. He granted the injunction requested by the State. Dearing immediately appealed the decision.

The last week of March, 1866, the Supreme Court of the Commonwealth sustained the Lower Court's ruling. It declared the O'Connell-Ring Company to be functioning as an insurance company. It enjoined the Company from selling funerals on the installment plan. It declared void all existing contracts.

Dearing took the three of them to *The Publican*, a men's grill located in the shadow of the Court House with its golden Bullfinch dome. The walnut paneled walls with carved capitals, the polished brass fixtures, the gleaming rolling silver steam tables, all boasted to the defeated trio that they were out of their element. Patrick, as usual, resorted to whiskey. Adam took rapid inventory of the rich furnishings and of the well-dressed attorneys and politicians at home in the polished surroundings. Dearing identified the important people.

Adam pointed to a table in the far corner which lay in the shadow of a potted palm tree. "Is that Tatlock?" he asked, "and the man with him? Is he who I think he is?"

Dearing peered myopically. He confirmed Brewster, Jr. seated with the Judge. Their conversation indicated more than just a casual relationship.

"Adam, stop!" Dearing was too late. Adam strode across the room. The men looked up in surprise. Tatlock tried to place the stranger. Brewster was more astute.

"Well, look who we have here?" The short prematurely balding prosecutor sneered. "Its our little scar-faced Jew from Cromwell." He burped out loud, "I would have thought you'd be on the first train back." His voice was mean and vicious. "Its all over, Ring. You and your drunken Irish friend are out of business. " He turned back to his plate. "Now ....if you will excuse me."

Dearing saw Adam make his fists into weapons. He was tensing on the balls of his feet, ready tear at Brewster's throat. His face was pure hate. How could one blame him ? "Don't Adam. Don't!" He held him back. "Come. Let's go home. Please. Leave them."

Tatlock had shrunk back in his seat, trying to remove himself from the distasteful scene. "Brewster," the Judge quietly offered, "there is no need. Let the man go in peace." He sought Dearing's help to separate the two. Adam ripped free from his lawyer's hold. To Dearing's surprise, he grinned.

If Frederick and Patrick had been despondent over the double legal defeat, Adam Ring had not allowed himself that luxury. Even before the Supreme Court ruling, his mind was examining options. He knew that even if he won this battle, the war would go on. Next year there would be more House Bills, more injunctions, more court cases. Sooner or later, he would lose. Or, if he won, the victory would be Pyrrhic. He and Patrick would be wasting their time and money on playing catch-up.

Dearing worried about what Adam was going to do when the immigrant leaned over the table. It was merely to shake the

Judge's hand and then the lawyer's. Both men were too startled to respond.

"Judge Tatlock," Ring bowed. "Mister Brewster. He repeated the mocking gesture. "Before we leave, I wish to thank you both." He pointed back over his shoulder at Patrick who was wondering what was going on. "My Irish friend and I owe you a debt of gratitude. He bowed again from the waist, inclined his head at both of them, turned on his heel, collected O'Connell, and left the pub. Dearing trailed behind. He was damned if he knew what his client was up to.

⚓ ⚓

Ring and Dearing took Patrick to the train station. While waiting, Adam quizzed the young lawyer.

"How long do we have before the Supreme Court's decision will go into effect?"

"I talked with the Clerk after the ruling was handed down. He said it would be at least forty-five days before the remitter is received by Tatlock."

"Then what will happen?"

"Usually, it takes a month after the official statement of the Court's ruling before the legal decision is put into effect. I suspect with Tatlock's new drinking partner, we can count on his expediting the ruling as fast as possible."

Ring leaned back on the hardwood bench in the Depot Waiting Room. The air was cold. The pot bellied stove at the far end of the domed room did little against the chill.

"Alright, then, we have about six weeks before the O'Connell-Ring Corporation can no longer sell burials on the installment plan. Six weeks, no longer."

"After that," Patrick said with bitterness, "we can't even deposit a check."

"He's right, Adam. In six weeks, you must close your books, or be held in contempt of Court."

179

"Alright, then. Six weeks. Let's make the most of them." Adam's voice was as determined as when he and Patrick faced their first crisis. "Patrick, get back to Cromwell. You have the books. Go over the customer lists with each branch manager. Make sure some agent sees everyone of those people. Reassure them they will not lose their money. Then talk them into paying several installments in advance. Lie, cheat, promise them the keys of heaven and hell, but, get the money. Cash. As much as you can squeeze out of them. Offer a discount if they will pay in advance. I don't care how you do it. Throw in one of your Irish Saints as a bonus. I don't give a damn if you get them drunk and sell each of them your immortal soul, but get the money. Don't deposit it in the corporate account. Put it in a locked vault in the Cromwell Mercantile Bank. Make sure no one knows what you are doing." He stood up as he heard the whistle of the train approaching. He could feel the dull rumble of the platform vibrating under his feet.

"I will do as you say, Adam, but why?" Patrick asked. "Frederick told me your conversation with Tatlock and Brewster, I don't understand why you thanked them,"

Adam stretched his short frame to the limit. His shoulder and head were arched back defiantly. "If those two sons of bitches had not won, you and I would be on our way back home right now to sell some more coffins on the installment plan. That is what we would be doing the rest of our lives. Selling caskets to some hicks. We can't any more. There is an old expression in this new country,' If you can't lick them, join them'. The Bay Staters have driven us out of undertaking business. Good. Now we are going to beat the bastards at their own game. Trust me, Patrick."

Adam gave the Irishman an affectionate clasp on the shoulder. Ring's last words were drowned out by the thunder of the train, the screeching of steel upon steel as the locomotive belched steam to the end of the track and stopped. Adam looked back as he left the terminal. He could see O'Connell boarding the train. His slight frame was almost erased by the clouds of white escaping from the brake cylinders. Adam clutched the young lawyer tightly by the arm. "Only six weeks, Frederick. We have work to do."

⊷⊶ ⊶⊷

Dearing did not have long to wonder what was in his client's fertile mind.

"Form me an insurance company."

"An insurance company!" Dearing protested. "Adam you may be bright and energetic, but you don't know the first thing about insurance companies. Neither do I." He kept shaking his head at the young man's audacity. An insurance company? The idea was absurd.

Adam would not be dissuaded. "Frederick, I want an insurance company. First of all, we can't function as we are. What the hell difference does it make if we sell a burial in advance on the installment plan, or we collect a weekly insurance premium and when the beneficiary dies give his estate the same money to spend anywhere they like for a funeral? It amounts to the same thing in the end. If you think about it for a minute, insurance is a damn better business than our own."

Dearing stared at his client, speechless, as Ring went on, determined. "With insurance, we don't need a factory to manufacture anything. We don't need wood, or machinery. We keep no inventory. Nothing ever goes out of style. All we need are some pieces of paper and a big drawer to collect the premiums. As long as we take in more than we have to pay out, we make a profit. Selling insurance is no different from selling caskets. The most important thing in any business is to have the customers. God damn it! We have thousands of them in five counties paying us every week. Frederick, it is a good idea. Make me an insurance company."

If Adam Ring's enthusiasm was boundless, so were the legal obstacles. Over the next week, the pair dissected laws regulating the formation of and conduct of such enterprises. They frequented the office of Thaddeus Bigelow and learned the requirements for a charter,

"Its hopeless," Frederick repeated each time he discovered another block to converting the O'Connell-Ring Corporation to what his client wanted. Each time, Adam thought out the problem and, with Dearing's legal expertise, patiently constructed a means of circumventing the provisions of the particular law. All their efforts were for naught. No matter how hard they tried, there was always the same obstacle. No way could the O'Connell-Ring Corporation manage to post a bond for one hundred thousand dollars, the legal requirement for a life insurance charter.

Ten days after the Supreme Court Ruling, Patrick visited them in their cheap hotel room where the two men shared a single bed. He immediately grasped the logic of switching the Corporation to selling insurance. They had the customers, the branch offices, the district managers and the salesmen. What difference caskets or policies? The money was the same. People still died and had to be buried. The idea was sound, but he, too, could not see how to come up with the hundred thousand dollars for the bond.

He showed Adam the results of his labors. He had collected over ten thousand dollars. "At this rate, we should have at least twenty thousand dollars by the end of the six weeks. But, that's all. We will never come even close to what you need." He returned to Cromwell that same day, leaving behind him two men whose pleasure at his success was dampened by the failure of their own.

They worked late as they had done each evening. The room grew crowded with legal books and documents. Adam Ring sat by the wooden table reading. His face was lined with worry. He would run his fingers nervously through his hair and throw back the black locks which had fallen over his forehead.

He was conscious of the dull ache between his legs. His testicles felt heavy and swollen. His penis was at a constant half-erection with a constant itch in the head which no amount of secret squeezing could help. What he needed was a good whore! Dearing was sitting primly on the side of the bed, carefully depositing each page in a neat pile. The man would never understand. To invite a woman up to the room? In their bed? Might as well suggest the Virgin Mary. The man was probably still innocent. With a sigh, Adam Ring turned back to his work. He now had another reason to hurry their search.

"Adam, listen to this, " Dearing rose from the bed and carried a thick legal tome over to the table. Adam could see the excitement beneath the usual calm veneer. He read the ruling. Then a second time, slowly and carefully, mouthing each word. It was right there, in front of them all the time!

"That's it, Frederick. Unless there is some trick which you lawyers use to take back with one hand what you give with the other." He hoped the look of elation would still be there. It was.

"No tricks, Adam," Dearing smiled. "It's true. I happened upon it yesterday. I didn't want to say anything until I had checked it out thoroughly. There is your insurance company. It may not be exactly the kind you had in mind, but it walks like an insurance company, talks like an insurance company, smells like one, will make money like one, and most important of all, is protected by the Commissioner of Insurance. Its your's, sweet and simple. The Bay State Funeral people will never be able to touch it."

Dearing was flushed with pride. It was not often, in his plodding way, he could top his employer. Ring urged the lawyer to return to Cromwell. He gave him no explanation why he wanted to stay behind an extra night. "Tell Patrick I will take the morning train. You get started on the special Charter application without me."

He stood on the curb without a coat or a hat, as he watched Dearing leave. The snow flakes scurried around him, landing on his hair and clothing where they instantly melted. He looked at the grey sky, savoring the tingle of the cold flakes landing on his upturned face. He took in a deep breath and held it a long time. All his fatigue was gone by the magic of the moment and the anticipation of success.

The guests entering and leaving the hotel jostled him as they rushed by. He did not care. He was still savoring the clever trick Dearing had found. A familiar scent of cheap perfume brushed by him. How many years ? Memories started to come back. He heard the high-pitched laughter of a female voice, A woman, face powdered white, was entering the hotel on the arm of a short grey-haired man. He looked closely. It was no woman. The girl could not have been more than sixteen or seventeen. The man, at least fifty, with a round face, covered with perspiration and red from alcohol.

Adam caught hold of the whore's arm, "How much?" he asked. "How much?" he repeated,

"Listen, sonny, I already paid for the whole night," the man objected.

The whore compared the two. The sweating pig, old and fat. The young man, lean and muscular. His face scarred, but interesting. She whispered in Adam's ear. Adam pulled out his wallet. He peeled off the figure and gave it to the man. He extracted an equal amount, then doubled it. He tore the bills down the middle and gave one half to the girl,

"There's twice what you asked for. In the morning, you get my half."

The jilted man tried to step between the negotiating pair. The girl patted him on the cheek. "Another time, father," she consoled.

Adam let the girl have all the liquor she wanted. He drank only moderately. He wanted to feel everything! He lay back on the bed. She worked his body with her mouth and tongue and fingers, and when he could stand it no longer, he emptied his need into the dark moist slippery warm hollow between her legs.

The perfume steamed off her skin. He thought he could never smell enough of it. The girl's flesh was tight and smooth and resisting. At the height of his ejaculation, he screamed in pain and pleasure as sperm shot out in burning jets through the scarred urethra. She repeated her name many times but he would never say it. All he would cry out was 'Sonja', 'Sonja', and drive deeper into her body. She ripped her fingernails into his back when he hurt her too much. It made no difference. She scratched and slashed his skin in vain. The pain only increased his passion, as breathing in the perfume of Chabot Street, he relived his past.

CHAPTER TWENTY-THREE

Whether it was the strong May sunlight streaming through the opened window (Billings had finally convinced John that night air was not poisonous) or that Kathleen stirred, but the young physician awakened with a start. At five thirty, the room was already light. He felt the warm shape of his wife lying next to him. He rolled over on his side. He fitted comfortably into her contour, knees pressed up against hers, the round of her buttocks pressing against his groin. His arms encircled her abdomen.

Kathleen gave a quick movement. John released his hold afraid that he had awakened her. She smiled and she settled back, burrowing into his body like a cushion.

The warmth, the peace of the new day, the memory of their love making, mingled in his hazy dream state. He could smell the odor of sex, mixed with the lavender from the linen pomander. His penis swelled like an arched rod between them. He squeezed tight to milk out the blood, instantly regretting a lost opportunity.

Kathleen wriggled free. Her head barely came up to his chin. Her lips brushed the curly red hairs on his chest. She stretched up and kissed him. Then before he could respond, she dove lower in the bed and hid under the quilt. Her hands found his erection and delicately stroked the smooth head.

"No, Kathleen," he protested without conviction, "I must get up." He looked again at the clock which had only a few minutes more to ring and shut it off. "Tonight," he promised, writhing under her persistent stroking. His wife could not be put off. Her hands caressed until he could resist no longer. He took her there. The act was immediate, rushed, frantic, unlike the leisurely coupling of hours before. The result was the same. Spent, each lay back, fingers intertwined. She could feel his panting subside and the dazed look in his eyes give way to purpose. He pouted as if angry by his weakness.

How unlike the maiden! Did all women change so easily from the blushing virgin to the passionate mistress? Whatever the answer, the winter of 1866 was the happiest in John's life. He kept his secret buried deep, hoping for some miracle. Kathleen gradually drifted off into slumber. Slowly, he eased out of bed. His wife's flaccid body flowed into the warm spot he had just left. It rested there without a sigh.

John dressed rapidly. He shaved, using the light from the window in the bureau mirror. He shivered as he lathered his face. The basin water was cold, but he did not waste time heating it. He inspected his reflection and sighed. That was one argument he had lost. Kathleen insisted he shave off his sideburns. Too much like kissing pillow stuffing, she teased. He had always considered the whiskers to enhance his dignity.

Finished, John viewed the soft shape gently molded under the quilt. Resisting the impulse for one last kiss, he left the room. Four months to go. The end of September. The baby would be born and die, or, she would die, or, both would die. He forced himself to stop thinking. He restarted the wood stove in the kitchen. He filled a pot with water, and set it on top. When it was boiling, he added ground coffee. He moved the pot to a cooler side of the stove and waited for the grounds to settle. He poured the coffee into a large cup, added cream from the zinc-lined chest which held the weekly block of ice. He sat back in the wooden kitchen chair to drink the steaming bitter draught.

The dawn was his favorite hour. The air was always clean and fresh. The house was quiet. The cares of the day had not yet started to pile up. When he was young, he would always find his father seated in the kitchen with a book, usually the bible, or writing his Sunday sermon, a large cup of coffee at his side. He was always dressed and shaved, prepared for the day, yet delighted it had not started. He always greeted his son with affection, but somehow, John always had the feeling he was an intruder. These few minutes were his fathers private slice of time, and he resented sharing it with anyone.

Sitting there this young May day, his pregnant wife sleeping scarcely feet away, a post-coital happiness cloaking him, John felt close to his father. It was a precious period of grace in which John felt at one with the world and at peace with himself. Through the window, the willow trees swam in the wind. He could hear the birds, staking out their territory for the spring fertility rites. If only everything in life were this perfect.

He snapped his watch open. He still had time before Billings's stable boy would come to take him to the Dispensary. He removed a letter from his jacket and carefully unfolded it. He chuckled to himself. If Guthrie could only see his domesticated student now. Content in the new spring day, he reread the letter from his former mentor.

Department of Materia Medica

McGill Medical School
Montreal
April 7, 1866

My dear Spencer,

It is difficult to believe that a year has passed since I advised you to test the waters of medical life in the Colonies south of us. The few letters I have received from you (please take the comment as a chastisement) and the many from Shaw Billings have confirmed the sagacity of my choice. It was never your calling to labor in the sterile halls of academe

Shaw told me his offer to you. It is a princely one. Even in our Northern Provinces one has heard of the incredible dam and canal system which have made your chosen domicile an industrial paradise.

I share vicariously in your marriage. Though I am loathe to preach on the state of matrimony (having feared it for a lifetime), it is a condition blessed by our Lord. My only regret is that your father, may he rest in peace, did not live through the winter to know of the pleasant fact.

I visited him shortly before his death. As usual, his only thoughts were on you and your happiness. Never berate yourself that you did not follow in his footsteps (I even echo his words having heard them so often). He was proud of you. That is the most a father can expect from his son. It is more than most ever achieve.

I have complied with your request that Britton Spencer's belongings be sold and the monies donated to McGill, It is an honorable action. I am afraid, however, that your fathers estate was an exceedingly humble one. You were his most valuable earthly treasure. The little realized has been given to the Library in the Student's Hall with an appropriate bookplate to commemorate the bequest,

I am most pleased that you have not abandoned your medical curiosity. I read with avidity your description of Shaw Billings' treatment of the patient with perityphlitis. I presented the case before the Quebec Medical Society monthly dinner in February. Tell my good friend that his diagnostic acumen and surgical prowess were received with universal acclaim. Some remembered Shaw from his days with us and send their sincere regards.

During the discussion that followed, the name of a Willard Parker of your adopted country was brought forward. One member there that night had the good fortune to be in New York City within this year. At a meeting of the Faculty of the College of Physicians and Surgeons, he heard Doctor Parker report a similar case.

I have thought hard about this problem as it relates to your patient Zebadiah Harcross. I do not know what to tell you. Your clinical description is certainly that of chronic perityphlitis. You in-dicate the increasing- severity of each attack. Should you open into the right lower quadrant over the cecum as did Shaw and Parker? What if the abscess is <u>not</u> walled off? Then the resulting peritonitis from your incision will cause his demise. Should you take the risk? If you are correct, you will save the patient. If you are wrong, he will die.

You may argue that he may die anyway. Remember, John, if you adhere to the traditional therapy and do not operate, he will die <u>of</u> the disease and you are blameless. If you wield the scalpel and you are wrong, he dies from what you did. You are young and just start-ing practice in the community. Zebadiah Harcross is a powerful man. The risks are great. Because they affect your future existence, I fear to advise you in this thing.

Your second issue concerned the new hospital, this same bene-factor is proposing for Cromwell. I must confess that I look upon such activity with an ambivalent feeling. True, we have need of temples of healing. Yet, I am reminded of our Lord's admonition that it is easier for a camel to go through the eye of a needle than for a rich man to enter the gates of heaven. I have reports of children stunted from a life sacrificed to unholy working conditions, of squalid slums which press up against the mills to prevent the workers from losing any more time or energy than necessary on living outside the factory gates.

Forgive the digression, but in years to come remember these words whenever you pass through the portals of the new Harcross hospital which, like most monuments, is certain to be of grandiose proportions. Do not forget those whose sweat has mortared the bricks like the Israelites of Moses.

Reports from the Royal College of Physicians in London indicate a growing predilection for the pavilion style of construction. Rather than a single building, compact and many floored, it is now considered salutary to raise many small buildings, separate from each other and connected only by an central hub, off of which the pavilions extend like fingers from a palm. In this fashion, the contagions and miasmas which afflict one pavilion can be kept away from affecting the others. The concept is sound. Certainly, you have seen erysipelas and puerperal sepsis sweep through contiguous wards like a fire in a wheat field. Wish that we have had built our own institution in Montreal in such an up-to-date manner. I will forward by fastest post all information on the subject. You can then broach the topic with your benefactor, armed with the most modern concepts of the Empire.

You must allow me to take umbrage at your third request. You asked the proper site for the Hospital. You apparently have forgotten my lecture on medical antiquities in your first year at McGill. Why are all young people in such a hurry to devour the mechanics of medicine without paying due heed and thanks to those who have created the history and heritage of our profession? Why are the lives of men who lived in the past so quickly forgotten in the haste to acquire their intellectual riches?

Offended by your lack of perspicacity, or of memory, I will say no more on the matter, except to commend you to Rhases, the Lute-Player of Baghdad who lived from 860-032 A.D. Inasmuch as you have forgotten my words on the great physician, I will refer you to Sir Bertram Lytell's excellent biography, (I assume that you have not forgotten your Latin as well.) The time spent will well reward you. Although the man was born a thousand years ago, he will show you how to select the healthiest site in Cromwell for the new Harcross Hospital.

I wish that I could respond to your last query with as confident a reply or in as light-hearted a mood. Nothing can be done for pelvic contracture. To save the mother, you must kill the child. A cesarean section will preserve the infant's life, if it is not premature, but the maternal mortality is 100%. I assume that the patient is the wife of one of your Cromwell patrons. All I would recommend is to state the alternatives and to support the decision. Unfortunately, as you know, the art of Obstetrics has not advanced one iota since the invention of the delivery forceps by Chamberlin in England. The irony that the birth of life is the female's greatest killer still haunts our profession and fills the cemeteries.

In conclusion, I must advise that any further letters will be unanswered. I leave in four days for Europe. This is my first trip to the continent in over forty years.

Spencer, there is a clean fresh wind blowing into the musty rooms and halls of medicine. It is a strong, vibrant wind. It is constant and increases in strength day by day. I hear it beat in my ears. I feel it on my face and in my hair. I stand in the corridors and see it stir up dust on the worn floors, tear asunder cobwebs above my head, rattle bones in the display cases and cause insects and beetles which have multiplied unbothered for centuries, to scurry away in alarm.

There is a new light shining on medicine. You may laugh and say it is the ranting of an old man. I say not. I am not wrong. I cannot be wrong. I may sit here in Montreal, but I listen. I look. I read. I talk. My mind inquires. A letter here. A letter there. The answers come, slowly but certain.

Something strange and rare and beautiful is happening. The magic is starting in England. In my own native Scotland. In Edinburg. It is growing in France. In Paris. It is spreading in Germany.

Wondrous things are happening at this very moment in history. Great deeds which, if true, will change medicine as it has been taught since the beginning of time.

I tremble. Sometimes, I fall asleep at night, terrified at what this new world will be. Remember God's warning to Adam and Eve. 'If thou shall eat of the fruit of the Tree of Knowledge, thou shall die.' Man disobeyed and was cast from the Garden.

Spencer. A new seed is planted. It has germinated and sprouted. The trunk is high and thick and strong. The leaves cast a wide shadow. The roots spread out far. The flower has dropped and now the fruit is ready. Will Genesis repeat?

Men in France and Germany and Scotland are reaching up for the fruit. They are hungry to taste of the forbidden promise. Nothing will stop them. When they have plucked the prize, I fear that medicine will never be the same. If you ask what the change will be, I cannot answer. I do not know. I only feel in my heart and soul that today, tomorrow, this month, next year, but soon, quickly, my world will be gone forever. A new one will be forced upon us by men with strange names like Koch, and Lister, and Pasteur. A dour German pathologist. A taciturn Scottish surgeon. A French chemist who plays with silk worms and boils wine.

I tremble for that future, but I am also greedy for that future. I must travel now to find the brave new world for myself.

I have heard of what these men say. I must see them for myself. I only pray to God that I do not die before the world has proved their findings.

Men may call me heretic, but if they are right we may yet reënter the Garden.

Spencer, how many more shall we kill in our sublime ignorance until that new day has dawned?

Your affectionate servant,

Professor Elias Guthrie

CHAPTER TWENTY-FOUR

I f Adam Ring's arrival to join Patrick O'Connell in the fall of 1865 was ignored by the ruling class in Cromwell, that was not the case in the Flats. There were few of his neighbors who were unaware of the Irishman's efforts after the War. When, without explanation, he converted his assets to cash and purchased lists of regional burial associations, some sagely warned of his failure. When he merged the fledgling societies into the Quabbin Valley Mutual Burial Association, these same persons predicted that his competition would crush him, if not in the market place, then in the courts. This Greek chorus watched with selfish satisfaction the death of his ambitious plans. Another few months, and he would be back to squirting embalming fluid into cadavers as he had done for twenty years in the filthy shed behind his tenement.

The initial reaction to Adam Ring was one of derision. His scarred face, manner of speaking, and foreign mannerisms were a butt of jokes. The Cassandras could not see how an immigrant Jew, a near bankrupt coffin-maker from Boston, could help the undertaker. Few expected the two men to form the O'Connell-Ring

Corporation and sell coffins on the installment plan. Like a phoenix rising from the ashes, the pair were successful, opening branch after branch. Each week, verging further out from Cromwell. The spectators thought they had the last laugh when the State brought suit to crush the Jew and the Catholic once and for all, and strip them of their gains. The addition of a pale impoverished lawyer to their midst did little to inspire confidence.

Judge Tatlock's ruling was received with a solemn shaking of heads. Most did not understand the intricacies of legal skirmish. All they knew was that those who raised their heads high to climb out of the disease-ridden canals would be struck down for their presumption. When the appeal was denied, the game was up! No one was prepared for the Byzantine maneuvers that followed.

Within weeks, all wagers were off as Cromwell saw the birth of a financial power undreamt of by those in the Flats. It was the damning of a new river of gold, a feat compared only to Zebadiah's chaining of the Quabbin. All now watched with rapt attention. All now voiced their long standing faith in the men from the very beginning.

All it took was a secret handshake!

Dearing discovered the fraternal benefit societies. Patrick had dealt with them before, when he had bought up their burial lists. These organizations with gaudy regalia, and symbolic handshakes, had names like the *Maccabees*. Others were *Knights* and *Crusaders*. *Orders of Slovakians*, *Moravians*. Others *Fraternities of Carpenters*, or *Masons* or *Lumberman*.

All of them had the right to issue life insurance <u>for their members</u>. The only State requirements were that they have at least one thousand members, each subscribing to an individual policy of at least one hundred and fifty dollars, and having paid up premiums of six months. If these simple conditions were fulfilled, the Commissioner of Insurance was mandated to issue them a charter.

"Jesus Christ!" Adam cursed during the busy weeks that followed. "It was right there all the time."

He quickly resurrected the Quabbin Valley Mutual Burial Association as a Fraternal Benefit Society. He sent Dearing and Patrick out into the countryside again. This time they sold life insurance policies instead of coffins to the members on the lists.

But not before Adam hired an actuary. "Frederick, we don't know the first thing about insurance. Go back to Boston," he ordered his exhausted lawyer. "Scout around the Old Colony Life or the Boston Mutual. There must be dozens of young actuaries whose mothers and fathers still speak Italian or Polish or Portuguese. Men with hungry bellies and dark skins. Men whose names end in 'ini' or 'iski' or'stein'. Men who will never get anywhere in those lily white companies. Find me one. A clever one. Offer him double what he is getting now. Bring him to Cromwell and tell him to set up our rate structure. I haven't gone this far to go bankrupt because I don't know how long some middle-aged Canuck with pleurisy from the woods of Maine will live in Zebadiah's mills"

Dearing was as good as his word. He came back with Frank Giordano. A young man in his late twenties, with a heavy black beard which no amount of shaving could lighten, and a perspiring olive face which would never allow the close comfort of a Cabot or a Lowell. The man was respectful. He listened to what Adam wanted. The kerosene light burned long hours. He covered reams of paper with neat figures in geometric columns. When he finished, he stacked the actuarial tables in a tight pile.

Adam could see the man's pride. He smiled and gave him another assignment. Giordano left that night for Boston. He returned in less than a week and immediately went to work covering more paper with more numbers. When he had finished, Adam's, smile was bigger. He warned Giordano not to say anything.

O'Connell rented a two story building next to the third canal. The warehouse formerly housed a grain merchant. The walls still held the nut-like scent of dry cereals. Dearing had an office on the top floor. He made it a world of paper. Paper policies. Paper tallies of the income and outgo each day. Paper bills. Paper circulars handed out on street corners. Paper bank deposits. Paper checks.

Adam and Patrick knew the customers, poor uneducated people, were confused by events which threatened to make worthless their payments up to then. These people were made happy by salesmen who credited past coffin payments towards an insurance policy which would guarantee a decent burial.

By March, Commonwealth had sold 1200 policies to their former Customers.

By April, the number was up to 2600 with face value of over $250,000.

By May, there were 6000 subscribers with insurance in force of $1,000,000.

In July, Adam made the dream come true. He was ready to convert the fraternal benefit society to a stock insurance company. He now had the money for the bond.

"The back door," Adam had exalted back in February in Boston, when Dearing showed him the loophole. "Those bastards left us the back door." They had given him the nettle to grasp. He had crushed it into gold.

The law was specific about the conversion. It was designed to prevent exploiting immigrants and their children. Stock had to be given to each member of the original fraternal organization in proportion to the face amount of each policy. One share for every $100.

The immigrants and the sons and daughters of the immigrants did not read fine print. Even if they had, what did it mean? They paid their premiums. They had their certificates engraved with Roman statues and rushing waterfalls. When they died, their heirs would have $150 in legal tender of the United States of America.

They signed away the stock options to the very nice young man who had sold them the original policy. Why not? In return Adam gave them a month's free premium. Cash in hand. Something for nothing. Why not? They were content. Adam and Patrick collected the options. Dearing converted the society.

July 4, 1866. A day commemorated by showers of fireworks set off from the roof of the Gatehouse.

A day John Spencer and his pregnant wife made love for the last time.

A day Elizabeth Harcross decided to travel to the continent in the fall, with no definite plans to return to Cromwell.

A day Shaw Billings lost consciousness during dinner.

A day the mosquito population in the valley exploded to critical mass.

July 4, 1866. A day that saw the formation of The Commonwealth Life Insurance Company. 200,000 shares of no-par voting common stock split equally between Adam Ring and Patrick O'Connell.

━◁┼ ┼▷━

The business of selling insurance consumed Adam Ring. Selling lumber, boxes, coffins, funerals, shoes, writing paper or potatoes. They were all tangible products of human labor. One could touch them.

Insurance was different. It had no substance. . It was intangible. …invisible. It was nothing more than mathematical equations of probability. A row of figures on a sheet of foolscap. It existed only by faith that the words on the paper would be honored. It was a magic machine by which one extracted small amounts of money from many in the present, in order to give back even less to fewer in the future. The difference was profit, accountable to no one. The profit was free to make more profit. The gold was power. Power was the slave of whoever owned it.

Power was what Adam Ring wanted. Could it erase a scar and the memories that went with it?

Adam conceived of the idea of hiring the sons of immigrants to go out into the counties to sell insurance. Giordano calculated the figures. Dearing couched them in legal terms. O'Connell trained the eager first generation Americans, promising them high commissions on each policy they sold.

Adam insisted the salesmen talk Polish to the Poles, French to the Canadians, Ukrainian to the Ukrainians. Adam had the translations printed on the back of the policies different languages. Cyrillic for the Russians. Hebrew for the Jews. The paper had to be thick and heavy, a rich creamy white parchment with the finest of engraving. At the top, the Goddess of Liberty spilling out her riches to those fortunate enough to own the policy.

Adam donated to each Church or Parish if they informed him of a marriage. The appropriate salesman was certain to call as soon as the honeymoon was over with a gift. One month's free premium on a policy the new husband was induced to purchase to protect his bride.

Adam paid the Clerk in each City Hall when notified of a birth. The Commonwealth Agent was among the first visitors when the mother was receiving. He was instructed to arrive when all the relatives were present. His task was to convince the new father of his added responsibility. Adam's gift to the newborn, a month's free premium,

Adam transferred the swelling funds to the First National City Bank of Boston. He had all the engraving plates changed. Each policy now listed, in large letters, the impressive title of the Hub bank as if it was a guardian of the fledgling enterprise,

Adam gave stock in the company to its key employees as an incentive. Not the voting common which was held equally by him and Patrick, but a new class of non-voting common.

On July 4, 1866, Frederick Dearing, Frank Giordano and eleven district sales managers were awarded shares in the Commonwealth

Life Insurance Company, The amount was small, but cost the recipients nothing. If they worked hard, the stock would make them rich. Adam took no chances. Upon the stockholder's death, or disability, the Company would redeem the stock at its increased value. If the employee left or was fired, the stock was forfeited. Adam was generous...... to a point.

July 4, 1866 was the hottest night of the summer. The moon was hidden behind the clouds. The air was still and saturated with a heavy wetness. A dense river of moist air had risen off the wetlands behind Pulpit Rock. It flooded over the Flats, drenching the human beings in their own sweat.

The windows of the conference room were wide open. The kerosene lamps seemed to attract every flying insect within miles. Flies and moths danced around the open lights, burning up in the flames or smearing their bodies on the glass lamps. The four men were soaked in sweat. Their jackets and collars were off, shirts open wide at the neck. They were still caught in the exhilaration of the moment. The branch managers were gone, leaving them alone. Each man was isolated in his own thoughts. Perhaps to wonder how it all came about.

Only Adam was thinking of how easily all of it could be lost. He walked around the room, touching each object in turn. If he had been drinking, he showed no signs.

"Come on, Adam. Relax. ."

Adam stopped in front of the Irishman. "Patrick, how many promissory notes did O'Connell-Ring hold at the time of the injunction?"

"Forty three hundred in Cromwell. Almost three thousand in the other branches."

"How many have been converted to policies in Commonwealth?"

"Almost ninety percent. It wasn't easy. We may have been the biggest chain of undertaking parlors in the four counties, but we are probably the smallest insurance company in the State."

"How many note-holders do you have left?"

"Jesus Christ, Adam. You can add and subtract as well as I can." Why was his partner was deliberately provoking him?

"How many?" Adam insisted.

Giordano did the calculation. "738, give 5 or 10, as of the close of business yesterday."

"Exactly," Adam replied, his face grim. "Tell me, Patrick. What happens then?"

"Happens?" Patrick sputtered. "Nothing has to happen. We just collect the premiums and hope that a big epidemic doesn't come along.

Adam walked over to the window and leaned out for a breeze. There was none. He thought he could hear, under the noise of the celebration, a faint rumble of thunder. God, he hoped so. What he would give for a cold drenching shower to wash away the heat.

Clouds of mosquitoes brushed by him, drawn to the lamps inside. Adam wiped his hands around his neck, squashing those that had settled there. "What if there is an epidemic?" He threw the challenge back. "What if the yellow jack comes like last fall, but worse? What if the frost is late this year, or more Negroes move in? " He circled the room, stopping in front of each man. "Where are the actuarial reserves to pay the claims?"

Adam had a point. But, what could they do about it? They would just have to pray for a dry summer and an early cold fall. Just pray.... and hope.

"Forget about the ague. The water fever. The bone-break fever. What about the competition? Do you think the Old Colony or the Boston Mutual are going to sit on their asses on Beacon Street? The only reason they never pushed hard before was because the pickings were too small. The big money was always in the cities."

" The big insurance companies will be out to get us, " he warned. "Those rich bastards are probably sitting in their paneled offices, with crystal chandeliers and soft carpets, with pink cheeks and neat quiet manners, sipping Madeira and listening to the Tatlocks and Brewsters making plans to deliver our heads on a silver platter."

The euphoria had vanished. Adam's made sense. He let them digest the unhappy message. His face then broadened into a grin, like a child who has pulled a trick on his parents.

"Gentlemen, I am not going to wait until they come sailing down the Quabbin. We are going to attack them!"

"How?" dumbfounded at his proposal.

Adam waited until they fell silent, then nodded to Giordano who suddenly understood the reason for his secret project.

"Have you ever heard of a Tontine?"

———◄╫ ╫►———

Frank Giordano was not the typical employee of the Old Colony Life Insurance Company. The hierarchy was all tested, refined, old New England stock. Lyall Prentiss, the founder and still Chairman of the Board, favored tall blonde fair-skinned men around him. The doggerel around Boston recited that when the gods of Olympus took to themselves the daughters of men, the result was Old Colony partners.

Frank Giordano looked more like a bastard son of Vulcan. His face was always shiny, a fact not helped by his habit of lavishing lavender-scented pomade into his black hair. He was thick of trunk and short of leg. His large head sat on his shoulders without benefit of neck. Two brown eyes squinted between fat folded lids.

He had only two assets. The first was an accident of birth. His mothers brother was Democratic Boss of Somerville. When the Boston Traction sought an extension into that expanding suburb, Mario Giordano requested a clerical position for his flesh and blood. The second was an amazing facility with figures. He could compute nine digit numbers in his head within seconds. Given a paper and pen, he could tally long columns without effort. The

Old Colony hired Frank Giordano to satisfy Mario Giordano. To keep him busy, they buried the young man in the Actuarial Department. He worked there for six years, his position and salary never advancing, as the Somerville franchise was issued in perpetuity. He saw others with half his talent climbing the ladder as the Old Colony quadrupled in size during the War. Nothing he did had any effect.

He studied the history of insurance. He devised ingenious ways to price policies. Once, in desperation, he wrote a memorandum on a revolutionary type of insurance tried only in Europe. All this effort got him a meeting with a very inferior assistant vice president. The man was pleasant, but distant. "You are doing a splendid job where you are," he assured. "Let us handle the sales. Besides", he scorned, "the Tontine is for crooks. It is dishonest." He looked down sadly at the standing clerk, comparing him to his own imposing physical image. "We, at the Old Colony, do not have to steal."

Frank could never tell exactly who the 'we' was.

Adam was not so particular. He liked the Italian, although he could never understand how the man could have married a woman who was a mirror image of himself, even down to the black moustache on her upper lip. He did not even care if Frank changed back to his real name of Franco. All he cared was that the man was ambitious and clever.

Adam motioned Giordano to speak. Giordano knew the Commonwealth was insignificant next to the Old Colony with their marble-lined hallways and uniformed guards. But, in this room, the men listening to him were the owners. His memorandum had never gotten even close to Prentiss. The Pole had given him stock in the Company. Giordano felt gratitude. His manner may have been hesitant, but his words were not

"The *Tontine* describes a lottery in which there is one winner. It is a French word dating from the Seventeenth century. During the reign of Louis XIV, an Italian financier named Lorenzo Tonti devised a plan to gain funds for the French Crown. He floated a series of government loans which were never intended to be repaid. Instead, the French government would credit annual interest on the loans. This interest continually reinvested until every subscriber in a series had died, but one. The single survivor received all the accumulated money which usually amounted to a huge fortune."

Dearing and O'Connell stole a side glance at Adam. He was sitting with a smug expression. The two men wondered what kind of chicanery he was up to. They did not have long to wait. Somehow the Polish immigrant had an intuitive grasp of Giordano's history lesson.

"What was the attraction of the *Tontine?*" Adam asked, then answered his own question. "It was the gamble. A chance to get rich from the contribution of others. Hundreds of thousands of people were willing to give money with no expectation of ever getting their small sum back. They took a chance they would make a killing at the end. They were betting that If they lived longer than the next person, then they would reap the reward. If they died earlier, then they were out of luck....but then, they had only lost a little."

Patrick and Frederick stared blankly.

"Look. What happens when we sell a $300 policy. We charge $3 a year for twenty years. If the policy-holder dies before the twenty years are up, we give the widow the full $300. If the man lives beyond the twenty years, the man gets nothing. We keep the full $60 he paid, plus all the accumulated interest. Suppose we change the rules. Let us charge the man $6 per year for the same policy. In twenty years, he will have paid $120. If he dies within the twenty years, his widow gets the $300, just as before. If he lives, we give him back the extra $60 he paid in."

He could see his associates shake their heads. So far they could not see inducement to the policy holder. Adam got to the core of the plan.

"We invest the first $60 in the usual mortgages and United States securities for our actuarial reserves and lock it away. But we invest the second $60 into higher paying investments. At the end of the twenty years, we divide the accumulated income into two portions. We keep one half. The other we give back to subscribers who survived their twenty years, dividing it equally among them."

Patrick was quick to see Adam's 'carrot.' Dearing was still puzzled.

"Look, Frederick, the man has the same insurance coverage. If he dies, his widow gets the same $300. If he lives, he gets back the sixty dollars he paid over and above the usual term policy plus his share of the invested income. If he lives, he will be a winner, not a loser with a drawer full of premium receipts. It is the *Tontine* all over again but wrapped up in an insurance plan."

"Even more, the man has an inventive for staying with us. If he switches companies, he loses his share in the pooled account, We get a lock on the policy-holder. We make our usual profit on the term policy. We keep half of all the profit on the premiums. No other insurance company has anything like this in the United States. And," he emphasized "there are no statutes on the books forbidding the *Tontine* in Massachusetts,"

"Its damn clever," Patrick was the first to comment, "It might just work. What makes you think the other companies won't do the same?"

"They could," Adam said softly, "although I doubt they are hungry enough to come down to our level to fight. According to Frank, they pride themselves on being 'gentlemen,'" He made the word sound dirty. "This will smack of the devil to them. Besides, they have already written thousands of regular policies. If they convert them, they are admitting they have been selling an inferior plan. That it took us, the Commonwealth, to give poor people a chance to get rich. No, Patrick," he boasted," the more they push a plan like ours, the more they show they have been cheating the public all these years. "

"This is what we are going to sell. We will call it the GOLD MEDAL PLAN. Use real gold foil on the seal. Real gilt along the edges." He touched his finger to his lips to caution secrecy, "We must not reveal the new policy until Frank has worked out the rates and Frederick has the certificates printed. Patrick will call in the district managers. We will break the news of the GOLD MEDAL POLICY throughout the State simultaneously. Frederick will see that the newspaper advertisements and the circulars are released at the same time. Patrick, your main job is to line up insurance agents in the big cities. Convince them to drop the Old Colony and Boston Mutual lines and take on the Commonwealth. We can offer double the commission, even triple. We will just take the extra money out of the pooled fund. The big boys can't do that. Commonwealth will use the policyholders' own money to pay the salesman to sell him the policy."

He stood up and stretched with nervous tension. "The War has ended. Immigrants are flooding in from Europe. Railroads are building out west. Mines and factories are expanding. Cities are growing buildings like forests. All this will take money. Over the next twenty years, you will see a shortage of capital. The industrialists, the financiers, must have it. We will have it to loan out. Every week. Every month. We can demand our price. With gold, we can be like Zebadiah Harcross and the rents he gets from the mills along the canals." He reached into his pocket and withdrew a gold coin. He spun it between his fingers. It picked up the light and shimmered with a life of its own. "Gold, gentlemen... just like the seals on our the new Commonwealth policies. Those little pieces of paper will make us rich!"

CHAPTER TWENTY-FIVE

O n July 4th, 1866, Willard Parker started at least a dozen replies to John Spencer's letter. Parker was sixty four years of age, medium height, with a square stern face framed in dark brown sideburns into which wisps of grey were beginning to intrude. His short stubby fingers were carpeted with tufts of the same wiry hair. After a lifetime of labor, Parker had finally attained the pinnacle of success in his field. Professor of Surgery at Columbia's prestigious College of Physicians and Surgeons, he was also New York City's most famous surgeon, his fame resting more on his careful clinical examinations and meticulous operative technique than on his popular talent of being ambidextrous. He was known to wield the scalpel equally with either hand.

Parker never denied that he was the creature of modern medicine. Up until the 1840s, before anesthesia, surgeons were rewarded by the speed of their operations. These men could sever limbs, remove tumors within minutes, even seconds, while the patient, narcotized only with liquor and laudanum, was immobilized in the iron lock of four assistants, chosen for strength and insensitivity.

Parker was slow in his operations. He paused often to consider his next move. In an era when blood loss was irreplaceable, and a successful operation ended by death from hemorrhage, he would carefully pinch off each spurting artery with his fingers and tie it with a silk or horsehair ligature before continuing. Only the invention of anesthesia allowed this slow painstaking technique. His clinical results were incredible in an era when surgery was considered a last resort. His practice was enormous. His fortune great. His fame increased year after year.

Parker picked up again the letter from Cromwell, Massachusetts. It was from some obscure physician, only a few years out of his training in Montreal. He knew why he had delayed his answer. Parker was a cautious man. Should he risk a reputation to reveal the truth to this unknown stranger? Parker walked over to the window and threw open the shutter. In the distance, he could hear the explosive sounds of the Independence Day celebration. Flashes of light speckled the sky as incendiary rockets flashed to their death.

His wife had gone to bed hours before. The servants were out on holiday. The house was quiet. He moved the kerosene lamp closer to the center of the table. He pushed away the crumpled beginnings of his answer. He hesitated. He rose from the chair and poured himself a half glass of brandy from a silver Tantalus resting on the sideboard. He was *a* relatively abstemious man. Tonight, though, he savored the strong liquor. He reseated himself, carefully placed the glass where it would not spill and slowly reread the letter from the expatriate Canadian physician.

May 7, 1866
Cromwell, Massachusetts

Dear Doctor Parker,

Forgive my presumption, but I write to you on the advice
of Professor Elias Guthrie, Chairman of the Department of
Materia Medica McGill Medical College. Doctor Guthrie was
my mentor during my training as physician and surgeon, and
remains my valued friend and preceptor. I place my query
with the hope that you may assist my partner, Doctor Shaw
Billings, and myself, in the treatment of a patient.

The man is in his late fifties. For the past year, he has
suffered recurring attacks of pertyphlitis. We have treated
him in the accepted manner with laudanum, appropriate
blisters and clysters. At present the patient is in a state of
remission. We fear that his constitution, hitherto vigorous,
may not survive another relapse. Professor Guthrie informed
me that you treated a similar case with incision into the body.
Laudable pus was found, drained, and the patient cured.
Shaw Billings has related a similar experience. He, too,
lanced an accumulation of sepsis with complete recovery.

Such a radical step is beyond the ken of my experience.
I know the danger of elective violation of the human cavity.
Yet, to do nothing in this case will, I fear, lead to certain
death. It is my earnest hope that you honor me with gleanings
from your store of clinical wisdom. I would travel to New
York City to see you in person. However, responsibilities,
personal and medical, preclude what I know would be a
richly rewarding experience.

With sincere thanks for your counsel, I remain Your
obedient servant,

John Owen Spencer, M.D.

Parker dipped the steel-nib pen in the ink well and then daintily teased the tip on the glass rim. He tested it several times until he had the exact amount he wished. He held the pen poised over the smooth writing surface. He suddenly put it down and reached for the humidor. He withdrew a dark-leafed Havana, clipped off the end which he deposited in a crystal ashtray. He rotated the end in the lamp, flaming the stump evenly as he inhaled deep breaths to create a perfect char.

Why was he delaying to write what he believed to be the truth for the over the past two years? He knew the answer. The white paper taunted him. He could hesitate no longer. He gave a sigh. Reluctantly he put down the cigar. He took one last sip from the brandy glass and picked up the pen again. There was a life at stake in a strange town he would never visit. An unknown patient whose survival depended on the words he was compelled to write.

July 4, 1866
New York City

My dear Doctor Spencer,

It is never a presumption when one physician inquires of another for aid to heal his patient. It is my duty, even a privilege, to respond to the limits of my ability. However, you must be aware that no literary effort can ever substitute for a clinical examination which I have not done.

From the earliest time, men of medicine have recorded deaths from that mysterious affliction which presents with fever, abdominal pain first starting in the right lower quadrant, accompanied by vomiting and obstipation. In 1642, Saracenus documented that fatal disease which has never varied during the two hundred years since then.

Have you never asked yourself why perityphlitis should always arise from one particular site? Why not from some

211

other part of the twenty feet of intestine which wind their slippery way through the abdominal cavity? What is so unique about the blind end of the cecum? Has not the answer to this enigma been staring us in the face all these centuries?

In the seventeen hundreds, Mestivier in France lanced a collection of corruption in the right lower quadrant during an attack of perityphlitis. The patient did not survive. At autopsy, the physician found at the bottom of the pool of stagnant pus a gangrenous appendix which had ruptured.

Yes, Doctor Spencer, that useless, innocuous appendage which juts out from the end of the cecum and named by Vidus Vidius the vermiform appendix.

Did you know that Parkinson, in England in 1812, examined a five year old child who perished from a cecal inflammation. He, too found not only the hallmarks of a peritonitis, but also an inflamed vermiform appendix which had burst. Again in France, Jean Baptiste Louyer-Villermay found the identical findings in two of his cases. He claimed a causal relationship between the fatal peritonitis and the suppurated appendix. His words fell on deafened ears.

Three years later, Mellier collected many such cases and shouted out to our colleagues that the appendix was the culprit. He argued to remove the offending organ <u>before</u> the corruption had spread. Like Jeremiah, his prophetic comments were ignored.

Finally, on April 5, 1848, Henry Hancock, a mere thirty nine (forgive me, but that age makes me feel ancient) had the daring to cut into an abscess cavity in the right lower quadrant. He drained the pus from a ruptured appendix and cured the patient. Like Mellier, he argued for immediate active surgical intervention. Drain the corruption before it spreads, he wrote. No one read his words. The patients continued to die.

I have taken the liberty of reciting this early history to place appropriate credit where it deserves. These men, Mestivier, Parkinson, Louyer-Villermay, Mellier, and Henry Hancock, all had the perspicacity to see the truth, They had the courage to speak out. The rest of us also looked and listened. We saw not and heard not. Generations of men have died because of our blindness.

Two years ago, I myself had such a patient. A man forty seven years of age. He had suffered many years. His last attack was the most violent. His family physician treated him as he had done successfully in the past. The patient was purged with forty grams of magnesium nitrate in lemonade each day. The cramps grew worse with vomiting. His abdomen was tensed and rigid, the skin edematous. He was given strong brandy and rum which he was unable to retain.

A consultation was obtained with another physician who changed the purgative to calomel without any salutary effect. Harsh blisters of Spanish fly were placed over the afflicted area to draw out the pus.....to no avail. Finally, excessive doses of quinine was administered per mouth and per rectum as a last resort.

When I was called to his bedside, it was evident the man was in extremis. His once corpulent frame was wasted. His pulse rapid. His breath fetid. His urine, dark-hued and scant and foul-smelling. His eyes were dulled. His respirations labored. The man had not long to live.

I dosed the man with laudanum until insensibility was reached. His abdominal muscles then relaxed sufficiently for me to feel a large fluid mass deep in the right lower quadrant. I placed the man under chloroform anesthesia and cut down to the lump I had just palpated. I was greeted with an immediate outpouring of thick creamy fecal smelling pus contained under great pressure. I completely evacuated the abscess cavity.

To my shock, at the bottom of the walled-off area, there came up in my hands the loose tip of a ruptured appendix. The other end was still attached to the cecum and could be seen spilling out bowel contents. I tied off the open stump with a heavy ligature. I packed the wound open. The man is alive and healthy. His major medical problem is gout which torments his right foot. I fear this contemporary affliction is the result of too much food and strong spirits, a combination which will probably precipitate his mortality as surely as the abdominal catastrophe God preserved him from earlier.

Parker rested his pen and relit his cigar. He refilled the glass of brandy. His expression was troubled. So far what he had written was history. What he was about to write was a theory. His direct challenge to the long-standing beliefs of his fellow physicians. They had heard it from others. From Mellier and Hancock. What made him think his words would receive a better reception? The risk was greater than merely to be ignored. What if they cast aspersion on his unblemished reputation? What then?

He looked around the room, relishing the affluence. He had climbed high since being impoverished student at the Harvard Medical School. He now had respect, privilege, rank, wealth. He was sixty-five. Should he risk them all on a theory he could not prove?

The pen lay there, challenging, daring, a silent gauntlet. He thought of the French physicians, and the Londoner. They had not hesitated. He could see the many who would die if men like him did not continue to speak out. Someday, a physician like himself would manage to fire into blazing truth the embers which Hancock and Parkinson and others had barely managed to keep alive.

He was a healer. Another of his fraternity had called upon him. Not for personal gain, but to save a human life. He knew what he must do. He picked up the pen.

Doctor Spencer, what I say springs from the crevasses of my soul. Up to now I have been loathe to express these words except in the most oblique fashion.

I do not accept the current concept of 'perityphlitis'. The disease is <u>not</u> a vague inflammation of the cecum. It originates from the harmless little 'worm'. When, for reasons we do not yet know, the appendix becomes inflammed, it will rupture spilling feces into the abdominal cavity. Death will result from peritonitis.

I believe the vermiform appendix to be this killer of men.

I believe that it <u>alone</u> is guilty for the symptoms we treat so ineffectually with our clysters and laudanum and purgatives and blistering plasters.

I believe that we physicians (my heart now lodges in my throat to consider the words) <u>must open into the human cavity</u> and remove this organ <u>before</u> the peritonitis has ensued, despite the risk.

That is my faith. I tremble at the enormity of what I tell you, of what you are thinking as you read these words. Perhaps in our lifetime, another will rise up in our midst to <u>prove</u> what is still just a hypothesis. However, we physicians living in the present must carry the burden without benefit of prophecy. Should one ever accept a belief without proof? As a man? As a healer? As a scientist? I do not know the answer. The dilemma was mine. Now, for better or for worse, it is also your's.

The baton of uncertainty, the tiny morsel of knowledge, like the bite of the apple, has been transferred to you. No longer will you be able to look at your patient with the same eyes. You now have a dilemma which did not exist before the post brought you this letter.

Whatever you do, please convey to me the results of your clinical decision.

I pray the Lord grant you guidance for a wise choice.

Your respectful servant,

Willard parker, M.D.

The physician's face was expressionless as he slowly reread the letter. He folded it, creasing the sharp edges with his finger nail. He inserted it in an envelope which he addressed for the morning mail.

The room was pitch black when he finally rose from his chair. He could see the last few fiery showers signaling the end of festivities. He thought again of what he had written. He wondered whether the truth would extinguish his own career as swiftly.

CHAPTER TWENTY-SIX

The summer sun beat down upon Cromwell, baking the land as if to balance the frigid winter. The burning white star rose each morning and set each evening undisturbed by cloud or storm. Workers dragged themselves to work each morning after restless nights. Each evening, they left the stifling brick mills where they sweated for Zebadiah.

Only the Master of the Quabbin seemed unaffected by the elements.

His illness was gone. For good, he hoped. Dormant, counseled Shaw Billings. Whatever the future for the perityphlitis, it had relaxed its grip. Zebadiah put aside the laudanum. He ate without fear. His frame filled out, muscles thick once again. It was as if the sun had given him a new life. Zebadiah was enthusiastic. It was a spirit Elizabeth thought gone forever. Now, in the full splendor of the summer, her father was happy.

During the terrible days of the winter when he lay uncertain of survival, thoughts for a future were deferred. The arrival of spring and the realization he had been spared, encouraged him to grapple with a business problem. Restored to vigor, his mind quick and alert, Zebadiah made the decision to commit his fortune to a project whose success would double his empire,

Tom Kennedy stopped the carriage on the east bank of the Manhan River. Zebeidah climbed down from the carriage, his arms full of papers and maps. His face had tanned from excursions into the country north of Cromwell.

The river contained only a weak trickle of water. The gravel bed of was dried everywhere except in the center where a weak current flowed. Zebadiah scrambled down the bank. He reached up to help Elizabeth negotiate the steep descent. "This is it," he pointed the length of the parched conduit. "What do you think?"

Elizabeth looked at her father's eagerness. During the summer, she had toured the area with him many times, cradling in her lap the rolled charts of soil borings and water elevations. She had participated in his project without complaint, but she knew that her enthusiasm was a façade. She could not disappoint her father. Watching him strut like a child seeking a forbidden prize, he seemed to be deliberately defying the gods.

' I am the Zebadiah Harcross who entered this valley a quarter of a century ago. I am not dead. I am not defeated.' How could she deny him? She did not have the courage to tell him she would be leaving after the frost. Perhaps all she needed was a short respite. She could not predict. There was no pleasure for her in Cromwell. Certainly nothing to match the love affair of her father with the river.

Zebadiah waited for an answer. She gave a smile for him to interpret as he wished. Zebadiah shouted to Kennedy to join him. The two men spread out their papers out on a large rock. Elizabeth quietly left them.

She picked her way around the bend of the river bank until the cover of alder and young birches hid her from view. She took off her bonnet and let her hair down. She unbuttoned the top of her bodice. She held her head high in the air to catch a cooling breeze. There was none.

Dense waves of mosquitoes flew around her. She swatted the biting insects with no success. She buttoned her dress and put the hat back on, trying to cover as much skin as possible. She closed her eyes, trying to imagine millions of gallons of cold water rushing past her in a wet roar. The river full and churning power The cooling spray bouncing off the boulders. The high-pitched whine of turbines. She tried to see her father's vision of another industrial city. It was difficult.

Zebadiah claimed that he had no choice. The magnates whose mills filled the Flats came to the Master of the Quabbin. They asked, begged, then demanded more land and more hydraulic power. The canals were drained of power. The brick buildings were packed cheek to jowl along the conduits. There wasn't enough free land to plant a tree. What could he do?

The industrialists threatened an alternative. Coal! Steam engines! They did not need him. They did not need his canals. They did not need Cromwell. They did not need the Quabbin! What could he do?

The question perplexed Zebadiah. He had more than enough money for his lifetime. Enough to endow his daughter and her heirs with riches in perpetuity. He would always be the Master of the Quabbin as long as he drew breath, even if the businessmen converted their mills to Corliss engines which drew their energy from coal.

He no longer had a son. Why should he fight any longer? He could sit back, count his gold, and enjoy the time left to him.

The challenge! He <u>was</u> the Master of the Quabbin. Should he let clanking iron and hissing steam pollute his valley? He knew what he must do. He must squeeze the river one more time!

How? Zebadiah poured over terrain maps. Teams of surveyors dissected the countryside. With Tom Kennedy in tow, he toured the valley, walking, riding, hiking, in the sweltering heat of day, probing, searching, seeking the magic fulcrum, like Archimedes, to make the miracle.

The only possible site for a fourth canal was where the neck joined the main land. Unfortunately, the land there tilted up towards the Highlands. The bedrock was solid schist. When the answer came, Zebadiah cursed his stupidity for not seeing it sooner.

At one time, the Manhan River must have been the main channel of the Quabbin. Then, the river changed course to flow in its present path. The Manhan remained a pale replica of its ancestor.

Zebadiah's fingers ran up the contour map until they found the spot where the glacier-uplifted granite ledges had abruptly severed the Manhan from the Quabbin five miles above Pulpit Rock. "There it is, Pride's Landing," Zebadiah called the spot by the local name. "Blast through that stone barrier, put in sluice gates to control the flow, and we can make the Manhan an industrial canal."

Kennedy slowly chewed his brown cud. "Your experts from Boston. How many horsepower do they calculate ?" He hawked the plug on the ground away from his employer, then wiped his mouth with the back of his shirt sleeve.

"Twenty thousand. Maybe more." Zebadiah stood back, proud. "It was there all the time. Who would have thought of using the poor old Manhan?"

"But, Mister Harcross, "if you drain the Quabbin above Pulpit Rock, you will lower the river level. You will simply be diverting the extra 20,000 horsepower down the Manhan instead of through the canals in Cromwell."

Tom was no fool. Robbing Peter to pay Paul was no way to make money. "No, Tom," Zebadiah laid his hand on the man's shoulder. "There will be no loss." He stood up straight, his chin thrust out. "We will raise the dam at pulpit Rock another twenty feet. The banks are high enough to increase the reservoir. Flood another hundred square miles to hold the extra water and we will have the power through the Manhan without loss downstream."

Kennedy's mouth dropped open. He gazed at the older man with awe. Make an industrial city along a prehistoric creek? Raise the dam another twenty feet? Flood more farms and forests upon which hundreds of farmers relied for their living. Just with a flick of his hand? A man who weeks before was one heart-beat from death. A man with no son. A man whose ambition would bury him, if not his pride.

It was obvious Zebadiah had thought through the plan with his usual care. He was determined. Tom Kennedy was not one to fight battles lost in advance. Whatever his faults, the Harcross was not niggardly in his pay. Tom Kennedy had no intention of jeopardizing his position for some upland farmers.

Elizabeth walked along the dried river bottom for over an hour before she turned back. Like the Irishman, she knew the project would go forward. Unlike Kennedy, her worry was on whether a fourth canal justified the financial risk. Blasting through the retaining rock ledge at Pride's Landing, dredging the Manhan, installing the sluice-gates, and raising the height of the dam at Pulpit Rock would cost over $350,000. Then, add the purchase of rights along the river and the land upstream for a reservoir....... Failure of the Manhan would put the entire Harcross empire in jeopardy. Would it not be better to put money in the Samuel Higgin's factory outside Worcester making the new steam engines? She would check it out. It would be a good anchor to windward.

Her father waved to her. He was impatient to ride up to Pride's Landing before sunset. Elizabeth wondered what this final gamble would cost him

CHAPTER TWENTY-SEVEN

"Rhases? When? A thousand years ago?" Billings confessed his ignorance. "Johnnie boy, when you get to be my age, its enough to remember to let out the piss before you go to bed, let alone recalling an ancient Arab. What in the world do you want to know about a flute-player for, anyway?"

"The plans for the new hospital cannot be completed until we select the site*"

"I thought Zebadiah had donated land at the junction of the second and third canals,"

"Its no good there, Shaw."

"What do you mean 'no good'? The location is four blocks away from the Dispensary. Most of the patients live in the Flats. And the Sisters will still be close to the Mother House. What could be better?"

"Shaw, all those reasons are sound. Yet, there is something......" "he groped for the proper word, " 'unclean' in the Flats."

"Unclean?" Shaw protested. "What in the hell is 'unclean' about where you and I heal the sick and needy of Cromwell?"

"That's just it, Shaw. I don't know, perhaps, 'unhealthy' is a better word. I have talked to people who have lived here their whole lives. They tell strange stories. I didn't believe them at first. I talked with to Patrick. Since the dam at Pulpit Rock was finished, the land along the canals has become diseased. I don't know why."

Shaw stopped objecting. When John followed his intuition, he was usually right, although in this case, he'd be damned to know what all the fuss was about the Flats. Rhases! Some damn Baghdad musician. Shaw realized he was getting old. The ways of the modern physician were too much for him.

Billings' library was filled with treatises on new nostrums and old remedies. Nothing by an Oxford scholar named Sir Bertram Lytell. There was no public library in Cromwell.

"Try Zebadiah's home," Shaw suggested. "His son, Matthew, was a great one for books. That was just one burr which rubbed his father the wrong way. Zebadiah never did truck with knowledge which could not turn a water turbine."

Elizabeth was at home when John came to search out the volume. She had not seen him since the night of the dinner. She found herself waiting for his arrival with an anticipation that made her feel ridiculous. Why the strange attraction to the married doctor ?

The day was hot. John carried his jacket over one arm. His collar was off. He was clutching his cravat in one hand. He had been perspiring heavily. His linen shirt clung to his chest. His sleeves were rolled up. Elizabeth could see the bronze-red hair covering his chest and arms. Spencer had lost weight. His face was scrawny with hollows under the cheekbones. He had no hips, and his waist merged into buttocks molded by the clinging wool trousers.

The foyer was dark and cool. Chilled damp rose from huge stone food cellars filled with ice blocks insulated with sawdust. He raised his arms lifting his shirt off his sticky skin. He tingled all over in the refreshing cold air.

The maid went to seek her mistress. John reflected on the tangible advantages of wealth. In the dead of winter, the Harcross mansion had been the warmest place in Cromwell and was certainly the coolest in the heat of summer. The Master of the Quabbin could bend the laws of nature to his profit and pleasure.

Spencer's own home was a sweltering oven, not quite high enough to catch the winds which swept the bluffs. It was hardest on Kathleen now starting her eighth month of pregnancy. The low back pains were constant from the growing burden. It pained even to use the narrow stairs. Her abdominal skin was stretched with large blue veins. Her breasts were swollen. The nipples had darkened to an unpleasant tan.

At night when he lay by her side, head on her breasts, his hands cupped her abdomen. If he was patient, he could feel the baby change position. If he was gentle, his fingers could sculpt the outline, the large head, the four miniature limbs. His fingers would trace their way down to the pelvic cage which could never open. If Kathleen stirred, he would apologize. His finger tips would quickly move to the skin between her thighs and linger there for a moment as if that was their original intent.

Those nights he was aware of a persistent discomfort in his groin. It had been some time since they had made love. Each time, he drew close to her, his sexual frustration grew. His penis was hard and sensitive. He felt his testicles ache. Kathleen was aware of his need. It was <u>his</u> insistence that they refrain from intercourse. When she found his genitalia at night, he unloosened her grasp. He had given in to sin of Onan when young. Now some superstition kept him celibate.

Spencer's eyes slowly adapted to the half-gloom of the hall. Elizabeth entered through the far door. She had on a pale green dress with delicate white embroidery over the bodice. Her arms were bare and the neck line emphasized the swelling of her breasts. John would have sworn she touched the highlights of her cheeks with rouge if he had not known better. Long auburn tresses hung free.

Whether it was his denied sexual needs long unfulfilled or the desirable woman next to him, but he felt an erotic urge. He became angry at himself. He was a married man, in love and contented. The woman of his choice carried his child. Why each time he saw Elizabeth Harcross did he have the emotion to take her in his arms and rub her smooth skin next to his? To run his hands over her naked breasts and tease the nipples? To crush his needs out in her body?

Elizabeth stood on the alternating diamonds of gleaming black and white marble. The man was disheveled, his hair tousled, his clothes wrinkled. She could smell his sweat, feel the heat. He waited for her, legs thrust apart, unashamed of the swelling where the two long limbs joined.

If only..... It was not his fault. There was a terrible logic to life. If she had been born with the delicate features of Kathleen O'Connell. If she had not even been Zebadiah Harcross' daughter, a mark which scared away half the eligible men and rendered the remaining suspect. If only.......

"Doctor Spencer," she broke the silence.

"Miss .... Harcross." John stumbled over the simple words.

She was at his side, coupling her arm in his. "Please call me Elizabeth." She held his gaze, "John.... If I may." Then, before he could mumble a reply, she led him into the library.

Matthew Harcross had never catalogued his collection. It took an hour of sifting through the packed bookcases until Elizabeth found the dust-covered volume. She was standing on the top rung of the library ladder. John stood below, supporting the stand with his weight. A scent of patchouli mixed in the air. It took all his willpower not to test the softness of her skin with his lips.

Elizabeth let go of the ladder to hand him the book. Her heel caught in her hem. She lost balance as the ladder twisted and fell to the floor. Spencer caught her falling body. Her face grazed his. He knew he should release her. His hands moved higher. His lips pressed her mouth open. Their tongues explored, saliva mixing with blood from animal bites. Her hands roamed freely over his back and buttocks. She pulled his head down, locking him in the kiss. Her pelvis writhed against his erection, deliberately causing pain. She felt a unaccustomed wetness between her thighs, which embarrassed her.

John wrenched free. He turned away, flushed with shame. She stood there, arms trembling at her sides. Neither said anything, as they waited for the passion to subside,

"I am sorry," he blurted out. "I had no right. It was unfair." What more could he say? He did not give her a chance to answer. He grabbed the book and fled as if the devil was pursuing him.

The following week was a busy confusing time for John Spencer. He continued work at the Dispensary, made house calls to the gentry. He worried constantly over Kathleen's imminent delivery. He made a strange detour to the slaughter house on the outskirts of Cromwell where he purchased ten young lambs and ordered them killed and skinned. Through it all, he could not stop thinking about Elizabeth Harcross. He wondered what would have happened if he had not left at that moment, or if she had held on to him just a bit tighter. His own father had warned that lust was a sin.

John knew he should not have asked Elizabeth to accompany him on the last day of his experiment. Yet, he could no more prevent the rash step than she could refuse him. Elizabeth knew she had done nothing to stop him that day. To the contrary she had led him on. Even how, she would do the same thing all over again.

Many nights she tossed in bed, unable to sleep, her heart beating fast.

She would throw off her nightgown and walk naked to the window. The air would brush her and dry the hollow between her breasts and in between her thighs. Her eyes were closed as her fingers ran up and down her body as she imagined another caressing her neck and teasing her nipples until they stood out sharp and sensitive and then descending with light pressure to her inner thighs. She spread her legs and allowed the breeze to penetrate that most private place into which she followed like Ariadne.

A coarse shiver sent ripples up and down her skin. The touch moved deeper. She bent her knees. Her fingers probed within the hidden place, and teased the secret spot. She could no longer help herself. Her body swayed in response to a silent beat. She made soft low moaning noises. Suddenly a plea echoed to the star-splattered sky above. The touch she craved was from another she could never have.

⚔

When John Spencer arrived at the Harcross mansion, Elizabeth was slowly crossing the broad green lawn. Her hair was gathered into two long tresses which wound around the back of her head in a particularly unattractive manner. Her arms and bosom were covered by a loose mauve dress. Her manner was correct as if nothing had happened between them.

John had borrowed a high-wheeled phaeton with matching blacks from Shaw Billings. The sun was just crossing into afternoon. For the first time in weeks, clouds were climbing over the horizon from the southeast. These were not filmy mares-tails nor fluffy cumulus formations. Today, large flat bottomed thunderheads rose high like masses of frozen black smoke. John checked his pocket watch. They would have to move fast to avoid the downpour.

John and Elizabeth said little to each other as the carriage entered the Flats. He gave her back the borrowed volume with a bookmark. "Read it."

Elizabeth opened the book and read the story. "Is that what you are going to do?"

"I have already done it. Exactly as a thousand years ago in Baghdad. When the Caliph asked Rhases, the Court Physician, where to build his new Temple of Healing, Rhases hung a dozen lambs on high stakes throughout the city. A week later, he inspected them. He chose as the healthiest site where the flesh had shown the least putrefaction. This afternoon, you and I will repeat the experiment.

"You mean to tell me that one part of Cromwell is more diseased than another?" Elizabeth protested. "I don't believe it. I have lived here all my life."

"I know it is a bold idea. which many will dispute. That is why I placed the ten <u>de</u>ad animals in random locations. Look here." He unrolled a map which was resting against the corner of the carriage. He had marked ten locations beginning at the canals and ending on the highest ridge. "Perhaps being an outsider gives me a perspective which a native could never have. I talked with Shaw and the Sisters. It is no secret that there is more cholera, dysentery, typhus along the canals than in the Highlands."

"But, John, look at the people. They are unclean. They do not eat properly. Their clothes do not protect against the temperature. They live crowded. Surely, the diseases must come in some part from living conditions, instead of an accident of geography,"

John stared at his companion. What she said was true. Damn her! She was smart. He thought of Kathleen and immediately felt guilty at making the comparison. "Alright, Elizabeth, forget the intestinal fluxes. What about malaria and yellow-jack? Certainly their numbers have increased each year since your father built the dam."

She grabbed the traces from his hand and stopped the carriage.

"Are you accusing my father of bringing death to the valley? I will not go with you any further."

John waited for her temper to subside. "Elizabeth, I have the figures. They do not lie. With each new canal, the cases of yellow-jack and malaria increased. Even worse since the dam at Pulpit

Rock two years ago, Cromwell has escaped an epidemic only by the grace of God."

Her impulse was to leave the carriage. Yet, Spencer was not a malicious person. She owed him the chance to present his case.

"Last year," John continued, "the Dispensary was so full, the Sisters refused to admit the dying. Shaw said in all his years, he had never seen such sickness. I know. I dissected the cadavers. Believe me." He swallowed hard before voicing his fear. "Elizabeth, Shaw and I have kept this privy, not to alarm Cromwell, but we dread a terrible epidemic this fall. Already the cases are climbing three weeks earlier than last year."

"John, couldn't those two plagues stem from the same conditions as the other diseases?"

"Poverty and hunger in Cromwell have not changed in the past two years. If anything, the people are more prosperous. The only thing that has changed is the dam and reservoir at Pulpit Rock. Elizabeth, all I know is what I see. The river brings wealth and life to Cromwell. It may also bring disease."

"You hope by means of ten dead lambs to convince my father that his river is at fault?"

"I do not know <u>what</u> the river brings. Perhaps just some miasma to weaken people. If there is such a possibility, the hospital must be built where this factor is least deadly. My quest is unprejudiced."

Elizabeth said nothing more as the carriage approached the first of the three canals. She automatically checked the water level. Despite two months of dryness, the current was fast and high. Zebadiah was right. The dam at pulpit Rock made all the difference. She could hear the turbines extracting the full measure of power. The river at fault? The notion was absurd. Here was clean power to support a modern city.

Mosquitoes swarmed in dense clouds around the perspiring pair. John held both reins in one hand, waving away the bugs with the other. Insects was one evil he had learned to accept with the coming of spring. He swatted and cursed. His skin was soon covered with bright red smudges from crushed bodies which only seconds before had sucked up his blood. The bites itched until he craved nothing more than to shed his clothes and dive into one of the canals to escape the torture.

As the carriage rolled through the deserted street, Elizabeth recognized a familiar sound. The thunder grew louder. Elizabeth sat bolt upright. The Gatehouse? Had Spencer placed one of his dead animals in the heart of Zebadiah's dominion, next to the huge Cromwell dam itself ? She thought she had been mistaken as the carriage rolled past the entrance. Then, it took a sharp turn to the rear of the tower and stopped. John helped Elizabeth down.

"The first one is here."

Elizabeth hurried to keep up as John disappeared around the back of the Gatehouse. He pointed to the gas lamp post. Suspended about eight feet off the ground, out of the reach of dogs, was a dark object swinging from a rope.

"How....? I don't.....? Elizabeth stammered, angry at the audacity of placing a dead lamb right below her fathers nose and in broad daylight,

"How did I get permission to put it there?" John laughed at her chagrin, "I knocked on the door and asked. A very coöperative man assured me it would be fine. He even volunteered that you would be pleased to be part of the experiment, I think his name was Kennedy, If you see him, thank him for me,"

Kennedy? That old fool. Probably was telling everyone in the Flats Zebadiah Harcross had been presiding over a rotting carcass for the past week. Wait until she talked with him! It was hard to remain angry, despite herself. She could not help chuckling.

"Kennedy? Short and ugly? Stinking from tobacco juice?"

John nodded.

"I have no doubt he was eager to help."

As the pair approached the lamp post, the foul stench of decaying flesh hit them. The mass had no shape, The surface moved as if it was alive with thousands of crawling insects. John picked up a stick and poked at the lump. It exploded into an swarming cloud. He spun the carcass around trying to normal tissue. There was none.

"You would agree that the process of putrefaction is complete?"

But Elizabeth had already fled back to the carriage. "I suspect the rest of your specimens will be identical." she answered,

"We shall see," John nodded sagely.

At first, it appeared that Elizabeth Harcross was right. The next three lambs had been placed at the ends of each canal. They were identical to the first. He noted his companion's smug 'I told you so' expression as the carriage left the Flats to ascend to the Highlands.

But Elizabeth Harcross <u>was</u> wrong. Even she could see the difference as they climbed out of the valley. The number of insects and grubs burrowing in the meat dramatically decreased. The smell was less offensive. There were even patches of dried yellow fat and white gristle to identify normal muscle.

Only by the horses' panting and the breezes which sprung out of nowhere could she tell how the carriage had climbed. She squinted against the sun. She could see ahead her own home. Only one wooded rise of land lay between them and the Harcross mansion. Was John was taking her to her own house? Was the last vile object under her bedroom window? What else had Tom Kennedy cooked up with the gullible physician? To her relief, the carriage stopped at the edge of the woods. He took her arm and led her to the edge of the hill.

In all the years she had lived in Cromwell, living less than a mile away, she had never been here. The ground fell away sharply as if a giant knife had sheared off the edge. It was the same sensation as looking through the glass windows at the top of the Gatehouse. She tried to talk closer to the edge, but Spencer held her back.

"I have never been here before, John. It is beautiful."

"Look behind you."

The woods were less than two hundred feet away. A dark forest island of evergreens had somehow been preserved. The peaks of the trees rose to the sky, each a perfect triangle. Below, the forest was dark.

"This is where the hospital should be built."

The last lamb. Where was it? The physician was clever She should have known not to trust his innocent manners. A hospital, full of diseased and dying people, right where she would see them each it she stood at her bedroom window,

"The tenth lamb?" Even as she asked, she knew what it would show.

"It is this way."

"John, you have been here before ? You knew what all the lambs would show?" She could see the twinkle in his eyes,

"Every day, Elizabeth, Every day," he laughed.

The forest was strangely cool and quiet. No buzzing. No noises. Not a bird. Not even an insect. There were no crackling twigs or crumbling leaves underfoot. The ground was covered with a slippery layer of tan pine needles, upon which one did not walk, but glided.

The last lamb was hanging from the bough of a large fir tree. The surface was dry and leathery as if it had been smoked. A few beetles and tree grubs clung to the surface. The lamb was as clean and preserved as the forest itself.

When the pair emerged into the clearing, they knew something was wrong. Instead of being blinded by light, it seemed that they had never left the gloom of the forest. The sun was blotted out by swirling thunderheads. The air was chilly and damp. A sharp piercing wind whipped them. Minute by minute, the blackness increased. Elizabeth shivered.

"I am frightened, John."

On the horizon, light was being extinguished with incredible speed. John weighed whether they should take the chance and leave before the rain struck. As he hesitated, the decision was taken away from him. A few fat drops of water condensed out of nowhere and landed on his face, making him blink. In the distance, the sky lit up with a brilliant white flare. They waited for the report of thunder to follow. There was only an ominous silence.

"Its lightening," John said. "I don't hear the thunder. The storm must still be far away."

Both horses reared up and strained and strained to break loose. John grabbed the leather traces and tried to calm them down..

"Your petticoat. Give it to me," he shouted over the deafening noise of the wind.

Elizabeth could not imagine what he wanted it for.

He shouted again. " The horses. They must think it is fire. We must blind their eyes of they will run away."

She turned away and stepped out of the long white garment. He tore it into two long strips and bound them around each black's head. He led the blindfolded pair into the forest out of range of the storm.

"It is too late to go back, Elizabeth. We are safe here. The trees will break the force of the storm. Let us hope the stallions do not panic and bolt out of the woods."

For two months, the Cromwell sky had been parched of moisture.

The few brief summer showers would scarcely moisten the ground. Now, with a vengeance, nature was compensating. The thunderclouds stretched over a mile wide and towered four miles high. Their bases were warm from contact with the hot earth. Their peaks climbed high into the chilled regions of the ether where hailstones were formed in infinite number. They fell, growing in size, colliding with one another, pelleting the earth.

John and Elizabeth stood at the edge of the forest, petrified by the energy which was clawed from the sky by the earth around them and given back as lightening. The storm was now closer, driven by powerful gales. Jagged white scars branded the sky, then disappeared. The clouds opened and emptied torrents of rain. The thunder grew louder, hitting at the same time as the flashes.

"The storm is upon us, Elizabeth."

The woman trembled as she clung to him. Her face was white. Her heart was bounding. Her skin was cold. One tree on the edge of the bluff stood out. Suddenly, it shattered as a blast of thunder shook the ground under their feet. The lightening hit was no more than a dozen yards from where they stood. They could see the trunk split down the center.

"A little longer," he comforted, "the storm is directly overhead. Soon it will pass on."

Even as he spoke, Elizabeth pulled on his arm. She could not get the words out, but pointed in the direction of the tree. Hovering a foot off the ground was a luminous sphere, eight or nine inches in diameter. It was slowly moving towards them. As they watched, it changed color from yellow to orange to red and back again. There was an eerie hissing sound and an strange pungent odor filled the air. It rolled closer as if it could detect their presence. They were frozen in place, unable to comprehend what was happening. Elizabeth gave a muffled shriek, a wave of nausea climbing in her throat, when, without cause, the ball of lightening vanished from view, as mysteriously as it had appeared.

With that sighting, the air around them quieted. The storm was now on the other side of the valley. On the horizon a light glimmering appeared as the clouds moved east freeing the sun. There was a freshness in the air,

John sucked in a deep breath and let it slowly out. His body was revived as the months of draining heat were washed away. He stretched his body with abandon. He felt an unusual physical tension. He was filled with the power of the storm. He squeezed Elizabeth in his arms. His lips found hers as she twisted to meet him. His hands ran up and down her body, pulling her in. Her fingers kneaded the muscles of his back and buttocks as tightened his hold.

"Wait," she whispered, then drew away. As he watched, she slowly removed her clothing, unashamed, proud of her body. She reached up to undo her hair. The tresses fell to her waist. He stared at her, his mouth dry. She began to unbutton his shirt. He caught her hands to stop.

"It is alright, John," Her lips grazed the side of his face, then worked their way down to his neck. She fell back on the ground.

He resisted no longer. He stripped off his clothing, now in a rush. His penis stood swollen and capped. His scrotum was pulled high into his groin. He positioned himself between her parted thighs, his only thought to satisfy himself. He felt her maidenhead and drew back. She sensed his doubt. Quickly, she tightened her legs, locking him in place. Her pelvis ground into him. He could not help himself. He lunged forward, burying himself in her body.

She felt a sharp, piercing pain, but she could no more release him than he could stop on his own. They were now moving as one as he violated her. Her heels dug into his back with every thrust, meeting every move with one of her own, forcing him in deeper and harder until they was no more he could give her. He had never made love to any woman who struggled to excite him as she did. Each time he relaxed, for an instant, she urged him on. Faster and faster they moved, pelvis bruising pelvis until he discharged with one violent convulsion. Over and over he came. But still she did not stop. Her nails slashed into his skin, scratching and tearing. Her arms and legs were a steel trap keeping him until she had what she wanted..

She continued to rock back and forth, carrying him with her. He had stopped thinking. The pelvic strokes heightened, draining him dry. When he thought he could stand it no longer, Elizabeth's body stiffened in a spasm....rigid....unyielding. Then came the rhythmic tremors as she moaned and rubbed her hands up and down his back. He moved with her, without a will of his own.

Spent, the young woman finally released her hold. She lay back and clasped his head between her breasts. Her fingers burrowed into the hair on his head as she waited for him to recover. He rolled on his side and reached out. for her. She entered his embrace, feeling his erection start again.

"Elizabeth.... Elizabeth...." was all he could murmur in a husky voice, as the terrible realization taunted him.

She touched his lips to silence him. She had no insight into the future. Despite her innocence, a feminine intuition told her he had never loved another as he had her. That was sufficient license for the moment.

Tears started in the corners of his eyes. She knew in her heart that the voyage of self-recrimination had started for him. She kissed away the drops. "No tears. Not now," she whispered.

Tomorrow was another day.

CHAPTER TWENTY-EIGHT

Over the next two weeks, John Spencer drove himself in his work hoping the fatigue would bury the memory of his love-making with Elizabeth Harcross. In his guilt, he even considered the tide of malaria and yellow fever flooding the Dispensary as punishment. In the closing days of August, he dispensed help, and where not possible, hope When he returned home at night, he undressed in the dark to hide the scratches on his back. No matter how soundly she was sleeping, Kathleen took him in a tight embrace which only increased his guilt.

He searched his soul to find the flaw which permitted the betrayal. What he discovered is that his affair with Elizabeth did not diminish his love for Kathleen. If the opportunity presented, he knew he would succumb again. The question plagued him. Could a person love two people at the same time? Was the affection of a man for two women like a mother for two children? Or was he rationalizing a blemish on his character?

When he lay next to his wife's fragrant body, the need for sexual release tore at him. Days, he would have violent erections which stunned him with their persistence. He wrestled with his carnal cravings like St. Anthony with the Temptations. Despite his repugnance, he was forced to relieve the frustration as he did when younger, hoping that the act would kill the desire for Elizabeth. It did not, and he felt unclean and ashamed.

The dilemma plagued him. He looked with love and pride at Kathleen and the child growing within her. Yet, whenever a thunderstorm came, he felt the passion of tearing through Elizabeth's virginity. There was no one he could turn to. The only treatment was a mind-numbing work. It was not a solution, but only the deferring of one.

Spencer reflected that his life was now complex and mystifying. The notions of love, fidelity, morality were no longer clear-cut. Where his future had been etched in black and white, it was now shaded in grey.

Kathleen was aware of the subtle change. He was morose at times. He no longer brought home amusing anecdotes to entertain her. In the early days of their marriage, he would stop in the middle of what he was doing and kiss her with a spontaneity which delighted both of them. No more. He was withdrawn, taciturn, isolated. It was doubtful in her innocence she could have imagined the reason.

Her approaching confinement was another source of anxiety. Although John had sworn on the holiest of vows, his denials held a hollow ring. His declaration that her mothers death in childbirth was coincidental did not satisfy her. Each morning she would take off her clothes and stand before the mirror in their bedroom. She would grimace at the swollen silhouette. She, who had once prized her doll-like dimensions, looked inhabited by a monster. She would lift the heavy breasts and sigh. What was it that worried her husband?

There was one person who had never lied to her. He brought her into the world. Shaw Billings would tell her the truth.

John was exploring the dormer under the Dispensary roof looking for space to put more beds. The cramped attic was dark without windows. Each step stirred up a choking cloud of dust. He made a mental inventory of what had to be done. The new hospital would take several years to complete. They could put the children up here, he thought bitterly. Their cries would be closer to God.

His inspection was interrupted by the black and white head which poked above the landing.

"Doctor Spencer. Come quickly," she called, then disappeared down the stairs.

Tom Kennedy was waiting on the first floor. The physician recognized him as the Harcross Superintendent who had helped with the diver. The man had no time to exchange pleasantries.

"You are wanted at the big house," he blurted out. His face was flushed and covered with sweat. Wet patches stuck under his arms and between his shoulder blades. His expression was somber.

"What's happened?"

"I don't know. Its Zebadiah. Miss Elizabeth said for you to come as fast as you can."

Sister Immaculata had already checked the contents of Spencer's medical bag. He whispered a few instructions to her, then followed Kennedy down the path to the waiting carriage. The horses were still panting from the drive down to the Flats, their flanks wet and covered with buzzing insects. The carriage moved slowly along the canals. John looked anxiously at Kennedy.

"If I don't let them get their breath, they'll never make it back. "

John was happy for the change from the heat and stench of the Dispensary. The ride even brought a fresh breeze before the mosquitoes found their prey them.

"Its the dam up at Pulpit Rock," Kennedy allowed as he watched his passenger swat and curse like a man possessed. Mosquitoes always seemed to avoid him. "Must sweat vinegar," he observed with a chuckle, then snapped the traces to increase the pace.

"What do you mean?" John stopped his frantic arm-waving long enough to stare at the older man with curiosity.

"Must taste bad to them, I guess. They never even come close."

"No. No. That's not what I meant. You said, 'the dam up at Pulpit Rock'. What did you mean by that?"

Kennedy looked at his companion as if he was an idiot. Being a doctor didn't automatically give one common sense, or, for that matter, the ability to use the eyes God gave him.

"The mosquitoes. We've always had them in the valley. At least as long as I've been here. But, they've never been as bad as since Zebadiah flooded the land above Pulpit Rock."

John remembered the ten dead lambs. Then, the rise in yellow fever and malaria with the dam at Pulpit Rock. There must be some piece he was missing. Maybe the pieces did not fit together because they were not supposed to. The river was the key. But how?

Kennedy could see the physician lost in thought. By the time the Morgans pulled up in front of the Harcross mansion, John knew how he could find the answer.

If John had concerns over meeting Elizabeth Harcross, the woman's distressed state banished that worry.

"John, I fear for his life. Come quickly."

John could tell immediately the patient's desperate condition. Bright kerosene lamps emphasized his deathly white pallor. He was severely dehydrated with his eyes sunk back in the sockets. He was breathing in short gasps through tightly clenched jaws. Most striking was the extreme rigidity. He wad terrified of the slightest movement.

John picked up Zebadiah's hand. The eyes opened, then slowly closed. The lips started to say something in greeting, but failed. The skin was burning from fever. The pulse racing so fast that the beats blended. John released the wrist. The hand dropped like a dead weight. He lowered the quilt and raised the man's bed shirt to reveal the severe distension. His fingers traveled lightly over the surface, tapping out the hollow sound of paralyzed intestines. He felt in the four quadrants. Each time he exerted the barest pressure, the patient screamed. John thought he felt a mass in the lower right portion. But it was only a suspicion.

He placed himself to block Elizabeth's view. He oiled his hand. He gently separated the man's legs and inserted his right index finger into the anus. Harcross whimpered. There was no stool. John replaced the coverlet and washed himself in the basin on the table. Except in response to pain, Harcross did not utter a sound. John whispered a few words of encouragement. He took Elizabeth's hand and left the room.

"How long has this been going on?" he demanded, angry that the patient was allowed to deteriorate this far before he was called. It was idiocy and would probably cost the patient his life.

"We tried, John. He has been like this for a week. We wanted to call Shaw earlier, but he wouldn't let us. He insisted that he was getting better. He's been busy with the Manhan Canal and was afraid Shaw would confine him to his bed. He hoped the attack would subside quickly like last time." A few tears moistened her cheeks, "He's very sick this time, isn't he, John?"

He nodded gravely. "Has he been able to eat anything?"

"Nothing. Every time we give him anything, even water, he vomits it back. Since yesterday, he has been vomiting steadily."

"How long has he had the fever?"

"The past three days. Before that he said he felt chilled and would shiver, but his skin was cool. Now he is burning up alive."

"Has he been able to relieve himself?"

Elizabeth indicated the chamber pot by the door. John inspected the few dark amber drops which clung to the bottom of the white bowl.

"That's all in the past twenty four hours?"

She nodded.

John suddenly realized something. "Why isn't Dr. Billings here?" he asked.

"I sent for him when Zebadiah's pain became extreme but his housekeeper said he had gone into Boston and would not be back for several days.

Boston? John had completely forgotten. Shaw had told him he was going to his new grandson's Christening. Even if they could telegraph him, it was doubtful Zebadiah could wait.

"That was a stupid thing for your father to have done. If Shaw had been able to treat him earlier, perhaps ...." His voice trailed off in a waver of uncertainty,

Curious, he asked, "How did your father stand the pain?"

"He had laudanum left from his last attack. I have been giving it to him whenever the spasms were too bad."

John reviewed the facts. The man had not eaten. The bowel was probably as empty as with clysters. The laudanum had slowed down the intestines and hopefully allowed the body to wall off the inflammation. He could see Willard Parker's letter as clearly as if it was in his hands. The words came back.

"I believe the vermiform appendix is responsible for this killer of men. I believe that it alone is guilty for the symptoms we treat so ineffectively with clysters and laudanum and purgatives and blistering plasters. I believe that we physicians must open into the human cavity and remove this organ before the peritonitis has ensued, despite the risk. Open into the human cavity. Before the peritonitis.

He wished he had never written to the New York surgeon, or never received an answer. It would be easy to know what to do until Shaw Billings returned. More laudanum. More clysters. A cantharid poultice. Perhaps hot cupping.

The vermiform appendix.

Killer of men.

What if he opened the peritoneal cavity and Parker was wrong? Better to wait. To watch. To hope for God to cure and for Billings to arrive.

John knew could not turn the burden of responsibility over to an invisible Deity or to a distant partner. Then, all doubt left him. He started to speak. How do you explain to a layman the mechanics of a disease buried deep in human body? If, by a miracle, one could teach this knowledge, how do you convince another of your belief in a theory? Faith is not a contagion. How to do all of this in a breathlessly short span of time, to an only child, whose father is dying in the next room?

John began bravely. Elizabeth said nothing. Why should he have expected anything ? He turned away in defeat when Elizabeth held onto his arm.

"John, I listened. I would not be honest if I told you that I understand everything you told me. Do you remember what I said when you amputated the young boy's hands?"

The scene was vivid, but the words escaped him.

" 'Trust Doctor Billings and Doctor Spencer. They know what they are doing.' I still trust you with my fathers life as with that boy. But, I again plead, that if that trust is misplaced, may God have mercy upon your soul."

━≺+ +≻━

John was not certain Zebadiah Harcross understood what he had agreed to. Spencer knelt down by the bed and explained the risk of doing nothing. When he suggested surgery to remove an obscure organ, Zebadiah managed to part his cracked lips. The words emerged in a hoarse whisper. "Do what you will, Doctor Spencer. I welcome death to spare me from this agony."

He scanned the room for his daughter, forgetting she was standing quietly at his side. He motioned her to come nearer. "I trust you, Elizabeth...." he stopped until the spasm passed,"...... with my life."

Elizabeth swallowed hard, her eyes tearing over. She had never felt as close to her father as now. Zebadiah was a proud man. The river, the valley, his power over men, were cherished possessions. Now when his mortality hung in the balance, he surrendered it all to his daughter. She squeezed his hand, as if she could infuse her own life's blood. Her head fell down upon his chest. He had given her life. Now, at the very end, his life was in her hands!

The Orientals always claimed that life was a giant wheel with the past rushing to catch up with the present to become the future. Somehow, with this last turn, went the bitterness of all those wasted years. The future would be different. Her father must live. Matthew 's ghost finally buried. She lifted her head to kiss his cheek.

John could see that the patient was sinking fast. Zebadiah was fighting to keep alive, but the effort was too great. Laudanum was numbing his will. He only saw blurred images. Sounds were indistinct scraps of noise, devoid of meaning. He was only aware of fragments..... Elizabeth..... a touch.... a voice....a shape... a color.....sprinkling through a fading consciousness. A son?...... it was no longer important.

He wanted to call out Elizabeth's name once more, but forgot how. He let go of her hand. He was now impatient to end to his pain. Faster and faster, it came. He let go.......as the laudanum engulfed him.

John was now able to feel the mass in the corner of the abdomen. Pressure now elicited only a weak moan. He opened the patient's lids. The eyes were moving aimlessly. Spencer knew he had to move fast if he didn't want to operate on a corpse.

The Harcross butler was instructed to drive to the telegraph office and send an urgent telegram to Shaw Billings. There was no time to move Zebadiah to the Dispensary. The Game Room in the East Wing contained a massive felt-covered slate billiard table. The other furniture was removed. Servants stripped kerosene lamps from the other rooms to supplement the gas jets. The Holbein was rolled up and removed. The make-shift operating theater would have to do.

Elizabeth watched the preparations in a daze, stunned by the rush of events. When the Sisters arrived and began to lay out the shining surgical steel instruments on the table, as the rolls of white gauze dressings were unpacked, as the room slowly changed to a surgical arena, she had new doubts. She saw the diver, his bloody hands. Her father gutted. She wanted to scream out, 'stop!'

Better to let him die a whole man, if that is what the Lord ordained.

John took of her hands. "Elizabeth. Find something to keep you occupied. Leave us." He could see her fright. "Trust me," he begged. The embrace was not between lovers.

"Thank you, John. I will be all right. I wish to remain here." She moved to the distant corner of the room and stood silent, folding and unfolding her hands.

Spencer was moving more rapidly. Tom Kennedy and two men from the household staff lifted Zebadiah off his bed and carried him downstairs. The trip made the patient to groan. John refused to give him any more opium, afraid of what the drug would do to his breathing.

"Only a few minutes more," he reassured her.

It was hard to tell what the servants thought of the scene around them. They did not have to be told their instructions more than once. They avoided looking at the doctor and Elizabeth. They cast quick glances at the Master of the Quabbin, dying in front of them. His daughter and heir cowering in the corner. The expected healer of Cromwell was in Boston. Only the red-haired stranger, like Jacob, waited to battle with the Angel of Death.

Somehow, the entire Harcross mansion knew exactly what was going to happen. Zebadiah's illness was no secret, and his remissions a source of wonder. But, to cut into living flesh, searching for an imaginary corruption was a brazen act. Even the most ignorant knew the surgeon's knife was reserved for amputating limbs, lancing boils. What kind of an unholy alliance had Spencer and Elizabeth made with the devil?

John checked the instruments. Sister Mary Magdalene, her movements limited by severe arthritis, had given anesthesia for Shaw Billings since its discovery in the late forties. She removed two large glass-stoppered flasks of sulfuric ether from their wooden casket. She placed the oval cloth cone and over the patient's face.

Zebadiah was naked with both arms and legs bounds by ropes to the legs of the table in case anesthesia failed. Spencer nodded to Sister Magdalena. Pungent drops of the oily liquid trickled on the mask. The volatile fluid evaporated, saturating the warm room with a heavy aromatic scent unlike anything found in nature,

John watched the patient's reaction. Zebadiah choked and bucked to escape the irritating fumes. John fell across his chest to immobilize him. He cautioned Sister Magdalena not to let up, hoping to bring the patient through this dangerous stage of excitement as fast as possible. Slowly, the limbs relaxed. The breaths were now deeper, regular. John pressed on the patient's finger tips. The skin blanched, then grew pink again when the pressure was released. His circulation was good. John thanked God, at least the man had a strong heart.

One last test. John drove his fist into the patient's belly. The patient never moved. His chest rose and fell with the same monotonous regularity. The Sister eased the flow of ether.

The time had arrived. John again urged Elizabeth to leave. She shook her head. "I'm alright, John. Do what you have to."

Spencer removed his jacket and rolled his shirt cuffs high above his elbows. He tied on the linen operating apron to protect his clothes. The stained gown reached to the floor. As he moved, it rustled from thick layers of dried blood and serum. He tested the edge of the scalpel with his finger, wincing at the sharpness. His head cast a shadow on the body. He stepped back and changed the position of the kerosene lamps. He moved to the right hand side of the patient. His fingers tightened around the scalpel.

He could no longer delay. His hand moved swiftly over the patient's abdomen. The scalpel blade etched a thin white line. For an instant, nothing happened. Then, beads of blood filled the cut. He hesitated. He could stop now. Make some excuse. Apply a linen binder and leave. No one would be the wiser.

The scalpel sliced down, dividing the skin. It bit deep through the yellow fat underneath. The edges of the incision bled. John packed folds of linen in the wound to seal off the blood vessels.

As he worked, John was no longer conscious of the room. He was back in the Montreal, dissecting under Elias Guthrie's careful watch, cutting tissue, naming each part in Latin, impatient to see what wonders lay next under the knife.

But, this was no cadaver. fresh from the grave. This bleeding tissue was a man whose daughter waited a dozen feet from where he stood. Sister Magdalena called his attention to the patient's condition. The respirations were jerky. The pulse was irritable with skipped beats.

"Stop the ether," he ordered, prepared to operate without anesthesia to prevent the patient's collapse, if necessary.

This decision meant he had little time left. He dug both hands into the wound, searching for the end of the large bowel. Adhesions blocked his way. He teased the scar tissue apart. The bowel appeared normal. He panicked. Where was the pus?

NOTHING!

No perityphlitis.

No pool of laudable pus to drain.

Had he and Shaw been wrong to diagnose perityphlitis all these months? Had he forced an unnecessary operation on a dying man?

Then, he remembered. The appendix. Willard Parker. He looked for the worm-like appendage. It was not there. His heart skipped a beat. It had to be!

He tried to lift it the bowel to look at the back. Something was wrong. It would not move. The cecum was stuck. Carefully, he freed it up. He met resistance. He forced his fingers in harder.... harder.... holding his breath. Suddenly, the tissue gave way. His fingers plunged through the wall of a deep abscess cavity. Thick rivers of yellow pus welled up in front of him. His nostrils were assaulted by the magnificent stench of fecal corruption.

He raised his head with a broad smile of triumph. He was barely able to restrain himself from shouting out.

LAUDABLE PUS!!

It gushed forth as if from an inexhaustible fountain. His hand moved deeper, cleaning out the cavity. There, sticking out from the bowel was the open end of the appendix, spitting out feces. John was breathing more easily. He tied off the leaking end with a long horsehair suture. He packed fresh linen strips into the wound.

Zebadiah was wakening. He stirred and groaned as John applied the last of the plaster strips to the skin. John did not care. The man could now have all the laudanum he wanted. Soon.... soon.... when the body purged itself of the last of the putrefaction, then Zebadiah would be freed of his pain and his sickness forever. Of that John felt as certain as of anything in his life.

He placed the specimen in a jar of formaldehyde. Sister Magdalena removed his apron and brought him a basin of water to wash his hands.

"Elizabeth, the appendix had ruptured as Parker predicted. He will live." He stood over her, tired but proud.

She pressed his hand to the side of her face. It was a miracle.

"It is all over," John continued. "You can stay with him until the ether has worn off. Then we will move him."

"Oh, John. Thank you." She lowered her head against his thighs and began to cry softly. His own eyes teared and he motioned to one of the nuns to relieve him. Embarrassed, he hurried about issuing instructions for the patient's post-operative care.

Sister Theresa remained behind after the other Sisters had returned to the Dispensary. She was young, twenty-two with a small round face and thick glasses which perched on a bud of a nose. She was small of frame and moved with the rustle of her habit. She changed the dressings every hour. When Zebadiah regained consciousness, she gave him water, wine, even brandy, but the liquids ran out of the corners of his mouth. The patient's fever climbed as his body battled the surgical trauma. The next hours would decide whether he would live or die.

John moved the wing chair next close to Zebadiah's bed and fell into it. Fatigue and nervous exhaustion swept over him. His head bobbed as he fought off sleep. Finally, he slumped back oblivious to the world. Sister Theresa gave his chair a wide berth, not to waken him.

Suddenly, loud screams tore through the room. John awoke to see the Sister Teresa part way on the bed, struggling to restrain Zebadiah. She was shouting for help. The patient thrashed about, crying incoherent noises. He had thrown off the bed clothes and was tearing the bandages. John managed to force laudanum down the patient's throat. He and Sister Theresa waited, pinning Zebadiah down until the opium took hold. Only then did John return to his chair. Almost instantly, he sunk back again into the same dream-less slumber.

He could not tell how long he had slept, nor what time it was, when he heard a familiar voice in the room. His eyes opened to see a fuzzy figure come into view. He tried to get up, but his muscles were slow to respond.

"Shaw...." he managed to get out. He awkwardly rose to his feet.

"Johnnie boy, I came as fast as that damn smoke-burner would go," he apologized. "I'm sorry I left you when I did. Damn child of Malcolm's anyway. No sooner did they sprinkle it with water, than the ugly little bastard pissed all over the Bishop and into the Christening Fount." He gave a raucous chuckle at the recollection, but immediately got serious again, "Johnnie you must tell me exactly what has happened. I have been talking to Elizabeth here, but I don't believe it. I want to hear it from your lips," He pulled a chair over.

John handed him the glass bottle containing the specimen. He held the jar up to the light, rotating it around several times to inspect the floating tissue. He went over to the patient and gently lifted up the dressings to inspect the incision. He smelled the discharge and carefully palpated the abdomen. He felt the pulse, opened the eyelids to examine the pupils. He listened to the chest with his stethoscope. He nodded his approval.

Finally, he opened his medicine bag and took out his own silver catheter. He liberally coated it from a small vial of oil and inserted it into Zebadiah's penis. He measured the several ounces of dark yellow urine which slowly dripped from the hollow end.

"I would insert the catheter every four to six hours to make certain his kidneys are working. Zebadiah has a touch of prostate trouble and could have difficulty voiding on his own. Other than that, Johnnie, for a refugee from Canada, I would say you have succeeded admirably."

Shaw accepted the glass of hard cider which Elizabeth poured for him.

"You know, Johnnie, I wonder on the fates that took me from Cromwell on this day of all days. Zebadiah is a very fortunate man, though he will never knew why."

"I don't understand."

"Had I been here, I would never have agreed to the surgery."

John protested. "You told me that once you did the same. You also read letter Willard Parker's letter."

"All that may be well and good, Johnnie. However, I was innocent and foolhardy then. With age comes a reluctance to challenge the gods. You, my boy, still have the faith of the young. May you never lose it. But, if you do," he patted John on his knee as he rose to leave, "be sure to do as I have done*"

" What?"

"Why, my boy, it is obvious. I took you," With that, Billings gave Elizabeth a hug, checked his patient once again and returned home.

The next day, John sat at Zebadiah's writing desk, pen in hand. His patient was sleeping peacefully across the room. He had survived the trial of the night. Though he still had fever, there were no further chills. The nausea and vomiting were gone, and the patient was swallowing water. He was alert. Through the stethoscope, John could hear the early sounds of intestines starting to work again.

John started writing, despite the fact he had not left the Harcross house for almost a day. Doctor Parker deserved that much from him.

The pen flew over the paper, as John related the clinical details and the operation. The words were more than black scratches on white paper. He could sense the New York surgeon by his side. The living ghosts of Saracenus and Mestivier were in the room with him. And Parkinson and Louyer-Villermay and Henry Hancock, and all the other pioneers. The men had been at his side. In some mysterious way, Zebadiah Harcross owed his life to them.

As John poured out his gratitude, an odd feeling came over him. He was more than just a country doctor in a small town the world would never hear of. He was a link in the chain of healers which began far back when man worshipped at the feet of the witch-doctor and medicine man.

For a brief instant, he had been annointed with Grace. If his father were alive, he would have understood.

For a single night, God had entered into Britton Spencer's son and helped him restore life to a dead man.

John Spencer laid his head down on his arms and cried. He knew that should he live to be a hundred, it was unlikely he would ever again be blessed with the Act of Creation.

One week later, John was finishing rounds at the Dispensary when Tom Kennedy appeared at the door. ckettsJohn could not understand why. He had made rounds on Zebadiah earlier that day and the patient was recovering well. The Irishman handed John a sealed envelope. He waited silently as John opened the envelope and withdrew two documents.

The first was a Sight Draught on the Cromwell National Bank, signed by Harcross. It was payable to him. The amount was left blank. The second and larger paper was a legal document, witnessed and sealed by the County Commissioners. It conveyed twelve acres, including a timbered copse, to the new hospital.

John read both sheets through a second and third time. John ripped the draught in two and handed the torn halves to the messenger.

Tom Kennedy laughed. "Zebadiah told me you would do that."

When John relayed the visit to Shaw Billings, the older physician saw nothing unusual. "You don't know Zebadiah as well as I do. Despite his faults and failings, of which he has many, in his own way, he is an honest man. I am certain he feels there is still the chance he will not live. Zebadiah will never die owing anything to any man. He always pays his debts. Remember that for the future, John. The Master of the Quabbin is a fair man. He prizes equity above all else of his earthly possessions."

John took out the deed many times over the following days.

Elizabeth must have told her father of the experiment with lambs and his preference for the windy site. He did not feel guilty for having extracted the land from the grateful patient, Zebadiah was a rich man and one piece of empty property was probably of little concern.

Over the following days, whenever John traveled on his rounds, he would look up to the western hills. If he concentrated, he could reach out and touch the woods. At such moments, he wished again for the storm and Elizabeth.

CHAPTER TWENTY-NINE

I n the private alcove in the Dispensary, the unborn child battered at Kathleen's body. For Patrick O'Connell, his daughter's screams brought back an old nightmare. First his wife, and now his child. The father had changed over the year. His frame had filled out. His face was now clean-shaven. Expensive tailored clothes hid his 'rickets-crippled bones. Thanks to Adam Ring, he was a wealthy man, far richer than those not privy to the secrets of the Commonwealth Life Insurance Company would have guessed. His lifelong time dream was within his grasp. He had the gold to raise his daughter as high as the heir of the textile journeyman who now claimed the Quabbin as his private fief.

Many times he had ridden with Kathleen to the bluffs overlooking Pulpit Rock. He had promised himself that one day his heirs would stand equal with the Harcrosses. Now, he stood within reach of that goal. To what avail? Kathleen waited upstairs, her life in the hands of an unborn child. He recalled the vow he had made. Kathleen must live. Her husband must respect that.

Eighteen years ago, Patrick had left the Church to keep its dogma away from his daughter. He had insisted that Kathleen's marriage be a civil one, immune from Papist demand for blood sacrifices. He had suffered the scorn of friends and neighbors all those bitter years when he rejected the Roman Catholic Church without explanation. Now, at the moment of truth, he felt vindicated. No black-frocked priest would come forth and kill his daughter in the name of an invisible God.

The husband facing the father was ashen-faced and scared. He had not expected the labor for at least another two weeks. He always knew the decision would have to be made. Just not now. When John left home before dawn, he had no suspicious that the delivery would be premature. All morning John moved among those dying of yellow fever, finishing his rounds to autopsy a puzzling case which had died during the night.

The patient, a man in his early sixties, had been plagued by an enlarged prostate. He relieved his bladder with a silver catheter. Its use was second nature to him, as were the chills and fever which followed. Three days ago, the metal tube slipped and perforated his pelvis. The next morning, the man came to the Dispensary in acute distress. John and Billings attempted to pass the catheter themselves, but were unsuccessful. The man's condition worsened. His abdomen was rigid and painful to the touch with severe cramps and vomiting. He developed a severe fever. He thrashed in agony. Other than laudanum, the two doctors looked on helplessly until he died.

This morning, in the basement of the Dispensary, John carried out the autopsy with Billings. The foul stench confirmed the diagnosis of peritonitis. Shaw examined the intestines. The odor was fecal in origin.

"There it is, Johnnie. " He pointed to a jagged rent in the bowel, still spilling out the contents. The metal catheter must have ripped into it." Shaw picked up the hollow tube and gave it a wry smile. "You forget, Johnnie, that I use one of these several times a day."

John was embarrassed.

"Its alright, my boy. Your day will come. I only hope that we both are more skillful than this poor fellow."

Their chat about the evils of the prostate gland was cut short by Sister Theresa descending the narrow stairs into the dank cellar room. "Doctor Spencer," her voice held a hint of alarm, "it's your wife. She's in labor."

Barely pausing to wipe his hands, John bounded up the stairs two at a time. He was surprised to find Patrick O'Connell in the Dispensary, He could see the man's anguish.

"She's in pain, John. The water broke while I was visiting. I took her here as fast as I could. The contractions are coming on slow, but she is in much pain."

"How fast are they?" Billings called out as he entered the room, wheezing from the exertion.

"About ten minutes apart, Shaw," Patrick replied.

Shaw knew why he had to separate the two men. " Patrick, John and I want to examine her. Afterwards you can go up and be with her." Before O'Connell could object, Billings had taken John by the arm and forcibly rushed him away from the father.

The Sisters had already put Kathleen to bed. She was lying still, perspiration drenching her face, her lips tightly clenched as she waited for the next contraction. It seemed forever before she would take a breath. John knelt down by the side of the bed and kissed her. She gave him a weak smile.

"Kathleen, do not be afraid. Shaw and I want to see how far the labor has progressed." Shaw oiled his right hand and carefully inserted it into the vagina. His naked fingers touched the cervix. He nodded to John. There would be no trouble there. The pelvis? It was still locked.

John repeated the exam, confirming that the head was stopped by the constricted bones. He laid his head on her abdomen. The baby's heart was beating so fast that it defied counting.

"Everything will be alright. The baby has far to go." He released her hand only when Billings told him to leave. To his surprise, Shaw stayed behind a few minutes talking in hushed tones to his wife.

He could not make out what they were saying. There were tears in Kathleen's eyes and she turned her head away. John recalled the strange scene, later, when he could make sense of it.

Patrick jumped up the moment the two physicians returned. "You have seen her? Is she well? The child. Will she deliver?" The questions rushed out in haste as he implored one and then the other.

"Kathleen is doing well," Shaw parried. "She is a healthy girl. So far, the labor is proceeding without trouble. The child lives." He could see John shrink back into the corner of the room.

"That is okay for now, Shaw. What about later?"

"For the moment, we do nothing, Patrick. During labor, there is always molding of the baby's skull. With enough time, and pressure, there is the chance that the vertex," He apologized for the technical term, ".....the leading portion of the skull will be shaped to fit through." It was a meager hope. Such things did occur. But never with this disproportion. What other option did they have? The mother or the child? He knew the breaking point had not yet been reached.

"Alright, Shaw, we will play your game a little longer," Patrick retorted sarcastically. "Your's and Spencer's, but what happens when your magic fails?" He walked around the room, pausing to taunt them, each in turn. "First, Rachel died. Now it happens all over again. What has your noble profession learned in the past eighteen years? You give good clysters and charge high fees. You amputate and lance. You give laudanum and hope. You are expert with cheap skills."

Billings made no effort to stop him. Better to let him drain his venom. Soon enough he would have ample reason to curse his God.

"You, Doctor Spencer," the father challenged. The physician sat hunched over in the chair, staring at the floor, unwilling to look the father in the eye. "I hear very little from you. You took my daughter. You knew that your love would kill her. Now you hide your face. It is <u>your</u> child which is ripping her apart. You could have prevented it!"

"I....I...," John stammered, stricken with guilt. He could not get the words out. O'Connell was right. He had done nothing to protect her. Only satisfy his needs. Did he really love her so little to risk her life?

"It is too late for silence," lashing out at the husband. "The deed cannot be undone. What will you do?"

John looked up blankly. What horrible thing was the man now asking?

"You cannot escape my question. Will you kill the mother or the child?" He saw Billings start up in protest, but waved him back. " It must be one or the other. <u>You</u> know that. <u>I</u> know that. <u>Shaw</u> knows that. YOU TELL ME!"

John stared at the distraught father. He wanted to give an answer. Patrick wanted to hear him say, ' save Kathleen.' That is what the husband and lover should say. But the words refused to come out. "Leave him be, Patrick. It is not his decision to make."

"No? Tell me, whose is it? Your's perhaps?"

"No, Patrick, not mine either, though I was the one who brought Kathleen into the world."

"I understand," the fathers voice was full of scorn. "Neither of you two great men wish the responsibility. Alright. I will take that burden. Kathleen is my daughter, I have the right."

"No, Patrick," Billings' words emerged in a whisper. "You do not."

Not the husband, nor himself. Who, then? Patrick wondered. Kathleen? The thought stunned him. To make the victim choose between suicide or murder? It was grotesque.

"Kathleen?" Spencer scrambled to his feet. "Shaw. It is not fair to make her choose."

"Not fair?" Billings shot back. His voice was sharp. "For whom is it more fair? I have sat here and listened to both of you. One ridden with guilt for the death of his wife. The other filled with guilt for have put his wife in jeopardy, now torn between desire for an heir and love for the mother. Which of you can made an unprejudiced decision? Who has more right than the mother herself?"

He rose to his feet with a labored sigh. "I may be old and fat and perhaps senile at times. I know many in Cromwell laugh at my ways. Unlike both of you, I have one grace which compensates for my failings. I have faith that God, in some mysterious way, will direct whose who believe in Him. Both you have forgotten, in your mutual self-pity, that we are talking about Kathleen. A mother and wife. She is not some glass bottle from which we will decant a child. She is a reasoning human being with all the passions of her sex. It is her child. Her life. It must be her decision,"

John spoke calmly. "Even if what you say is true, how can you expect a decision from someone suffering as she is?"

Shaw's eyes took on a hard glint. "Is that the real reason you refuse to let Kathleen decide?"

There was no fooling the old physician. Through the half-closed lids and lethargy, lay a brutal insight. Shaw had his finger on Spencer's jugular and would not let him escape. He made John look deep into his conscience.

"When we made love for the first time, I saw Kathleen's fear. She knew her own birth had been accompanied with tragedy. " He could see Patrick sitting bolt-up, as unforgiving as the wrath of Jehovah.

"Yes, Johnnie?" Shaw gently urged his confession.

"I told Kathleen to trust me. I let her believe her mother had died of childbirth fever. I.... I...." he choked on the simple words. "I lied to her. "

"And now, Johnnie, you must go upstairs and tell her the truth."

"Shaw....Shaw...."

Billings put his hands on his shoulder. "That's all of it. Isn't it Johnnie?"

The silent nod told him what he wanted to hear.

"You, Patrick," Shaw turned to the father. "How many years have you lived with Rachel's death? Is sacrificing your grandchild your an act of atonement? Do you see Rachel lying upstairs? Is saving Kathleen what you should have done 18 years ago?"

The father could not reply.

"No, gentlemen, neither of you is fit to decide." Shaw continued. "However, I agree with Johnnie that it would be cruel to ask Kathleen <u>at</u> <u>this</u> <u>time</u>."

Was Billings accepting their position?

"Kathleen came to me almost a month ago. Patrick, your daughter is an intelligent girl. I don't know what made her suspicious, perhaps your constant denials. Whether she detected a change in John's behavior ? Maybe female intuition. She knew l would tell her the truth, and I did."

"Kathleen?" John blurted out. "She knew a month ago? She never said a word."

"Nor to me either," Patrick added..

"Kathleen swore me not to tell either of you until today."

Suddenly, Sister Theresa burst into the room. "You had better come quickly," she begged. "The pains are two to three minutes apart." Tears were in her eyes. "Please Doctor Billings. You must do something. The pain is too much for her."

John caught Billings' arm and held him back. "What was Kathleen's decision?".

"She said she would tell you when the time came. That time is now. Johnnie, go to your wife."

Spencer repeated the pelvic examination after Shaw. The head had not budged. The skull still floated high, unable to pass. The condition of mother and child was rapidly deteriorating. The contractions were so close and prolonged it seemed Kathleen's body was frozen into one continuous spasm. Her lips were bitten raw as she waited until the last possible second to shriek out. Her fingers tore into the palms of her husband and father. Billings tried to hear the fetal heartbeat, but each spasm clamped off the blood supply to the placenta, and the beat weakened.

"Kathleen," John's lips grazed her face. "How can you forgive me for lying to you?

"Hush...." she whispered. "If you had told me earlier, you would have deprived me of the happiest months of my life. I am glad that you did not." She was forced to stop until the next wave of pain had faded. "John, do not blame yourself for loving me as a husband. To have done otherwise would have been unnatural and false."

"Kathleen, we must...." he groped for the words, "remove the child to save your life. We do not have much time."

"It is the only way," Patrick was barely able to speak.

"No. No." Kathleen tried to lift herself off the bed. "You cannot. John. Hear me out. I know the alternatives. Shaw told me. You cannot destroy the child."

"There is no other way," John insisted, "if we are to save your life."

"There is another. You must carry out the Cesarean operation." John looked at Shaw.

"Johnnie, I told her the risks of surgery. She knows she was delivered by that method and her mother died."

"The risks," John insisted. "I don't know of anyone who has survived."

"There is always the chance. The hope," Kathleen persisted.

"Hope...." John made a deprecating gesture. That was for <u>other</u> patients. How could he offer such hypocrisy to his own wife?

Nothing John or Patrick said made any impression. She held to her wish. Kathleen could see John rebel. How could she convince him before she succumbed to the laudanum?

"John, listen to me. Shaw has told me we have little time if the baby is to be saved. I know the duty a daughter has to her father. But, Patrick can find others to fill that place. I have a responsibility as a wife, too. You are young. You will forget, if not forgive. You will find another to love as you have loved me and she will be a fortunate woman. You will have another child." The tears in her eyes streamed down her face. "I am more than a daughter to Patrick. More than a wife to you. I am a mother. There is a life within me. It has no one else to speak for it. I cannot kill my child. No mother can do that, even at the cost of her own life. That is the way God made us. That is why we carry the child and not the father. Men would always decide selfishly to save their lover. God in his wisdom gave the child to us. And as it grows inside our body, so grows the love."

"My mother gave me life. I have lived eighteen years. Can I deny my own child that same chance? I am not that selfish."

With that she sank back onto the bed, exhausted and surrendered her body to the poppy.

Patrick was sobbing softly in the corner. John fought no longer. He moved like a sleepwalker.

Only Billings was able to act. "Come, Johnnie," he gently ordered. "We have much work to do."

"Damn you!" John flung out at him. "Damn you to Hell!"

Billings ignored the outburst. "Johnnie, there are two lives which need you. I cannot do this thing by myself. I need your help."

Kathleen was brought to the Operating Surgery. Light anesthesia was cautiously administered. The pair put on their operating gowns and waited patiently on opposite sides of the narrow metal table until the touch of the scalpel blade caused no reaction.

John's hands were shaking. He fought off the waves of light-headedness whenever his eyes strayed from the naked abdomen in front of him to Kathleen's face.

Billings appreciated willpower that kept his partner at the table. He talked to John in a matter-of-fact tone.

"Johnnie, there are two hazards to the Cesarean technique. The first is hemorrhage from the uterus. Second is peritonitis."

Even as he was talking, the bistoury sliced in one broad horizontal sweep. The wound grew deeper. John quickly pinched them off the spurting arteries until Shaw tied horsehairs around the ends. Sister Theresa smiled to reassure that the patient was doing well. The respirations were still slow and steady. John took his hand out of the incision and pressed the neck. The carotid artery pulsed with a fast but strong beat.

"Johnnie, we will use the technique of Physlck in Philadelphia to avoid opening the peritoneal cavity."

"Can that be done? The uterus lies in back of the cavity."

Billings was pleased to see John alert and attentive once again, "If we are careful, we may succeed," Shaw answered.

With delicate teasing movements, the older physician dissected down. John saw what Shaw was aiming at. He reached in to help him. Maybe…..possibly….. they could avoid …….. It might just be possible. The uterus rose huge and magenta swollen with John's child.

Billings could see Spencer hesitate, "No, Johnnie, not now. Keep your head. We must move quickly,"

This was the time of maximum danger. Once the scalpel cut through the wall of the uterus, it would bleed fiercely and lose blood they could never replace. The child must be instantly extracted, the umbilical cord cut and tied, the placenta stripped off and cast out, the hemorrhage somehow stopped. All to be accomplished within brief minutes.

John could see the outline of the child. It was upside down with the head at the bottom where it should be. Billings cut through the wall of the uterus, taking care not to injure the baby itself. A slash of blood welled up, hiding everything. Billings dropped the knife. His fingers dug into the uterus and grabbed the baby.

"Johnnie, help me!" he called out. They had passed the point of no return!

The umbilical cord was wrapped twice around the neck, trapping the infant. John automatically clamped his fingers around the cord and cut it. Billings swiftly lifted the child out, holding the other end of the cord between his fingers until he was able to tie a ligature. He handed the blood-drenched body to the father.

"Hurry, John. It must breathe."

Without another glance, he turned back to stopping the hemorrhage. He removed the placenta and began to knead the uterus between his palms, praying it would go into spasm and compress the bleeding arteries. Slowly, but perceptibly, the desperate maneuver worked. Shaw held his breath. He relaxed his grasp. The uterus stayed collapsed in a tight spastic ball.

The child! In his haste to control the bleeding, Shaw had completely forgotten about the baby. Then he heard it! A loud piercing cry of anger as the new life sucked in its first breath and then another and another. Shaw cried to himself at the miraculous sound. John's face told him everything he needed to know. The child would live.

" Its a boy, Shaw. Thank you," was all the father could say. He realized he had forgotten about Kathleen.

"The bleeding has stopped. The uterus is contracting."

John did not leave Kathleen's side for the next several days. The uterus remained in spasm, with minimal bleeding. Although the patient had lost much blood, she was young and could tolerate the loss. Her mind remained clear and alert. She required steadily decreasing amounts of laudanum. By the fourth day, John permitted her out of bed.

The baby was healthy with a strong suck reflex which made Kathleen smile the first time she fastened it to her breast. Through her tears and laughter she asked, "Should I have taken its life? Could you have denied it the chance to live? Tell me, John. Wasn't I right ?"

He had no answer. She lived. The child lived. It was a miracle. Only Billings said nothing. He smiled as did the rest and offered the same blessings and thanks, but his enthusiasm was guarded. He was too old to believe in miracles.

Something was wrong.

By the fifth day, he was certain. Kathleen's pulse became weak once again. Her eyes glazed over. Her color flushed high from a sudden fever. The vomiting started. The temperature climbed relentlessly. Shaking chills racked her body. Her abdomen became exquisitely tender. Billings removed the linen plaster covering the skin incision. The wound drained foul brown pus. Billings wondered where he had smelled that same odor just recently. The signs were unequivocal. Puerperal sepsis. Childbirth fever.

On the sixth day, the wound opened..

"It has drained," John reported with guarded optimism. Maybe...maybe... if the abscess emptied, there was still a chance. Hope.

It was too late. The purulence in the pelvis sped through rest of the body, There were times when Kathleen could recognize John and her father and the child. John held his breath, praying that it was a sign of remission. Then the infection burned her alive.

On the eighth day, her heart stopped.

On the tenth day, Kathleen was buried next to her mother. That night, Patrick rode to Pulpit Rock, He climbed down from his carriage and viewed the line of silver reflecting in the moonlight. He did two things. First he cursed God. Then he sat down and cried for the end of his dream.

John, too, had tears, but the luxury was not for long. Shaw Billings saw to that. The epidemic of yellow fever and malaria was at the peak. Billings claimed a recurrence of his dropsy. For three days he took to his bed, pushing the dying on John until his mind and body were crushed with fatigue. During those days, Shaw had time to reflect on what had happened. He had no doubts that the right course was taken, despite lingering reservations of John and Patrick. The wonderful thing about age, he convinced himself, was the serene confidence of early senility.

On the last day before returning to work, he was sitting in his study sipping brandy when he looked at his hands and realized where he had smelled the odor of Kathleen's drainage. The patient with the perforated bowel he and John had autopsied that morning. It was a strange coincidence considering there had been no other similar cases in the Dispensary. He pondered the facts, unable to fit them together. He decided it would be unwise to take any chances.

The next morning, when he reported to the Dispensary, he ordered large cast-iron tubs of vinegar boiled in each Ward to expunge the evil miasma which had cost Kathleen Spencer her life.

CHAPTER THIRTY

Kathleen Spencer's death caught Elizabeth by surprise. John had never indicated his wife's life had been in jeopardy. Learning by rumor of the Cesarean section, and the childbirth fever, Elizabeth felt the sorrow of her sex as well guilt for her infidelity. She knew the self-recrimination which must be racking him.

Such considerations were quickly swept aside by the responsibilities of the Harcross Water Power Company. Day after day, she rose to spend long hours in the heat supervising conversion of a sterile creek into an industrial conduit. The construction contracts, the dredging, the specifications for sluice gates, turbines, brick embankments, and, most of all, for raising the dam at Pulpit Rock, all passed through her hands. She saw the financial blood-letting the risky enterprise was demanding. She now learned that to raise funds, Zebadiah had literally mortgaged his soul.

Capitalization of the Corporation was simple. Zebadiah held over 80% of the common stock. Small amounts were still in the hands of the original backers. They had the pleasure of seeing the value of their holdings rise year after year. However, the satisfaction was hollow. The Corporation never paid any dividends. Each year, Zebadiah reinvested the profit back. Zebadiah had a standing offer to buy them out. The price was far below actual value. It was a stalemate. The minority shareholders fumed and threatened. By imposing Draconian measures, Zebadiah extracted from internal funds slightly over $200,000.

How to raise the extra $600,000? Promissory notes or bonds were risky. The bankers insisted upon a short maturity, high interest rates, and a sinking fund fed by annual profits to redeem the debt. He was prepared to pay the interest, but not a rapid pay back. Elizabeth wondered whether his objection stemmed from a desire for funds to build a fifth and even sixth canal.

Brokers in Boston and New York eagerly offered to float a common stock issue. They promised huge profits. In return, they demanded majority representation on the Board of Directors to protect their investment. For the Master of the Quabbin, control was not a negotiable item, and this tack quickly discarded.

The solution was a compromise. The brokers formed a syndicate to float $600,000 of 7% cumulative convertible preferred stock. Not just preferred for the first claim on profits, but structured so that any failure to pay the dividend would be a perpetual lien on future earnings. Zebadiah accepted this restriction without a battle. The real threat lay in the last clause in the Prospectus.

Zebadiah fought it. At the end, he was forced to give way. In the event that the dividend was passed, holders of the majority of the issue had the power to elect 50% of the directors of the Harcross Water power Company. Not enough to impose their will, nor to oust Zebadiah, but enough to block working control if he did not pay the omitted dividend.

It was a sword of Damocles which the money crowd on State Street held to her father's throat. Skip one dividend, and the Monarchy would pass to a Directoire. Men who would dismantle the Corporation and sell its off assets. It was a gamble.

I could succeed... if......

If the water released from Pulpit Rock could keep the Quabbin full at the so that the turbines ran at maximum speed

If the construction costs were held firm.

If the manufacturers took up their options along the Manhan.

If these, and a million other factors fell into place.

If nothing unexpected happened.

If not, the power and gold of the Quabbin would flow through another's hands.

Each day, at the Gatehouse, she met with engineers to determine the flow needed for the canals. She then ordered Pulpit Rock to release the water from the reservoir. Too much water sent down to the main dam and the excess would be wasted. Too little, and the turbines would slow down and the ground rents fall. Zebadiah was an expert with skills honed over a lifetime. Soon, they were saying that his daughter was his equal, if not his superior.

Each day, on her instructions, a messenger would ride out to Pulpit Rock and the impounded water freed.

Each day, the Quabbin received a little more of the spring rains which had waited all summer to increase the Harcross fortune.

Each day, another several hundred square acres were converted to stagnant pools of festering vegetation.

Each day, the Aedes and Anopheles found new breeding ponds to nurture their young.

Each day, the female mosquitoes raced to suck blood for one last meal. The days were growing shorter. They mated and multiplied as if the devil was driving them. They descended into heart of Cromwell and attacked and attacked and attacked.

Nobody could not recall a summer when the biting insects seemed to possess the very air around them. It must be the canals, some muttered. The dam at Pulpit Rock, others cursed. They all agreed, though, it was like the plagues of the Pharaohs. But, what did Moses want? No one came to make a trade. The affliction continued.

The sickness lay heavy upon the valley. Those who were lucky, shook and chilled and vomited and pissed black blood until they recovered. Those who were unlucky, shook and chilled and vomited and pissed black blood until they died. The bodies fell in the streets and homes. How could one tell the difference between the malaria or the bone break fever? It was simple. If one lived that summer, it was the ague. If not, the death certificate reported the yellow-jack.

Each day, carts passed through the street carrying bodies to mass graves. The wagons paused at the Dispensary door to pick up the dead. Then, to the schools and churches which served as temporary facilities.

John and Shaw worked day and night, catching only glimpses of sleep on a cot in the Dispensary. There were no favorites in this battle. Men and women and children died equally. Those who survived shut themselves up in their homes, burning foul chemicals to scorch the air. They refused to leave for work. They emerged for food and water and then raced back to their sanctuary.

Nothing the two physicians did seemed to arrest the disease.

The mills became deserted hulks. The turbines continued to turn. The leather belts and pulleys flapped and whirred through the silent spaces.

The Boston and Albany Railroad took the side spur to skirt the city whenever possible.

Trams stopped their horse teams on the boundaries of the city.

The prosperous sent their wives and children to visit other cities where relatives and friends were not too scared to take them in.

The rich rested in their mansions in the Highlands. They waited out the sickness on their wind-swept bluffs, receiving loyal retainers who came to tell of death along the canals. The poor stayed in the Flats with their families and died.

Each day Tom Kennedy drove Elizabeth to the Gatehouse to release more water. The drained flood-lands became mosquito ridden bogs. But, the canals ran full! The ground rent linked to water flow continued unabated although fewer hands worked the looms. The manufacturers looked at their competitors who could shut down their steam engines, and compared their turbines still turning for the benefit of Zebadiah, and pondered the lesson. They considered the Manhan. They priced the Corliss engines.

Each day, John cried out in desperation, "Shaw, we must do something."

Each day, Shaw gave the same answer. "Quinine for the malaria and laudanum for the yellow fever. Pray, Johnnie, that the supply lasts until we can get a shipment from Boston. Pray for that and the frost."

The hot weather held on. The sky cloudless. The plague continued.

John had long since given up house calls. Some days he did not have the strength to drag himself to Patrick's home to visit his son. The child had been named Elias Britton. "I would have tacked on a 'Shaw'," John apologized, "but two 'Shaws' in Cromwell is one too many."

"Think of all the fun you will have someday making a 'Shaw' for me," Billings replied. It was a feeble attempt to break through the gloom.

John would hold child in his arms, marvel at the tiny arms and legs, the delicate fingers and toes, so perfect in miniature. The inquisitive eyes, darting from side to side to every change in light and sound. The black hair which made John cry every time he cupped his palm over the head and thought of Kathleen. As the days passed, as with most mortals, his wife's death settled in proper perspective, so that the business of living could continue.

When he thought of Elizabeth, he had no prurient urge. Was natural for a man to have his physical desires banked like dying

271

embers. Shaw would have considered his concerns petty. He shelved the dilemma for happier times.

Elias was a godsend for Patrick. He watched the child at play. He knew that time would harden him to Kathleen's death. There was now a future. He could still have his dream.

He held the child, whispered to it the secret promise. His own blood flowed in the small creature which sucked on the wet-nurse. Like the rainbow, little Elias was a sign from God.

In the second week of September, Patrick O'Connell died from relapsing malarial fever. The limbs were straightened and the corpse clothed. Patrick O'Connell was buried next to his wife and daughter.

One week later, dead from yellow-fever, young Elias joined him between his grandmother and his mother. The stone-masons were too busy to keep up with demand for headstones. John visited the mass grave. The smallest rectangular patch of overturned earth was his son's resting place. Kathleen's he knew, was where the grass had grown back.

Shaw Billings accompanied John to the cemetery. John recalled Antietam. There men killed one another. After all, man was imperfect and mass slaughter just another example of his imperfection. In Cromwell, Death walked like a thief in the night. It was a perfect God who killed here. Was not His sin the greater?

The anger did not leave. Neither did the yellow fever. John remembered Rhases and the dead lambs. Tom Kennedy and the vinegar sweat. He wrote letters. He waited. When the replies came back, he studied the answers late into the night. They were not the proof he had asked for, but then again, neither was the letter from Willard Parker. Common sense and faith had saved a life there. Surely Zebadiah was a reasoning man. He must see the logic. Shaw said he was a fair man. He would do what had to be done, if Cromwell was to be saved.

What if rejected the theory and laughed at the doctor? John saw the thousands who were yet to die. This was no time for scruples. Before leaving for Zebadiah's house, John opened his surgical case, He withdrew two letters. They crackled from the dryness. He reread them. There was no choice. Zebadiah must drain the reservoir behind Pulpit Rock. John offered up a prayer to forgive what he was going to do.

━≪· ·≫━

John did not tell Zebadiah Harcross why he wished to see him. Night had long since fallen. Still the hot earth gave off rivers of heat which suffocated the physician as he travelled along the deserted streets. The smells of rotten vegetation and sewage were everywhere. A sudden breeze cooled the sweat on his skin. He held his arms wide for more, but it had already fled and the torrid air closed in again.

Zebadiah was pleased to see Spencer. Shaw Billings had been visiting him daily. The wound was slowly healing. As before, Zebadiah rebounded with his usual resilience As he stood in the foyer, holding on to Elizabeth for support, he was once more the Master. Zebadiah Harcross had no doubt that the final victory over the Manhan would be his. Did not his survival prove man's dominion over Nature?

Elizabeth often thought of how she would react to seeing John. The fact that he was free. If a single ember remained, which of them would be the first to blow it into flame? Their meeting, she predicted, was destined to be awkward.

Elizabeth was wrong. John did not respond to their condolences nor to Zebadiah's delight in seeing the physician who had saved his life. Spencer's greeting was flat, almost muted. His clinical duties had sapped his energy. He had lost much weight, though Elizabeth would have sworn his spare frame never had any excess to begin

273

with. He was pale, much too pale. His gait was slow, requiring an effort he did not have. When he spoke, his eyes wandered around the room. His lips barely parted. The words emerged in a low tone.

"Zebadiah, the epidemic of yellow fever cannot go on. Even you must know what has been happening down in the valley."

"John," Elizabeth interrupted, "I go to the Gatehouse each day. The people believe it is a plague from the Dark Ages, I pass burial carts piled high with bodies. I hear the families wailing behind the funeral wagons. ." She moved closer. "John, isn't there anything you can do? Cromwell will become a city of the dead."

" Will become 'city of the dead' ? I disagree, Miss Elizabeth." She could not mistake the anger. "Cromwell is a city of the dead. I know better than most. For whom? Certainly not those high in the hills. " His strides made thumping sounds which echoed in the two-story hall.

"The death you see from your carriage belongs to those who cannot leave the Flats where the miasmas come to kill. There, along your canals, the river, the reservoir... there... there is where people die."

Elizabeth was unprepared for the vehemence. The physician was tired, exhausted. The burdens of the dying were on his shoulders. She could understand his frustration. He could be excused. .

"Sit down, John. Let me get you some brandy."

John ripped himself away, "Brandy to numb my pain. What about those in the Dispensary? All the spirits in the world won't help them."

"Doctor Spencer." Zebadiah commiserated. "This is my valley, even more than your's. My life is in every brick. In every street. My blood runs in the canals along with the water. Someday, my death will be here, too. Is there anything I can do, that we can do? Money? Men? You have but to ask."

"John," Elizabeth repeated, "we know how you must feel. It is a terrible thing"

"Do you really know what I feel, each time another child dies in my arms, like my own son? How could you? Any more than what the people are saying about your father?" "What do you mean? You had better explain, Doctor Spencer," Zebadiah demanded.

John realized that the purpose of his visit could no longer be put off. "It is no secret. Even the school children point to the Gatehouse as responsible for the epidemic."

Zebadiah's face turned red. "That is just foolishness," he scorned. "Malaria and yellow fever have been in the valley long before I came."

"But, the cases have increased since the dam was built at Pulpit Rock and the waters backed up in the reservoir."

"That is just coincidence, Doctor Spencer, and you know it. Look at the number of Negroes who have moved in since the War. They bring the fevers of the West Indies. How can you blame the canal system? The water brings work and wealth and life to this valley. Remove the canals and Cromwell would return to the Indians. " His voice grew softer, "When one loses a loved one, it is normal to look for someone, something to blame. However to accuse the dam system is unfair. Unjust."

"Is it, Zebadiah? Are the people so far from the truth?" He withdrew a sheaf of papers from his pocket. " I have been told you are a man of logic, of reason. I expect you to judge these reports without prejudice." He held the letters out to him. "Please read them." For an instant, he was not sure whether Harcross was going take them. The eyes went from the papers to the physician's face, suspicious. In the end, he extended his arm for them as John hoped. He remembered Shaw Billings' words, 'whatever else his failings, the Master of the Quabbin is a fair Man'.

John watched Zebadiah move the arm chair to catch the light from the gas sconce over his head. He slowly read each of the odd dozen letters in turn.

"What is in those letters, John?" Elizabeth asked.

"Elizabeth, you were with me when we tested the dead lambs. You were with me the night I operated on your father. If I come here tonight to ask for something, please accept that my request is sincere."

"I believe you, John. You have yet to explain."

"Cromwell is not the only city with canals and dams and reservoirs. There are towns along the Merrimac River, like Lowell and Lawrence. Along the Connecticut like Holyoke. In Rhode Island at Pawtucket. In Vermont and New Hampshire. Wherever there are rapids, men like your father have dammed rivers for power. I wrote to physicians in each of these communities. I asked them to search for similar epidemics and when they started. The replies are all the same."

"The Negroes are not to blame. Nor is it coincidence in a dozen cities. In each place, the cases soared each year as the dams grew higher and the reservoirs larger. None of these men know any more than Shaw or myself what provokes the sickness. Whether the water poisons the earth or causes the air to form the deadly miasmas? The actual cause is still a mystery, but the numbers cannot be disputed."

"I do dispute them, Doctor Spencer." Zebadiah waved the papers at the doctor. "This is all conjecture. Fairy tales from old men. Proof, Doctor Spencer. Proof! Show me that."

"Proof? I have no proof. Where was the proof when you accepted the knife?" he challenged. " I had only a letter. Only stories from other old men. You accepted their findings then, didn't you?"

"Doctor Spencer, the 'vermiform appendix,' as you physicians call it, can be seen and felt. It could be cut out and put in a bottle. It is a physical fact. It is not the same with the yellow fever and the malaria? Where is their physical being? You cannot see them, nor taste them, nor cut them out. You cannot place them in a bottle. Where is the link to connect the plagues with the water? We still drink the water and bathe in it as we have for years. We baptize in it. Why is the water suddenly pure at some seasons and dangerous at others? It is the same river. You cannot see nor cure the yellow fever and the malaria, and now you claim they are caused by water in a way you do not know. No, Doctor Spencer, do not compare a reservoir full of water and power with a rotted organ two inches long, filled with pus."

Zebadiah fell back into the chair, exhausted by his speech. John felt trapped. This man of logic was driving him to do the unthinkable. If <u>only</u> Zebadiah would accept on faith..... and test the theory?

Zebadiah read his mind. "Even if all these conjectures were true and the sickness caused by the water, what would you have me do?"

"Break the dam at Pulpit Rock. Yes. Open the gates. Drain the reservoir."

There was a gasp from both father and daughter. They looked at each other in shock. Release the impounded waters? Waste the spring rains so that the three canals would run half empty during the fall? There was even more at stake. The new Manhan Canal. Its very existence was contingent upon raising the dam at Pulpit Rock to create a larger reservoir. What the physician was asking would destroy them.

"No, Doctor Spencer," Zebadiah was the first to speak. "That cannot be. Ask anything else, but not that."

"You cannot ask that," Elizabeth said. "Especially without proof that it would be of value."

"Proof?" John protested again. "<u>That</u> is the proof. Break the dam. See yourself if the sickness does not disappear. Unless you do that, the epidemic will continue."

"No, John. You are wrong. The epidemic will stop as it has each year with the frost. Wait for the cold air from the north."

"You must release the water now," he pleaded, "or else you will kill many more than you have already murdered."

"Murdered!" Zebadiah jumped to his feet. He raised his arm to strike him. Elizabeth had never seen her father so angry. She tried to restrain him, but he would not be stopped. John drew back to ward off the blow.

"Murdered? How dare you come into my home and accuse me of murder? If I did not owe you, Doctor Spencer, I would have the servants throw you out of this house into the street like a dog. Instead, I ask you to leave this very minute and never to return. That final courtesy will cancel out my obligation. Remember, no matter what kind of evil men accuse me of, I have never taken the life of a single human being."

John was afraid. Not fear of bodily injury, but for the blow he must deliver. He had hoped that faith, generosity, even intellectual curiosity would have persuaded Harcross. His arguments had fallen upon deaf ears. He had <u>no</u> choice. John gently removed Zebadiah's hands.

"I am sorry for what I said," he apologized, "I will leave your house, and if you wish, never return." There was a stricken look on Elizabeth's face. She <u>must</u> have faith in him. Their future depended upon what would happen in the next few minutes.

"You said that you have never taken the life of a single human being. That is not true."

Zebadiah started up again in anger.

"No. Please. Listen to me. Just this once. Than I will go away. First," he looked at Elizabeth, "your daughter must leave us."

"No, father. I won't," she objected.

Something convinced him to do as the physician wished. "Nothing will happen. Please, Elizabeth, leave us."

The young girl reluctantly left, unsure what was going to happen. John waited until the door closed behind her. "Just a few minutes, Zebadiah. I have a story to tell you. It is a short one. Please listen to me. It is all I ask."

Zebadiah took his seat, caught by the man's sincerity.

"It was four years ago, in 1862. During the War of the Rebellion. There was a battle with armies shredding each other to pieces. All trying to see how many lives and limbs they could win as if it were a child's game with a prize for the highest score. Nothing even now in Cromwell can ever compare with those horrors."

"I took care of many. I could not keep count. I remember one particular boy. I do not know why. Out of all the countless numbers I treated, I think of him alone. He was a handsome lad with dark hair, a strong chin. He had a quiet pleasant almost ingenuous manner about him. Yet, he was dignified and intelligent. He had stepped upon a land mine."

Zebadiah slowly edged forward. Something in the doctor's words made him uneasy.

"Both legs were shattered above the knee. I had to amputate at the mid thigh." Zebadiah held his breath. "There was a greater injury. The explosion had destroyed his manhood. His penis and testicles were gone, leaving only a brutal scar."

Zebadiah was staring at him with fright. His hands gripped the sides of the seat until the knuckles blanched.

"There was more. The leg stumps and groin were covered with crawling maggots until the surface ran alive with them. I talked with the boy. I tried to reassure him that he would heal and, one day, he would find his loved ones at home to welcome him. What was important was that he should live. His family would and bless God that he had survived. After all, I assured him, life was the most precious possession a human being could have."

"Matt.... Matt....hew....?" Zebadiah stumbled over the name.

"I did not know of you at the time. I knew only the boy's first name was Matthew, not his Christian name. I found that out later when my aide gave me a letter you had written to your son,"

There were two letters in his hand, Zebadiah wondered why he had not noticed them before. John handed the longer one to the father. Zebadiah rubbed his fingers over the dark brown smudges of old blood. His hands shook as he read his own words over again,,,,,

> **You will find that my influence is great and there is no place where you can escape my will............ You are my single fragile link with posterity......... The fruit of your loins will issue forth.........I shall not appeal..........out of love. You will obey me."**

The letter dropped from his hands. He made no attempt to pick it up.

"There was another letter," John continued, tapping the second shorter paper against his palm, "Matthew died before he could send it to you,"

Zebadiah reached out for it, driven to follow the nightmare through to its end,

Forgive me.... Forgive me... Forgive me

The words repeated over and over.

John knelt down before the older man. He squeezed his hands in his own.....as he gave the father one last hurt.

"Matthew pulled out his sutures and bled to death. Now, Zebadiah, you will never be able to say you have not killed a human being."

Harcross did not move. The man sat carved out of stone. Suddenly, he rose from his seat and without even looking at Spencer, went to the door. His voice cracked as he cried out for Elizabeth. She came running into the room, shocked by her father's appearance.

Zebadiah did not give her time to ask what had happened. "Elizabeth, open the gates." She did not believe her ears. "Open the gates," he repeated, "release the waters. Tonight. Have Tom Kennedy ride out to Pulpit Rock. Now! Now! Elizabeth."

"But, father," she protested, trying to make some sense out of what had happened in the room without her. "You can't. The dam! The canals."

"Damn you!" he swore, his eyes wild, expression ugly with self-hate. "Open the dam! FOR YOUR BROTHERS SAKE!" He sank back into his seat with his head between his hands, shaking like a man doomed.

John saw Elizabeth eye the letters in her fathers hand. Before anyone could stop him, he thrust them into the nearest gas jet. He held them there until they had burned down scorching his fingers. He dropped the ashes into the cold hearth and ground out the char with his heel. He saw the father's look of gratitude.

In the days to come, Elizabeth pondered the events of that night, a mystery on which neither her father nor John would enlighten her. She recalled something she had completely forgotten. She could still see Zebadiah sitting in the Library, long after John had left, his face turned up to the portrait of Matthew. He had done that often. Never in her life had she seen her father cry.

CHAPTER THIRTY-ONE

John was at the main dam when the flood crested. Everyone in Cromwell who could walk or be carried had gathered around the Gatehouse to see the rare sight. Within hours of news that Zebadiah was planning to release the impounded waters in the reservoir, wild rumors were circulating. Some people claimed that the magnate's recent illness had unbalanced his mind. Others who learned from the servants of Spencer's nocturnal visit to the Harcross home claimed a conspiracy plot. All knew, whatever the reason, that the decision would be costly.

Those who had escaped personal tragedy from the epidemic remembered the years before Pulpit Rock when the canals ran half-empty for part of the year. The shifts on half-time and short pay envelopes. The merchants recalled dry goods in their stores staying on shelves till the canal waters rose. It was going to be a long hard winter the Cassandras warned.

The bore drove down the Quabbin with pent-up force, swirling and twisting like an angry beast. It was thirty feet high, one hundred and fifty feet wide and moved at a steady eight miles an hour. The early morning sunlight backlit the opalescent greens and blues in the moving wall. Clouds of white foam exploded as the churning water hit rocky embankments and crashed on the boulders.

The huge swell was preceded by a dull roar which increased in pitch as the tide approached. The avalanche overflowed its banks, ripped into the side and creeks and streams, flooding brooks and ponds. Always tearing loose and shattering millions of delicate rafts of germinating mosquitoes. Within a single hour, almost all of the next generation of incubating and Anopheles were washed away, along with boats, logs, docks, wharfs..... all sucked into the surging maelstrom. It was a sight few had ever seen and all would to tell their grandchildren.

The crest grew closer. Men on horseback rode back and forth, shouting to the noisy crowd how close it was. Suddenly it was upon them! The air changed into water as the cliff pounded past, drenching those foolhardy enough to stand near the edge. The bore spilled over the dam, piercing the newly constructed apron in the center. The mighty hammer of liquid sent huge geysers of stone and flying timbers high into the air, as the crushing weight of tons of water cracked into the river bed below the high dam.

"There will be the devil to pay," dam workers muttered to themselves as they saw the construction of the previous year destroyed in the flash of an eye.

Elizabeth Harcross was visibly shaken as she made her way from the Gatehouse to her carriage through the dense thicket of milling people. The reservoir first. Now the apron. The loss of revenue. The cost of repairing the apron in addition to the Manhan Canal. What had possessed her father? All because of some emotional impulse of his.

She could still hear his angry words ringing in her ears. ' Damn you!... Matthew!..... For your brothers, sake!' Matthew again! Would his ghost never stayed buried? Was the wanton act a laugh from the grave? Damn him and damn John Spencer! What had the man showed her father to have provoked this insane act?

In the wake of the vortex, the water suddenly became placid. The floating debris would eddy for days now that the water level was too low to top the dam. She swore a silent oath. Never again would Matthew's dead hand rise to cripple her future. She would rebuild the apron. Finish the Manhan, Raise the reservoir even if it meant flooding half the State!

By chance, she picked out the familiar figure of the red-haired physician. How could she have lain naked in his arms, lost her innocence and heart to him? Love was a terrible thing. It blinds. Her eyes were now open. She vowed they would stay that way. How quickly love could turn to hate,

John caught her glance. He breasted the crowd, trying to make his way to where she stood. He waved, happy, wanting to share the moment with her. She waited until he was close enough that he could have touched her arm. Then, she deliberately turned away, mounted her carriage and left without so much as a backward glance.

Over the two weeks, John made up his mind to call on Elizabeth and try to heal the rift. Each day, he delayed, hoping for a break in the epidemic so that he could prove that by their generous act the Harcrosses had preserved the life of the city. For the first week, there was no change. Then, within the fortnight, as the sun dried the drained hinterlands, the number of new cases took a definite drop.

The Culicidae flew madly, trying to breed another generation before the fall, but the watery link in their life cycle, the wet breeding grounds, were no more. The females, laden with parasite-rich blood, looked in vain where to lay their rafts. Exhausted, swollen with eggs, they fell to the dry ground and died.

John showed the statistics to Shaw. The older man tried hard not to show his enthusiasm. He had seen cycles too many times when the next day's figures would bring a heart-breaking rise in the deaths. But, the numbers continued to fall. Slowly. Slowly. Then faster and faster as the Aedes and Anopheles aged and died and did not replace their immortality.

John was exultant until, as if to punish his hubris, Nature tricked him! Almost simultaneous with the drying of the Quabbin valley, the wind shifted. It swept out of the northwest. Overnight, the temperature dropped thirty degrees. The sun remained in force. The sky itself remained a pure cerulean blue. But, the air was now chilled by the frigid Canadian air which entered the valley and rested.

The ground grew cold. In the morning, with the first rays, a light mist hovered over the land as heated air touched the night-cooled ground. The frost froze the fall vegetables still in the ground, reducing them to pulp. The insects now flew with a dull lethargic pace, close to the ground to capture heat. The Aedes and Anopheles rose later each morning and rested earlier with the sunset. Finally, the morning when pitchers and porcelain basins in bedrooms held a thin crackling layer of ice, Cromwell knew that the summer had ended, life preserved for another year.

John saw the yellow fever and malaria creep away like surprised thieves in the night. They would not return until the spring. He was sad. Not that the epidemic was gone. Nor that it would come back as it had for generations. He had lost forever proof that breaking the dam was responsible for ending the plague. He did not bother to return to the Harcross home. There was nothing he could say to Zebadiah or to his daughter. The frost, they would retort angrily and with good reason. That was the magic you needed. Destroying the dam was an expensive folly.

Next summer when the burial carts were full again, Spencer would have no more letters for Zebadiah.

CHAPTER THIRTY-TWO

That Adam Ring was a scavenger was probably the kindest thing said about the rising insurance lord in the fall of 1866. The curses hurled at the Polish Jew covered the full gamut from his religion to his scarred face to his lack of morals. The object of the scorn was not a hypocrite. He would have been the last to deny the charges. However, as he pointed out to his associates, he had no sympathy for those who preferred to die with honor than live with dishonor, especially when dishonor was accompanied with gold. He had not come this far to lose everything to black piss!

They had sat in the Commonwealth Life Insurance offices in the early summer of 1866 and weighed the odds whether in the fall there would be an epidemic. They worried over the growing pile of policies taken out in a frenzy by panicked families who feared the worst. .

The Commonwealth Life Insurance Company had expanded, exploding out of the central counties into untapped areas stretching from the Berkshires in the West to Cape Cod in the East. The Gold Medal policy had captured the imagination of the public. The hard-driving advertising campaign emblazoned a gold seal against a map of Massachusetts on every billboard and barn siding the length and breadth of the State.

The insurance in force sky-rocketed. The cost of starting up consumed almost all of the first year's premiums, causing a temporary, but alarming drop in the actuarial reserves. Adam and Patrick threw into the breech the entire accumulated surplus earned so far to stave off bankruptcy which the unexpected success threatened,

"Adam," Patrick warned as he spent anxious days with Giordano examining the balance sheets, "go slow. Cut back on the advertising. Don't sign up everyone who can breathe. Wait."

Ring had heard those words before. In the summer of 1865, Patrick had urged similar caution. 'We must stop seeking new business until the winter stops the sickness or the numbers will drive us under.' Adam had ignored the worry then. He had laughed at the Irishman's panic. Patrick managed to squeeze the extra money out of somewhere to pay the bills. There was no epidemic. Adam had been proved right. Now, it was different. Patrick's fears were echoed by Frank Giordano and even Frederick Dearing about whom Adam felt the earth could open up at his feet without more than a passing comment.

Adam Ring truly was a scavenger. However, he was not a fool. He had an instinctive sense of when not to go too far. Despite his compulsive drive and a deceiving nonchalance about risking his all on a throw of the dice, he was not reckless. He insisted that he would not stop selling policies, even in Cromwell. "I will never let the Old Colonial or the Boston Mutual take over the valley," he swore. However, in deference to his three associates and his own intuition, he decided to hedge,

"Frederick," he asked, "an insurance policy is really nothing more than a legal contract? Isn't it?"

It was obvious Ring was leading up to something. Knowing his employer, Dearing nodded and waited for the Pole to get to the point.

"You lawyers are clever. I can't imagine any contract that you folks draw up that cannot be voided."

"You can always go to court to break a contract by suing, claiming misrepresentation, fraud, or improper performance of the stipulated terms."

Adam wondered it the lawyer talked this way during sex. "That's not what I am after. What if I wanted an insurance policy that would give the Commonwealth Company the right to cancel the contract, at our option? Can such a policy be written?"

Dearing turned red and flustered at the proposal.

"No, Frederick. Nothing illegal. I don't want to go to Court to break each policy on the vague terms you suggested. I would like to add a legal clause which allows us to avoid paying the claim. .... if we so desire."

"Adam, you are asking for something which runs contrary to the very heart of what you are selling. When a person buys your policy and pays his first year's premium, he is really purchasing your commitment to carry out your part of the contract, to redeem the face value of the policy and pay his widow or estate upon his death. He is placing his life on one side of the balance scale. On the other side is trust in the contract. Void that faith, unilaterally, arbitrarily, and you shatter the sanctity of the legal bond. Even if the law would back you up, what you have done is sinful and unethical."

Adam listened with a tolerant expression. He had heard Dearing's vows of morality many times before. The pleas for ethical business conduct. He had chosen Dearing not only because he was smart. There were plenty of other lawyers in Cromwell with brains his equal, perhaps even superior. Dearing was poor. So were others. But Dearing was a hypocrite. A hungry hypocrite. The best combination.

Two years ago, there were shiny patches on his trousers. Now he held 6% of the non-voting capital stock of the Commonwealth Life

Insurance company. He lived in the Highlands, in an impressive red brick Georgian home with a white pillared colonnade, purchased with a mortgage extended by the Commonwealth Corporation. He was a bought man, and Adam Ring held the key to his golden chain.

Adam's favorite recreation was reflecting on the ease by which men's souls could be bought. Even easier and cheaper than a whore's cunt. Dearing would sputter and protest, but in the end, he would come around. If Adam was correct in his interpretation of Frederick's impassioned speech, the deed could be done.

Adam was not mistaken. He had an ability to sniff out scruples of those about him. Dearing. Giordano. The District Managers. A growing handful of State Legislators. All of them. Just like Jacob Kowalski, bartering his daughter for a handful of silver. Casmir Landsteiner, for his perversions. He had beaten them all. The trick was not worrying whether a man had a price. They all could be bought. The trick was to have a purse large enough to close the bargain. It was an article of faith which Adam Ring was shortly to put to its harshest test against a red-haired doctor with whom he had once viewed the autumn colors of the Quabbin valley.

The clause Frederick Dearing came up with was contained in two regal-sounding, sweet flowing French words.

" 'Force majeure', Adam. That is what you want,"

Adam did not know French. Even O'Connell who had learned a smattering of the language could only offer a translation which did not make any sense. "It means, 'superior force', Adam," Patrick tried to help,

Dearing explained, "It is a term employed in law to connote a physical catastrophe, something beyond the measure of either human initiation or control. It refers to an Act of God. An earthquake, A flood. A conflagration from lightening. A war."

"An epidemic?" Adam asked, cautiously. His eyes were now alive,

"It has never been tested as such before, I searched for a legal case which would establish natural disease as a 'force majeure '. There are none," he confessed. "However, in my opinion, there are ample precedents with other natural disasters to cover such a contingency. The least it would do is provide a reasonable basis for voiding the policies. If you should eventually lose in the Court, it would buy time, even years, before we exhausted all possible appeals. You know how the law works," referring to Adam's own tangle with JUSTICE the year before.

Untried, unethical, but hopefully legal, all policies written by the Commonwealth beginning in the summer of 1866, carried such a rider buried in the small print. Few bothered to read it. Even fewer questioned its meaning. If pressed for an explanation, the agents were instructed by Adam to tell the truth. The fancy phrase, the coöperative salesmen explained, referred to the unlikely occurrence of certain rare events in Nature, such as a volcano erupting in the central hills of Massachusetts or a locust plague of biblical proportions. Of course, the salesmen offered, the clause could be removed, but the premiums would be higher. Their fears allayed, the clauses, for the most part, remained intact.

The sickness raged through the Quabbin valley. The claims piled up in the offices of the Commonwealth Life Insurance Company. Letters went out daily, excusing the crush of paperwork for the delay in payment. There was no crush of paperwork. Adam was just marking time until the fact of an epidemic was incontrovertible.

On September 11, 1866, the Massachusetts Legislature on Beacon Hill was asked to vote on a very strange law. It was House Bill #10670. It declared in legal tones that the epidemic in Cromwell was an 'Act of God'. It voted money to children orphaned by the catastrophe. It requested that all charitable persons within the Commonwealth search their hearts and respond to the crying needs of the stricken community.

Nobody really knew why the Bill was introduced in the first place, or by whom. The lobbyists were evasive. There were unproven rumors that the Commonwealth Life Insurance Company was behind the measure. However, what good Christian could refuse the vote on such a humane measure, especially when at the last moment, those who wavered or were suspicious, received midnight visits and open bank draughts.

The Act was passed, duly noted, and sanctified by a Minute of standing, with bared heads, in silent prayer, by both Chambers of the Legislature, asking God's mercy for the plagued city.

Twenty-four hours later, the Commonwealth Company sent out notices voiding all policies of those signed out as victims of malaria or yellow fever, Dearing insisted that the decedent's estate receive back a pro-rated refund of the remaining portion of the current calendar year's premium, Adam Ring did not object. It was the only proper thing to do.

━╬ ╬━

Like the other inhabitants in Cromwell, John Spencer was aware of the meteoric rise of the Commonwealth Life Insurance Company. He remembered his meeting with Adam Ring the year before. He was not surprised at the man's success. He also knew that his father-in-law was Ring's partner. The combination impressed him as odd, yet he realized that the world of business was foreign to him, and he was no one to judge what qualities made for commercial compatibility. Kathleen had been unable to shed additional light on the pair. In the fall of 1866, John Spencer suddenly found himself involved with the world he had but glimpsed in passing.

The growing entrapment by Adam Ring started in an oblique fashion. Shortly after the Commonwealth Company sent out notices cancelling the policies, John and Shaw were besieged by widows who came to them in tears, clutching the voided contracts.

"It was your death certificates," they accused unfairly. "You put the diagnosis of yellow fever or malaria. Why didn't you write the flux or the pleurisy or consumption. Here. Look at these," They thrust the Commonwealth notices into the physicians' hands, clamoring for them to do something.

John could see the justice of their cause. The Commonwealth Company had perpetrated an out-and-out fraud upon the unsuspecting people. But, what could he, or even Shaw do for that matter? The doctors went so far as to seek legal counsel. The results were as they would have predicted.

"Ring and Dearing are damn clever. Sure, you could fight them, but it would take forever and a day, and cost a fortune, which is what these poor people don't have."

The wise lawyers shook their collective heads and stroked their collective beards, and uttered the same collective vows that the Lord would punish the guilty and then they closed their collective doors on the physicians. Insurance companies need lots of lawyers. It would not be wise to offend Adam Ring. It was not every day that such a fountain of gold gushed in Cromwell.

In the most desperate cases, John dug into his own pocket and offered what he had to help. It was a drop in the ocean. He ended by closing his heart and ears to the countless number of similar tales he heard in the fall of 1866.

When Adam Ring and Frederick Dearing came to call one evening, the two physicians imagined that it was concerning their fight against the Commonwealth Company. John had moved back into Shaw's house. The housekeeper ushered the delegation into the Library where Spencer and Billings received them with cold formality. They did not ask them to sit down, but remained themselves standing themselves. There was an awkward silence. Ring indicated to Shaw that his presence was a hindrance. Billings started to leave when John strongly objected.

"Please, Doctor Spencer," Adam said, "let him go. Our business tonight does not concern Dr. Billings nor the insurance policies. It is a private matter between you and me."

John was puzzled, but could not find any excuse to hold Shaw who quietly left the room. With a curt nod, John motioned the two men to seat themselves. In contrast to Dearing's tenseness, Adam Ring was relaxed. He noted the sideboard holding brandy and glasses which his host refused to provide for his guests. The room was cold. The two physicians had been readying the fire with kindling stacked in the hearth. Spencer made no effort to warm the room. He stood by the mantle, hostile, waiting.

Dearing took advantage of the pause to open a flat leather case and remove several long legal documents. The thick parchment-like sheets crackled as he checked to make certain they were all there.

"Doctor Spencer," Dearing began softly, "Adam Ring and I would first like to express our sympathy at the unfortunate deaths in your family. It is hard for a layman to realize that doctors suffer misfortune from disease as do the rest of us."

John appreciated that the young man was trying to be civil. He acknowledged the attempt, but still remained silent. Ring was staring intently at the young doctor. His fingers were interlocked in front of his face where they made a curtain which hid what he was thinking.

Dearing continued, "I am here tonight in my capacity as sole executor of the estate of the late Patrick O'Connell. As you know, your father-in-law lived beyond the life of his only child, your late wife, Kathleen O'Connell Spencer."

John stirred impatiently at the labored foreplay. Dearing speeded up his delivery.

"Your wife died after giving birth to your only child, a son named Elias Britton Spencer. Patrick O'Connell's will was a very fastidious one and provided for most eventualities. In the event of his death during your wife's lifetime, his estate was to descend outright to her. If she predeceased him, the corpus would pass to her living issue in equal parts. When Patrick O'Connell died last month, your son, Elias Britton Spencer was alive and became the sole inheritor under Patrick O'Connell's Last Will and Testament. Upon Elias Britton Spencer's death, the estate passed into your hands, minus, of course, the usual fees and taxes."

John was struggling to follow the Byzantine tale. Dearing held out a group of papers for the doctor to take. "Your father-in-law, despite his humble way of life, was a rich man. Very rich. He had extensive holdings of real estate, and of course, assorted personal property. However, the bulk of his estate is contained in 100,000 shares of voting common stock of the Commonwealth Life Insurance Corporation out of an authorized and issued 200,000 shares. These shares carry a par value of one dollar a piece, although their value today is probably in excess of $6 each. The Will may be contested, of course. I have no doubt that you will be confirmed in your new possessions."

Adam Ring watched the unsuspecting beneficiary. He could not repress the bitterness that here was a fortune being handed over to a man who had not been obliged to lift a finger for it. A man respected by the community in his own right. A man who had the love and body of a beautiful woman at one time, and would, no doubt, obtain another. Adam quickly moved off the unprofitable path of self-pity. He had planned long and hard for this evening. He could not afford personal feelings, not if he was to preserve his stake in this land of milk and honey.

John riffled through the papers, unable to come to terms with the unexpected chain of circumstances. The documents were undecipherable and he returned them to the lawyer.

"You mean to tell me," he asked Dearing, "that I control the Commonwealth Life Insurance Company?"

Dearing laughed at the naive question. "No, fifty percent of the voting stock does not confer control. For that, you need fifty <u>one</u> percent. Mr. Ring owns the other 100,000 shares, an amount equal with your own. What it means......" Dearing looked at his employer for a signal to go on. Adam nodded.".....what it means is that you and Mr. Ring must agree on how to run the company."

Adam saw the change come over the physician. Spencer's eyes squinted as if he had been handed some prize. Then, he smiled. Adam Ring knew that the time had come!

Ever since Frederick had acquainted him with the 0'Connell inheritance, Adam lived the nightmare of having the young doctor as his partner. He knew John Spencer had no sympathy for his philosophy. Not even grudging respect for what he had accomplished as a penniless immigrant. With the unsavory scandal involving the insurance policies, he was certain the physician held him in contempt. Yet, if he was to survive, if the Commonwealth Company was to survive, he must have the physician's cooperation, his vote. He struggled with the challenge. How could he obtain Spencer's consent when the man despised him?

The dilemma seemed insoluble. Adam Ring researched his prey with a diligence he had never demonstrated before. Where was that wizard's box to cage the physician? Half of the profits? Fine. Adam had no use for dividends. What he wanted was control and the power that came with it. The Commonwealth Company had many more States to conquer. He would spread it across the nation, driving West with the railroads, sucking out gold to ship back East. He must be left in charge of its destiny. The Canadian idealist must surrender the veto power in his inherited block. The solution was at hand.

Adam Ring anticipated John's question.

"What Frederick means is that you can force me to restore all the policies voided during the epidemic. You can demand that we pay off the face value of the contracts."

How did the Pole know what he was thinking? Could he read men's minds? Owning half an insurance empire meant held little attraction for John. What he valued was knowing that he could correct a gross injustice. Providence did act in mysterious ways.

"Yes, Doctor Spencer, you could do that, although it would bankrupt the company. I know the Commonwealth has little value to you. The fact that it has great value to me and my associates does not matter when weighed against a chance to correct a injustice." His voice was deliberately sarcastic.

Frederick handed him two separate documents. Adam walked over to Spencer and held out the first one.

"These are Minutes of a Board of Directors Meeting of the Commonwealth Life Insurance Company. It contains a unanimous vote to restore the voided policies. I have signed my name as you can see. It needs only your signature to give it the force of law. By tomorrow morning, the bank draughts will be issued and circulating through the mails. Here," he thrust it at him, "sign it, or...." He handed him the second document, "or, Doctor Spencer, you can sign <u>this</u> one in its place."

John took both papers, and scanned them rapidly, his head going back and forth from one to the other, and then to Ring and Dearing.

" The second document is an alternate set of Minutes of the same Board of Directors' meeting. It confers upon me working control of the company for the next 12 months. It pledges to use all Commonwealth resources to guarantee that the dam at Pulpit Rock remains open forever."

Adam Ring took his seat. He had played his hand exactly as planned. The fingers rose again to hide his face. The lids dropped. The words were barely audible as if he no longer cared what the physician would do.

"The decision is your's. The Commonwealth Company is rich from money taken from the poor. Half of that stolen wealth belongs to you. You can give back the money and destroy the Company. Or, you can use the money to cleanse valley from epidemics. Give me the company and I promise you the lifeblood of the Harcrosses, <u>their</u> holy river. Look down into that valley as we once did long ago….when you desired nothing. Then, John Spencer, tell me what you will do."

The Pole opened his eyes. He had never been wrong before. Would this doctor be the first? John stared back, frightened by what he saw ….in himself. The man offered an unholy pact with the devil. But, the price!

Adam Ring laughed as he held his hand for John's soul.

CHAPTER THIRTY-THREE

I mmediately following upon Spencer's decision to block refilling the reservoir behind Pulpit Rock, the citizens of Cromwell were treated to the rare spectacle of a fight between the Commonwealth Life Insurance Corporation and the Harcross Water power Company. In October, Zebadiah Harcross died in his sleep and Elizabeth was installed in the Gatehouse as his successor. If Adam Ring entertained hope that his task would be easier, he discovered that the mantle was inherited by one of equal fiber. Despite the transient belief that the new mistress of would abandon the reservoir, she took up the gauntlet. She started repairing the damage at Pulpit Rock. The Pole had pledged his word to John. He had to find a way to stop her. The battle was joined.

Overnight, John became an outcast. It had not taken long for the terms of Patrick O'Connell's will to become public knowledge. Many owed their lives to the doctor. Others heard of his reputation by hearsay. There were few, however, who had not been grievously wounded by the Commonwealth Company in which the Canadian doctor was a powerful stock-holder and the equal of Adam Ring.

Why didn't he use his power to correct the wrong, they wondered? Earlier, he and Shaw Billings had tried to help the beneficiaries. Now, he was silent. Had he, like everyone else in Cromwell, sold his birthright to the Jew for a mess of porridge? And, if so, why? Was he addicted to the gold, now held in joint possession with the thief?

John's practice dwindled. Patients would enter the Dispensary and shy away from his greeting. When he approached them, they would avert their eyes, mumble some inappropriate excuse and ask for the older physician. At first, John ignored the danger signals. He soon realized that he was becoming a pariah in his chosen home.

"Shaw," John pleaded, "What can I do? Nobody will believe the dam is responsible."

John had explained the results of the lamb experiments. Shaw agreed that putting Hospital on the Bluffs, instead of down in the Flats, made common sense, even if was unconvinced of the scientific merit. Second, he had been impressed by John's daring to operate on Zebadiah, again an act resulting from medical research. When John showed Billings the yearly statistics he could not deny the relationship to the reservoir backed up behind Pulpit Rock. He read the letters from physicians in other New England mill towns. Despite the evidence, his reaction was like Zebadiah's. Where was the proof? John had none.

Billings marveled when the Master of the Quabbin ordered the dam at Pulpit Rock broken. He did not believe John's explanation that Zebadiah had accepted the letters from the other mill cities. Yet, he probed no further. His unassuming partner had had a mysterious hold over Harcross, which he refused to reveal. Shaw knew that the time was not ripe to press for the truth. After the reservoir was drained, Shaw watched John scan the daily statistics. His excitement when the sickness curve was shattered. His bitterness when the frost destroyed his proof.

Adam listened to rumors the Harcross Water power Company would default the semi-annual payment on the new loan. The bonds were selling for forty cents on the dollar. Adam had the Commonwealth take up a dominant block of them. He contacted the other minority share owners who had been slighted by Zebadiah. The Annual Meeting of the stockholders was scheduled for the end of December. Ring did not anticipate any trouble placing at least half of the directors on the Harcross Board.

Elizabeth was equally determined to preserve the heart of the Company, even if it meant sacrificing one of its limbs. She immediately voided contracts for the Manhan Canal, eliminating future losses. She moved to raise the ground rents on the three existing canals, squeezing mills for money to satisfy the bondholders. She insisted that the reservoir behind Pulpit rock be filled by the spring rains. She would need every dollar.

"One good year," she grimly assured Tom Kennedy, "and we will have the Board back again for ourselves."

"It will drive the mill owners towards steam," Kennedy warned.

Elizabeth thought of her silent holdings in the coal carrying railroads which she had coerced her father into buying, and smiled. From her own resources, she took up the options on the Higgins Steam Engine Company in Worcester.

In a grudging sort of way, Adam admired the young woman. Zebadiah never would have jettisoned the Manhan. His ego was too great to give up the project, even if it meant losing the entire Company. 'This daughter of his was a cold-blooded bitch,' he swore.

Whatever his admiration for Elizabeth, her unexpected tactic of abandoning the Manhan cancelled his trump card. Several profitable fiscal quarters, and the skipped dividend would be paid off. With the Manhan a dead issue, how was he to obtain leverage to fight her? He had until spring.

"Riparian rights!" he ordered Dearing. "Find out about riparian rights. The river is the jugular. Cut the artery and the Harcross Power Company will bleed to death."

Dearing knew nothing about riparian rights. He learned fast. In New England and other eastern States, the riparian rights followed Old English Law. The owner of the river had total control, regardless of any hardship to others along its banks. The law was different in the Western States. There, the Courts protected those downstream against those upstream who wanted the water for their own exclusive use. Dearing immediately filed for an injunction to keep the river open at Pulpit Rock, and to prevent rebuilding at Pulpit Rock. He appealed to the Courts to apply to the western code to eastern rivers. It was a gamble. There would be appeals and more appeals, hopefully continuing until the frozen ground would be too hard to work at Pulpit Rock.

It did not pay to underestimate any Harcross, even one with breasts and skirts. Ring and Spencer would ride to out to watch Elizabeth's determination to erase her father's tragic error. Until the courts would stop her, she would rebuild. From the busy activity at the dam site, the legal battle would be long and difficult. It was too late to withdraw. John had cast his lot in with his unscrupulous partner and, like his female adversary, there was no going back.

Shaw and John had planned the trephining for weeks. The young boy of fourteen had suffered recurrent spastic seizures which rendered him unconscious and incontinent. The attacks started after he had fallen off a dray cart the year before. The two physicians easily felt the depressed bone fracture which pressed into the brain. The mother, an uneducated Italian woman, who communicated through one of the Sisters, was frightened at the suggestion that her son's skull be opened.

"There is no other way," they insisted.

The last attack convinced the mother. She was on the Ward when the boy choked with saliva running out of his mouth, and his left side was drawn up in a rigid contortion. When he recovered, he had no memory of what had happened. The doctors knew what was passing through the mother's mind. Better to be dead than to live among people like this. She fingered her rosary beads, tears in her eyes, and agreed to the operation.

Although he was scheduled to assist, John did not show up for the surgery. Despite the risk, Shaw was determined to proceed. He knew that any hesitation might let the mother change her mind. The case was long and bloody. Several times anesthesia had to be halted to preserve a fluttering heart beat.

Where was John? More than once Billings cursed when John's skillful fingers were not there to stop hemorrhage. He had no right to abandon a patient! Finished, Shaw removed the blood-drenched operating apron. As he stretched his cramped muscles, the room suddenly swam before his eyes. He sat down in the corner of the room gasping for air. Thank God he had been able to complete the surgery. But, where was Spencer? Damn the man! He had never been this irresponsible before.

Billings' anger was tempered by concern that something untoward had happened to his partner. John did not show up at the Dispensary the remainder of the morning. When Billings returned home for the noonday meal, John was not there. The housekeeper greeted him, worried.

"Something is wrong, Doctor Shaw. Doctor John received a letter this morning. I do not know what was in it, except it had foreign stamps on the envelope. He was excited when he first opened it. Then, after he finished reading it in the Library, he went to his room and stayed there. I thought I could hear him crying, I knocked on the door. He wouldn't open it. I asked if there was anything I could do, but he did not answer.

Shortly before you came home, he left his room. He was in a terrible state. He had not shaved. His clothes were soiled. I could tell he had been drinking. The liquor was spilled all over him. He rushed right past me and left in your carriage with the grey bays without saying where he was going."

Letter? From abroad? It wasn't like Spencer to be drinking in the middle of the day. The young man was certain not a teetotaler and many was the night the two of them had finished more than one bottle of claret. However, he would never have deserted Surgery unless there was something terribly wrong.

John's bedroom reflected whatever turmoil had possessed the physician. The smell of sweat and stale bedclothes. The chamber pot left full since the maid was not allowed in the room. The odor of whiskey where it still puddled on the carpet. John had not bothered to open the drapes and the kerosene lights did little to pierce the gloom.

Next to several empty whiskey bottles on the desk, Billings saw the crumpled sheets of a letter. The stamps were English. The mailing address, Edinburgh. John had never spoken of anyone he knew in Scotland. Shaw tried to understand what was going on. The pages rustled in his hand. He was torn between reluctance to read another's private mail and his desire to help his friend. Against his better judgment, he closed the door and sat to read the letter from Elias Guthrie.

September 2, 1866
The Black prince Arms
Princess Street
Edinburgh, Scotland

My dear Spencer,

How many times have I hesitated to pick up my pen fearful you would attribute these words to the ranting of a senile old man, perhaps one even afflicted with some foreign malady affecting his reason. I had considered waiting until I arrive back in Montreal (I leave from Liverpool on the eighteenth of this month) or even travelling to the Colonies to convince you that sanity has not left this ancient abode. I can delay no longer. What I have to tell should not hinge upon the vagaries of time or place. Read these words, John, and laugh or cry, for what I have seen should fill you with humility and gratitude... and sorrow,

I have traveled these hot summer months on the continent, arriving just a fortnight ago in this northern vestige of my ancestral Anglo-Saxon land. Unfortunately, most of what I have observed here, in the Dispensaries, the medical institutions, the hospitals, convinced me that my tour was a futile exercise. I often closed my eyes and imagined I was back in Montreal, or even worse, back in the days of Galen or Da Vinci, for all the progress medicine has made in the long intervening years.

Certainly, in Berlin, in Milan, in Vienna, Budapest, our fellow physicians seem dedicated to the proposition that hallowed rituals of the past should remain enshrined for future generations, unchanged and immutable. Those days I longed to be back in our own fair land, away from these inhabitants of the Mediterranean and Central Europe with their strange ideas of courtesy and food and drink and hygiene.

Then, Spencer, my legs took me to France. There I found a quiet unassuming little man. He is short of height, stutters slightly when excited and suffers the same 'mal de tête' which afflicts your poor old mentor.

This Louis Pasteur does not even practice medicine. He has made his mark in his native country by finding out why silkworms die and wine grows sour. Do not laugh, as I did, and all else who heard of his strange reputation at first knowledge. Spencer, he has shown that silkworms perish and wine spoils from the same cause that makes good milk go bad and meat fester and putrefaction of any kind occur. Yes, Johnnie, the laud-able pus of the physician, the gangrene of the battlefield, the peritonitis of the surgeon, the fecal corruption, child birth fever, cadaveric poison. All of these share a common property with the dying silkworm and the tainted wine. I looked into Pasteur's heart and work, and know that there truly exists a tribute to God's generosity.

Pasteur claims that decay is not an inherent defect of tissue whether it be animal or vegetable. Pus does not arise by vague un-known miasmas or by the mysterious confluence of humors in the body. The larvae and grubs which grow in decaying flesh are not produced from the tissues they inhabit by some rare unseen alchemy. This meek man has proved that there are floating in the air around us invisible particles of life which evoke decay and rot and corrup-tion of any kind.

I can see you laugh and rattle the paper in my absent face. 'How ridiculous' you retort. 'How insane'. I know how you react, for did I not the same in my turn? But, bear with me, my doubting friend, for what I shall reveal will sweep away everything we know like cob-webs in a strong gale. This provincial little man has replaced our Old World with a New one of his own making.

Pasteur eagerly demonstrates his experiments to anyone who comes. He takes food and heats it to kill these 'microbes', as he calls them, and then sets the dishes in the sun. Where the food has been exposed to air, it disintegrates with decay and insects.- But, where he excludes the microbes by sealing the food under glass, the food remains pure and fresh for an indefinite time.

He is a magician. He is the first man in history to arrest the elemental process of corruption. Heat the item, keep away these in-credibly tiny organisms, and the process he calls fermentation but which we know as putrefaction, will never occur.

Now, you say, alright, let us accept this Pasteur and his ex-periments. Let us believe in his impossible vectors of disease and their omnipotent power to rot. 'I will take on faith that heat will destroy them,' But, of what use are these prescient observations to me? I have before me a peritoneal cavity or an amputated limb. I cannot put them in a boiling cauldron to protect. You have given me but one link in a tantalizing chain whose next coupling I have no knowledge. So be it with your Frenchman, you proudly conclude.

I agree, my hasty friend. That is why I traveled to Scotland. There, Johnnie, is a country to ravish your senses. No wonder the lairds fought to keep it free from the malevolent English. The hills and lakes are beauty personified. The ladies virtuous. The malt spirits invigorating. If I were ever to leave my native land, it is here among the bones of my ancestors I would return. However, let us leave the reveries of an old man before you consign the remainder of my story to a fairy tale.

There is in Edinburgh a rough-hewn, abrupt, perhaps even coarse surgeon, every bit the antithesis of our gentle French scientist. His name, is Joseph Lister. I went to visit him, as have those few enlightened of our profession in Europe and indeed, in the world, over the past six months. The first time I met him, he was making rounds in his Surgical Ward, surrounded by an appropriate retinue of awed medical students and clinical clerks. I could see him at first glance at the far end of the large room filled with his post-operative patients.

Although the meeting was only days ago, I do not remember the sight well enough to describe the surroundings. I do not recall his greeting words to me as I drew close. I cannot feel the warmth of his firm handshake with which he clasped my own. All that will forever remain in my memory is the strange sensation that came over me as I walked along the iron beds. Something was wrong! THERE WAS NO SMELL!

I felt like walking in a dream, sightless and soundless, as if cushioned in cotton wool so that my very senses were muffled.

Spencer, here too was SILENCE! There were no cries of patients in agony, suffering as their flesh rotted off their bodies. The air was fragrant. Where was the vile stench, that belligerent hallmark of every surgical ward on this earth? Where were the foul odors of purulence? The pungent stigmata of pus and corruption? The sweet scent of gangrene? The air here was clean and pure, except for the faint medicinal smell of an odd acrid chemical.

In France, one attributes to Louis Pasteur the wonderful saying, 'Chance favors the prepared mind'. Here, in a dimly-lit hall, in dour Presbyterian Scotland, an ebullient surgeon has proved himself worthy of those perspicacious words. Lister had reflected: Perhaps the putrefaction in a peritoneal cavity after surgical exploration, and, the pus at the end of an amputated limb, are caused by these same French microbes. If so, we should be able to prevent putrefaction if we can exclude them.

You must admit, the concept has a certain appealing simplicity. Yet, the logistics of implementing the philosophy seems insurmountable. We cannot place the human being in a glass flask and seal him away from air. Nor can we boil the limb and destroy with heat the offending germs. Lister thought hard on the problem. The solution was ingenious and therein lies this man's claim to greatness. The means to kill the microbes was readily at hand. A weak solution of a cheap common salt.

Edinburgh is now afloat in a sea of bichloride of lime. The walls and floors of the hospital are scrubbed hourly by attendants with buckets and brushes of the solution. The tables and surgical instruments are soaked in the solution. Every drain and suture and packing is drenched in the fluid. When surgery is carried out, the skin is first shaven and then washed with the chemical even as the air is constantly sprayed with a fine mist of it. The surgeon literally operates in a cold fog of the odd-smelling liquid.

But, the results! Lister has brought the mortality of amputations down from 70% to 2%. Yes, Johnnie, two percent! Protest, but believe! When this man opens the abdomen, the wound stays fresh. The edges adhere to each other and heal by PRIMARY closure. No more open cavities with drainage and packing for weeks and months. The scars are thin and fine,

The wounds pink and clean.

Spencer, I have seen that most tragic of accidents, the compound fracture of a limb, treated without amputation. Yes, with just simple splinting as if the skin was never pierced and the bone never perforating into the air. Lister purifies the wound with his lime solution. He saturates the ligatures and packings with it. The limbs heal perfectly.

Spencer, I have seen a maternity floor without a single case of puerperal sepsis! Lister places a basin of the lime chemical by each mothers bed. All that he does is insist that the doctor wash his hands thoroughly in the chemical before inserting them into the mothers pelvis. Thirty years ago, in Hungary, Ignace Semmelweiss told of such a feat, but the world ignored him. Think, Spencer, on the millions of women who have died needlessly because we physicians refused to cleanse our hands of the corruption we transmit from a septic patient to the sacred womb of another.

Spencer, I have seen this and more. I tremble with excitement at the thought of how the world will benefit from the work of these two men. Now, there will be others, many others, to follow their torch. Johnnie, Lister and Pasteur have shown us the way back into the Garden. I only pray that I live to see our children reenter. Your affectionate servant, Professor Elias Guthrie P.S. Your letter telling me of my Godson's birth and his name was forwarded to Edinburgh. My heart grows warm at the generous gesture. I hope in the spring to visit young Elias and his lovely mother. Perhaps then, there will be a sister, now that Shaw tells me you know the way.

Billings replaced the letter back in its envelope. Broken phrases kept repeating.

The limb has healed perfectly without amputation….the doctor wash his hands thoroughly. … not a single case of puerperal sepsis….women who died needlessly.

He thought of his friend who had read the pages before him. Any rancor towards John's strange behavior was now replaced by the fear whether it was too late to save the physician…. from himself.

Like John before him, he left the house in haste. The housekeeper stood in the doorway, watching Shaw Billings ride off in his carriage. She drew upon her endless supply of ancestral saints to protect the two physicians in her household.

Billings did not stop to tell her where he was going. He could not be certain. Putting himself in the place of the stricken husband, he felt there was only one possible place for him to be. But, first, he made a short, but necessary stop in the Highlands.

───

It was a weekday and the Cromwell Cemetery was deserted. Shaw asked the caretaker if he had seen John Spencer. The young doctor was well known since the summer epidemic. He pointed the way to the 0'Connell family plot. John was standing next to the triple grave. He did not hear Billings' muffled footsteps on the soft turned-over earth and gave a slight start when the older man greeted him. Billings could see that John had been crying. Even now his gait was unsteady.

"Come, John," Shaw gently urged. He motioned him to the stone benches at the far side of the field. The urns of wilted flowers stood on graves waiting for their headstones..

"No, Shaw," John resisted, "there is nothing you can say. You read the letter from Elias?"

"I have, Johnnie," he still held onto his arm. "But, come anyway. Sit with me." John allowed himself to be led. "I read the letter," Billings said. "Is that why you came here today?"

"Why else?" John cried out. "What else could I do?" He held his hands up. "You read what Elias wrote. These hands...." waving them in Shaw's face. "... killed Kathleen. " He grabbed the older man's arms and pulled them up. "You are as guilty as I am. Have you no shame? No guilt? No sorrow?"

"Sorrow? Yes, Johnnie, I have that. But, guilt? Shame? No! I have none of those. To accept them would make me less a physician to those who need me."

Shaw waited.

It was cruel, but it had to be done.

And, it came out. In a torrent.

A confession which purged the young man as violently as ipecac and magnesia for his bowels.

"What have I done, Shaw? I came into your house and fornicated with your servants. I married a young girl and I killed her, first with my cock and then with my hands, while saying I loved her. I blackmailed Zebadiah into opening the dam at Pulpit Rock." He could see Shaw's expression. "Yes, blackmail. You knew there was more to the story than the letters from the other mill towns. I hurt him badly. Do not ask me how at this time. I stooped to that despicable act to drain the reservoir. Even worse, I made a pact with Adam Ring. I gave him the monies he stole from Cromwell in order to fight the Harcrosses and keep the dam open. What if the waters do not bring malaria and yellow fever? Then, I have sinned twice...... for naught!"

" But always, Shaw, I had something to hold on to. I could heal. I could take away suffering. That balanced my errors. Now, you read Guthrie's letter. In our blindness, we have torn off limbs which could have been preserved. We have opened the womb and let in death."

His voice shredded his conscience. "What have I left? I came here and stood by the grave. I have been here for hours. My tenure here has been no good, Shaw. I will stay until you find a replacement. Then, I will return to McGill and join professor Guthrie in the laboratory." His head hung in shame. "There is nothing here for me anymore."

Shaw Billings suddenly turned on him, angry. "That is not the all of it, Johnnie, is it? As long as you are crying like a spoiled little boy who hurt his finger and now wants to run home to his mother, why not tell the rest?"

"I don't understand."

"I do, my dissembling friend. What is the <u>real</u> reason you came to Cromwell? You were in the War. You saw men, like yourself, lead others to their death. You saw soldiers and generals glory in the slaughter. And..... you....said.... to.... yourself. 'How horrible. How can men do such things? ' You wrote to Elias Guthrie. You could not wait to rush back to your monk's cell and convince yourself that you were <u>not</u> like those men. You were different. A physician. "

John shrunk back from the accusation.

"For God's sake, Johnnie, do not lie to yourself any longer. As a doctor you know you cannot cure if you deny the diagnosis?" He continued, his voice more compassionate.

"You came to Cromwell. You found that without any urging you could fornicate like other men. You could take advantage of ignorant chambermaids in my house and when they became pregnant ship them north with thirty pieces of silver. You found that you could love two women at the same time. You knew the sexual act meant death for one.......and you <u>knew</u> how to prevent it. You wanted an heir. You closed your eyes and excused your sin with faith in a miracle you knew would <u>never</u> happen."

"Johnnie, you became a man in more ways than with your cock and balls. You blackmailed Zebadiah and bribed Adam Ring. Now you feel dirty for having soiled your virgin conscience...... and,........all for a quest you have lost faith in."

"Today, you learned that physicians are only human. We are not born with infinite wisdom. We learn a little more year by year. In the process, we must treat patients with the limited skills we have.

The lay person knows_this. He does not condemn us. He knows we are not infallible. You thought you were. Your crime is hypocrisy."

"A letter from Guthrie tells you that you are just a speck in the cosmos and will always be so. Your father would have accepted what it says in Ecclesiastes, 'Dust to dust', and still not lost faith. But not you! You run off to hide in Montreal like some petulant child. Stop crying. Grow up. Be a man."

He still had one more blow... and he would be finished.

" Do you think you are some sort of angel that God placed upon the earth? You bleed. Angels don't bleed. You bleed because God made Adam and Eve see their nakedness. Angels don't have pain because they don't suffer. We do. But, angels don't have what we have. Wives. Children. Lovers. These bring pain. They also bring up the kind of love angels will never know... and that you been blessed to have. Human love comes with a price.... suffering. That is why we bleed and the angels do not."

"Johnnie.... you are a man. Behave like one." Billings wondered if he had gone to far. The physician was visibly shaken.

" Shaw, what is to be done? How can one live with such a burden?"

" Think, Johnnie. " Use your reason. Kathleen. She had a happy life. She loved you. She enjoyed passion with you. She married you and saw her own child alive and well. She lived happy and died happy. How many can say the same?"

" Guilt? The desire to procreate is not a sin. Without it, you and I would not be here. To deny another life, that is a sin."

" As for blackmail and bribery, as you so quaintly characterize your adventures into the world of commerce, If the choice was made without rancor or prejudice, to help others, then you must use the tools which Providence gave you."

" Most of all, do not feel shame for your ignorance. Glory that you are alive at a time when knowledge is advancing. What about me? I will die without ever seeing the scales balanced."

"Johnnie, when you get to my age, all you will have to look forward to is a cock that is limp, veins from which I must lance two pints a week, and a bladder into which I insert a silver tube three times a day and hope not to die like our patient. These are burdens of the <u>flesh</u>, but we do not commit <u>physical</u> suicide. One cannot abdicate from life because of pique. Life is too precious."

He pointed to the hills. "Johnnie, Someone there needs your love. She has loved you from the first day she saw you. I know. I have always known. Go to her."

John see the wooded bluff where the new Hospital was to be built. "Elizabeth? How can I face her after all that has happened?"

"Johnnie, she too, has her burdens. She grew up loving a father who denied her. She loved a man who racked himself with guilt when he made love. The rest of her life, half of her fortune is in trust for an institution dedicated to the memory of a brother who stole her father for nineteen years. She is struggling, alone, to preserve a business in a changing world which despises her for her sex and ability. She has only unhappy memories, and little to look forward to. Those are <u>her</u> burdens. But, she persists! All she has left is a love for you."

It did not take long for the young physician to reach the windy copse. He saw Elizabeth's hazel stallion tied to a tree, snorting and sweating from the climb. On the opposite side of the clearing, the young woman stood, catching the breeze. Their fingers felt and clasped.

Dusk was falling rapidly. A luminous ribbon still clung to the far horizon. One last beam of sunlight skimmed across the land to capture the Quabbin River in a flash of brilliance.

"John, I will fight you at Pulpit Rock."

He smiled as he bent down to kiss her. He heard the words and did not object. As Shaw would say….. ' just another burden.'

He held her close. They followed the twisting white curl of the Quabbin disappear north.

Only one thing mattered. Someday, their children would live... and love…. and suffer...

It would be their burdens in their struggle for the world.

That was all that anyone could do.

It was sufficient.

THE END

Made in the USA
Middletown, DE
06 July 2016